SELECTIONS
FROM THE
WRITINGS
OF
'ABDU'L-BAHÁ

SELECTIONS
FROM THE
WRITINGS
OF
'ABDU'L-BAHÁ

Compiled by the Research Department of
the Universal House of Justice
Translated
by
a Committee
at the Bahá'í World Center
and by
Marzieh Gail

BAHÁ'Í
PUBLISHING

EVANSTON, ILLINOIS

Originally published by the Bahá'í World Center,
Haifa, Israel © 1978 The Universal House of Justice

Bahá'í Publishing, 1233 Central St., Evanston, Illinois 60201

Copyright © 2010 by the National Spiritual Assembly
of the Bahá'ís of the United States
All rights reserved. Published 2010
Printed in the United States of America on acid-free paper ∞

26   25   24   23   6   5   4   3

Library of Congress Cataloging-in-Publication Data

'Abdu'l-Bahá, 1844–1921.
  [Selections. English. 2010]
  Selections from the writings of 'Abdu'l-Bahá / compiled by
the Research Department of the Universal House of Justice ;
translated by a Committee at the Baha'i World Center and by
Marzieh Gail.
      p. cm.
  Originally published: Haifa : Bahá'í World Centre ; Wilmette,
Ill. : Distributed in the U.S. by Bahá'í Pub. Trust, 1978.
  Includes bibliographical references and index.
  ISBN 978-1-931847-74-2 (alk. paper)
  1. Bahai Faith. I. Universal House of Justice. Research Dept.
II. Title.
  BP363.A3 2010
  297.9'3824—dc22

                                        2009054202

Selections from the Writings of 'Abdu'l-Bahá was first issued in
1978 in both hardcover (ISBN 0-85398-081-0) and softcover
(0-85398-084-5) editions. A lightweight edition (0-85398-136-
1) was issued in 1982. By permission of the Bahá'í World Center
the first pocket-size edition was released in 1996.

Cover design by Robert A. Reddy
Book design by Patrick Falso

CONTENTS

PREFACE

'Abdu'l-Bahá's exposition of the Bahá'í Revelation is recorded in His written works, in the many compilations of His recorded utterances, and in His correspondence. The written works such as *The Secret of Divine Civilization*, *A Traveler's Narrative*, the Will and Testament, are available in English translations. Likewise many compilations of His recorded utterances, among which may be mentioned *Some Answered Questions*, *Memorials of the Faithful*, *Paris Talks*, are kept in print. Not for sixty years, however, has any large compilation, in English, of His innumerable letters been made; the three volumes of *Tablets of 'Abdu'l-Bahá* published in the United States between 1909 and 1916, although running into second editions, have long been out of print.

The present compilation attempts a much wider selection than was made for those early volumes, and its perusal will give some indication of the vast range of subjects dealt with by the Master in His correspondence. Included are a number of Tablets translated by a Committee at the World Center using early drafts made by Shoghi Effendi during 'Abdu'l-Bahá's lifetime, and a large number by Marzieh Gail, sent to her from the World Center's collection of more than 19,000 original and authenticated copies. Some famous Tablets, such as the correspondence with Auguste Forel, or the greater part of the Tablet to the Hague, have been omitted since they are available in separate publications.

The happy and blessed recipients of the vast majority of the Tablets here included were the early believers of the east and west, whether individuals, groups, organized committees or assemblies of the friends, and their value to the nascent communities of the west in those days when Bahá'í literature in English was meager in the extreme, cannot be overestimated.

It is believed that publication of these writings of the Master's will serve to increase the fervor of His lovers in responding to His call and add to their perception of that wondrous harmony of the human and divine which He, the Mystery of God, so perfectly exemplified.

REFERENCES TO THE QUR'ÁN

In footnotes referring to the Qur'án the súrihs have been numbered according to the original, whereas the verse numbers are those in Rodwell's translation which differ sometimes from those of the Arabic.

INTRODUCTION

'Abdu'l-Bahá (23 May 1844–28 November 1921) was the eldest surviving son and designated successor to Bahá'u'lláh, the Prophet-Founder of the Bahá'í Faith. Though he was known as "'Abbas Effendi" outside of the Bahá'í community, Bahá'ís often refer to him as "the Most Great Branch," "the Mystery of God," and "the Master"—titles bestowed on him by Bahá'u'lláh. After Bahá'u'lláh's passing in 1892, he chose to refer to himself as "'Abdu'l-Bahá," meaning "Servant of Bahá."

The Bahá'í Faith originated in Iran in the middle of the nineteenth century, and owes its origin to the labors of two successive founding Prophets: the Báb and Bahá'u'lláh. As the former explained, His mission was to prepare the way for "Him Whom God shall make manifest," the Manifestation of God awaited by the followers of all faiths. During the course of successive waves of persecution that followed this announcement and that

I

claimed the lives of the Báb and several thousands of His followers, Bahá'u'lláh declared Himself to be the fulfillment of the Divine promise.

As a child 'Abdu'l-Bahá recognized his father's spiritual station even before it was revealed publicly and accompanied Bahá'u'lláh in his banishment and exile beginning at age eight. 'Abdu'l-Bahá often served as his father's deputy when dealing with officials and with the public. Upon Bahá'u'lláh's passing in 1892, 'Abdu'l-Bahá became the head of the Bahá'í Faith in accordance with provisions made in Bahá'u'lláh's writings.

As Bahá'u'lláh's successor and chosen interpreter of his writings, 'Abdu'l-Bahá holds a special spiritual station of his own. Bahá'ís consider him the perfect exemplar of the Bahá'í Faith, endowed with divine knowledge, although he is not a prophet.

During his remarkable ministry 'Abdu'l-Bahá corresponded with Bahá'ís all over the world, providing them with an abundance of practical and spiritual guidance. Although many of the letters compiled in this volume were addressed to individuals in response to specific questions, the guidance they impart contains universal truths worthy of study by all. The correspondence and written works collected here cover a wide range of topics and contain a deep spiritual wisdom that remains as relevant and vital today as when it was first committed to paper.

SELECTIONS FROM THE
WRITINGS OF 'ABDU'L-BAHÁ

1. O peoples of the world! The Sun of Truth 1.1
hath risen to illumine the whole earth, and to spiri-
tualize the community of man. Laudable are the
results and the fruits thereof, abundant the holy
evidences deriving from this grace. This is mercy
unalloyed and purest bounty; it is light for the
world and all its peoples; it is harmony and fellowship, and love and solidarity; indeed it is compassion and unity, and the end of foreignness; it is
the being at one, in complete dignity and freedom,
with all on earth.

The Blessed Beauty saith: "Ye are all the fruits 1.2
of one tree, the leaves of one branch." Thus hath
He likened this world of being to a single tree,
and all its peoples to the leaves thereof, and the
blossoms and fruits. It is needful for the bough to
blossom, and leaf and fruit to flourish, and upon
the interconnection of all parts of the world-tree,

dependeth the flourishing of leaf and blossom, and the sweetness of the fruit.

1.3   For this reason must all human beings powerfully sustain one another and seek for everlasting life; and for this reason must the lovers of God in this contingent world become the mercies and the blessings sent forth by that clement King of the seen and unseen realms. Let them purify their sight and behold all humankind as leaves and blossoms and fruits of the tree of being. Let them at all times concern themselves with doing a kindly thing for one of their fellows, offering to someone love, consideration, thoughtful help. Let them see no one as their enemy, or as wishing them ill, but think of all humankind as their friends; regarding the alien as an intimate, the stranger as a companion, staying free of prejudice, drawing no lines.

1.4   In this day, the one favored at the Threshold of the Lord is he who handeth round the cup of faithfulness; who bestoweth, even upon his enemies, the jewel of bounty, and lendeth, even to his fallen oppressor, a helping hand; it is he who will, even to the fiercest of his foes, be a loving friend. These are the Teachings of the Blessed Beauty, these the counsels of the Most Great Name.

1.5   O ye dear friends! The world is at war and the human race is in travail and mortal combat. The dark night of hate hath taken over, and the light of good faith is blotted out. The peoples and kindreds of the earth have sharpened their claws, and are hurling themselves one against the other. It is the very foundation of the human race that is being destroyed. It is thousands of households that are vagrant and dispossessed, and every year seeth thousands upon thousands of human beings weltering in their lifeblood on dusty battlefields. The tents of life and joy are down. The generals practice their generalship, boasting of the blood they shed, competing one with the next in inciting to violence. "With this sword," saith one of them, "I beheaded a people!" And another: "I toppled a nation to the ground!" And yet another: "I brought a government down!" On such things do men pride themselves, in such do they glory! Love—righteousness—these are everywhere censured, while despised are harmony, and devotion to the truth.

The Faith of the Blessed Beauty is summoning 1.6 mankind to safety and love, to amity and peace; it hath raised up its tabernacle on the heights of the earth, and directeth its call to all nations. Wherefore, O ye who are God's lovers, know ye the value of this precious Faith, obey its teachings, walk in this road that is drawn straight, and show ye this way to the people. Lift up your voices and sing out the song of the Kingdom. Spread far and wide the precepts and counsels of the loving Lord, so that this world will change into another world, and this darksome earth will be flooded with light, and the dead body of mankind will arise and live; so that every soul will ask for immortality, through the holy breaths of God.

1.7   Soon will your swiftly passing days be over, and the fame and riches, the comforts, the joys provided by this rubbish-heap, the world, will be gone without a trace. Summon ye, then, the people to God, and invite humanity to follow the example of the Company on high. Be ye loving fathers to the orphan, and a refuge to the helpless, and a treasury for the poor, and a cure for the ailing. Be ye the helpers of every victim of oppression, the patrons of the disadvantaged. Think ye at all times of rendering some service to every member of the human race. Pay ye no heed to aversion and rejection, to disdain, hostility, injustice: act ye in the opposite way. Be ye sincerely kind, not in appearance only. Let each one of God's loved ones center his attention on this: to be the Lord's mercy to man; to be the Lord's grace. Let him do some good to every person whose path he crosseth, and be of some benefit to him. Let him improve the character of each and all, and reorient the minds of men. In this way, the light of divine guidance will shine forth, and the blessings of God will cradle all mankind: for love is light, no matter in what abode it dwelleth; and hate is darkness, no matter where it may make its nest. O friends of God! That the hidden Mystery may stand revealed, and the secret essence of all things may be disclosed, strive ye to banish that darkness for ever and ever.

2. O my Lord! I have drawn nigh unto Thee, in the depths of this darksome night, confiding in Thee with the tongue of my heart, trembling with joy at the sweet scents that blow from Thy realm, the All-Glorious, calling unto Thee, saying: 2.1

O my Lord, no words do I find to glorify Thee; no way do I see for the bird of my mind to soar upward to Thy Kingdom of Holiness; for Thou, in Thy very essence, art sanctified above those tributes, and in Thy very being art beyond the reach of those praises which are offered Thee by the people that Thou hast created. In the sanctity of Thine own being hast Thou ever been exalted above the understanding of the learned among the Company on high, and forever wilt Thou remain enwrapped within the holiness of Thine own reality, unreached by the knowledge of those dwellers in Thine exalted Kingdom who glorify Thy Name. 2.2

2.3   O God, my God! How can I glorify or describe Thee inaccessible as Thou art; immeasurably high and sanctified art Thou above every description and praise.

2.4   O God, my God! Have mercy then upon my helpless state, my poverty, my misery, my abasement! Give me to drink from the generous cup of Thy grace and forgiveness, stir me with the sweet scents of Thy love, gladden my bosom with the light of Thy knowledge, purify my soul with the mysteries of Thy oneness, raise me to life with the gentle breeze that cometh from the gardens of Thy mercy—till I sever myself from all else but Thee, and lay hold of the hem of Thy garment of grandeur, and consign to oblivion all that is not Thee, and be companioned by the sweet breathings that waft during these Thy days, and attain unto faithfulness at Thy Threshold of Holiness, and arise to serve Thy Cause, and to be humble before Thy loved ones, and, in the presence of Thy favored ones, to be nothingness itself.

2.5   Verily art Thou the Helper, the Sustainer, the Exalted, the Most Generous.

2.6   O God, my God! I beg of Thee by the dawning of the light of Thy Beauty that hath illumined all the earth, and by the glance of Thy divine compassion's eye that considereth all things, and by the surging sea of Thy bestowals in which all things are immersed, and by Thy streaming clouds of bounty raining down gifts upon the essences of all created things, and by the splendors of Thy mercy that existed before ever the world was—to help Thy chosen ones to be faithful, and assist Thy loved ones to serve at Thine exalted Threshold, and cause them to gain the victory through the battalions of Thy might that overpowereth all things, and reinforce them with a great fighting host from out of the Concourse on high.

O my Lord! They are weak souls standing at 2.7 Thy door; they are paupers in Thy courtyard, desperate for Thy grace, in dire need of Thy succor, turning their faces toward the kingdom of Thy oneness, yearning for the bounties of Thy bestowals. O my Lord! Flood Thou their minds with Thy holy light; cleanse Thou their hearts with the grace of Thine assistance; gladden their bosoms with the fragrance of the joys that waft from Thy Company above; make bright their eyes by beholding the signs and tokens of Thy might; cause them to be the ensigns of purity, the banners of sanctity waving high above all creatures on the summits of the earth; make Thou their words to move hearts which are even as solid rock. May they arise to serve Thee and dedicate themselves to the Kingdom of Thy divinity, and set their faces toward the realm of Thy Self-Subsistence, and spread far and wide Thy signs, and be illumined by Thy streaming lights, and unfold Thy hidden mysteries. May they guide Thy servants unto gentle waters and to the fountain of Thy mercy that welleth and leapeth in the midmost heart of the Heaven of Thy oneness. May they hoist the sail of detachment upon the Ark of Salvation, and move over the seas of Thy knowledge; may they spread wide the pinions of unity and by their aid soar upward to the Kingdom of Thy singleness to become servants whom the Supreme Concourse will applaud, whose praises the dwellers in Thine all-glorious realm will utter; may they hear the heralds of the invisible world as they raise their cry of the Most Great Glad-Tidings; may they, in their longing to meet Thee, invoke and pray unto Thee, intoning wondrous orisons at the dawn of light— O my Lord Who disposest all things—shedding their tears at morningtide and even, yearning to pass into the shadow of Thy mercy that endeth never.

2.8   Help them, O my Lord, under all conditions, support them at all times with Thine angels of holiness, they who are Thine invisible hosts, Thy heavenly battalions who bring down to defeat the massed armies of this nether world.

Verily art Thou the Mighty, the Powerful, the 2.9 Strong, the All-Encompassing, the One Who hath dominion over all that is.

O holy Lord! O Lord of loving-kindness! We 2.10 stray about Thy dwelling, longing to behold Thy beauty, and loving all Thy ways. We are hapless, lowly, and of small account. We are paupers: show us mercy, give us bounty; look not upon our failings, hide Thou our endless sins. Whatever we are, still are we Thine, and what we speak and hear is praise of Thee, and it is Thy face we seek, Thy path we follow. Thou art the Lord of loving-kindness, we are sinners and astray and far from home. Wherefore, O Cloud of Mercy, grant us some drops of rain. O Flowering Bed of grace, send forth a fragrant breeze. O Sea of all bestowals, roll towards us a great wave. O Sun of Bounty, send down a shaft of light. Grant us pity, grant us grace. By Thy beauty, we come with no provision but our sins, with no good deeds to tell of, only hopes. Unless Thy concealing veil doth cover us, and Thy protection shield and cradle us, what power have these helpless souls to rise and serve Thee, what substance have these wretched ones to make a brave display? Thou Who art the Mighty, the All-Powerful, help us, favor us; withered as we are, revive us with showers from Thy clouds of grace; lowly as we are, illumine us with bright rays from the Daystar of Thy oneness. Cast Thou these thirsty fish into the ocean of Thy mercy, guide Thou this lost caravan to the shelter of Thy singleness; to the wellspring of guidance lead Thou the ones who have wandered far astray, and grant to those who have missed the path a haven within the precincts of Thy might. Lift Thou to these parched lips the bounteous and soft-flowing waters of heaven, raise up these dead to everlasting life. Grant Thou to the blind eyes that will see. Make Thou the deaf to hear, the dumb to speak. Set Thou the dispirited ablaze, make Thou the heedless mindful, warn Thou the proud, awaken those who sleep.

2.11   Thou art the Mighty, Thou art the Bestower, Thou art the Loving. Verily Thou art the Beneficent, the Most Exalted.

2.12   O ye loved ones of God, ye helpers of this evanescent Servant! When the Sun of Reality shed its endless bounties from the Dawning-Point of all desires, and this world of being was lit with that sacred light from pole to pole, with such intensity did it cast down its rays that it blotted out the Stygian dark forever, whereupon this earth of dust became the envy of the spheres of heaven, and this lowly place took on the state and panoply of the supernal realm. The gentle breeze of holiness blew over it, scattering abroad sweet savors; the spring winds of heaven passed by it, and over it, from the Source of all bestowals, were wafted fruitful airs that carried boundless grace. Then the bright dawn rose, and there came tidings of great joy. The divine springtime was here, pitching its tents in this contingent world, so that all creation leapt and danced. The withered earth brought forth immortal blooms, the dead dust woke to everlasting life. Then came forth flowers of mystic learning, and, bespeaking the knowledge of God, fresh greenery from the ground. The contingent world displayed God's bounteous gifts, the visible world reflecting the glories of realms that were hidden from sight. God's summons was proclaimed, the table of the Eternal Covenant was readied, the cup of the Testament was passed from hand to hand, the universal invitation was sent forth. Then some among the people were set afire with the wine of heaven, and some were left without a share of this greatest of bestowals. The sight and insight of some were illumined by the light of grace, and there were some who, hearing the anthems of unity, leapt for joy. There were birds that began to carol in the gardens of holiness, there were nightingales in the branches of the rose tree of heaven that raised their plaintive cries. Then were decked and adorned both the Kingdom on high and the earth below, and this world became the envy of high heaven. Yet alas, alas, the neglectful have stayed fast in their heedless sleep, and the foolish have spurned this most sacred of bestowals. The blind remain shrouded in their veils, the deaf have no share in what hath come to pass, the dead have no hopes of attaining thereto, for even as He saith: "They despair of the life to come, as the infidels despair that the dwellers in the tombs will rise again."*

2.13   As to you, O ye loved ones of God! Loose your tongues and offer Him thanks; praise ye and glorify the Beauty of the Adored One, for ye have drunk from this purest of chalices, and ye are cheered and set aglow with this wine. Ye have detected the sweet scents of holiness, ye have smelled the musk of faithfulness from Joseph's raiment. Ye have fed on the honeydew of loyalty from the hands of Him Who is the one alone Beloved, ye have feasted on immortal dishes at the bounteous banquet table of the Lord. This plenty is a special favor bestowed by a loving God, these are bless-

---

* Qur'án 60:13

ings and rare gifts deriving from His grace. In the Gospel He saith: "For many are called, but few are chosen."* That is, to many is it offered, but rare is the soul who is singled out to receive the great bestowal of guidance. "Such is the bounty of God: to whom He will He giveth it, and of immense bounty is God."†

O ye loved ones of God! From the peoples of the world, against the Candle of the Covenant discordant winds do beat and blow. The Nightingale of faithfulness is beset by renegades who are even as ravens of hate. The Dove of God's remembrance is hard pressed by mindless birds of night, and the Gazelle that dwelleth in the meadows of God's love is being hunted down by ravening beasts. Deadly is the peril, tormenting the pain. 2.14

The beloved of the Lord must stand fixed as the mountains, firm as impregnable walls. Unmoved must they remain by even the direst adversities, ungrieved by the worst of disasters. Let them cling to the hem of Almighty God, and put their faith in the Beauty of the Most High; let them lean on the unfailing help that cometh from the Ancient Kingdom, and depend on the care and protec- 2.15

---

* Matthew 22:14
† Qur'án 57:21

tion of the generous Lord. Let them at all times refresh and restore themselves with the dews of heavenly grace, and with the breaths of the Holy Spirit revive and renew themselves from moment to moment. Let them rise up to serve their Lord, and do all in their power to scatter His breathings of holiness far and wide. Let them be a mighty fortress to defend His Faith, an impregnable citadel for the hosts of the Ancient Beauty. Let them faithfully guard the edifice of the Cause of God from every side; let them become the bright stars of His luminous skies. For the hordes of darkness are assailing this Cause from every direction, and the peoples of the earth are intent on extinguishing this evident Light. And since all the kindreds of the world are mounting their attack, how can our attention be diverted, even for a moment? Assuredly be cognizant of these things, be watchful, and guard the Cause of God.

2.16　　The most vital duty, in this day, is to purify your characters, to correct your manners, and improve your conduct. The beloved of the Merciful must show forth such character and conduct among His creatures, that the fragrance of their holiness may be shed upon the whole world, and may quicken the dead, inasmuch as the purpose of the Manifestation of God and the dawning of the limitless lights of the Invisible is to educate the souls of men, and refine the character of every living man—so that blessed individuals, who have freed themselves from the murk of the animal world, shall rise up with those qualities which are the adornings of the reality of man. The purpose is that earthlings should turn into the people of Heaven, and those who walk in darkness should come into the light, and those who are excluded should join the inner circle of the Kingdom, and those who are as nothing should become intimates of the everlasting Glory. It is that the portionless should gain their share of the boundless sea, and the ignorant drink their fill from the living fount of knowledge; that those who thirst for blood should forsake their savagery, and those who are barbed of claw should turn gentle and forbearing, and those who love war should seek instead for true conciliation; it is that the brutal, their talons razor-sharp, should enjoy the benefits of lasting peace; that the foul should learn that there is a realm of purity, and the tainted find their way to the rivers of holiness.

2.17 Unless these divine bestowals be revealed from the inner self of humankind, the bounty of the Manifestation will prove barren, and the dazzling rays of the Sun of Truth will have no effect whatever.

2.18   Wherefore, O beloved of the Lord, strive ye with heart and soul to receive a share of His holy attributes and take your portion of the bounties of His sanctity—that ye may become the tokens of unity, the standards of singleness, and seek out the meaning of oneness; that ye may, in this garden of God, lift up your voices and sing the blissful anthems of the spirit. Become ye as the birds who offer Him their thanks, and in the blossoming bowers of life chant ye such melodies as will dazzle the minds of those who know. Raise ye a banner on the highest peaks of the world, a flag of God's favor to ripple and wave in the winds of His grace; plant ye a tree in the field of life, amid the roses of this visible world, that will yield a fruitage fresh and sweet.

2.19   I swear by the true Teacher that if ye will act in accord with the admonitions of God, as revealed in His luminous Tablets, this darksome dust will mirror forth the Kingdom of heaven, and this nether world the realm of the All-Glorious.

2.20   O ye loved ones of the Lord! Praise be to Him, the unseen, welling bounties of the Sun of Truth encompass you on every side, and from every direction the portals of His mercy stand ajar. Now is the time to take advantage of these bestowals, and benefit therefrom. Know ye the value of this time, let not this chance escape you. Stay ye entirely clear of this dark world's concerns, and become ye known by the attributes of those essences that make their home in the Kingdom. Then shall ye see how intense is the glory of the heavenly Daystar, and how blinding bright are the tokens of bounty coming out of the invisible realm.

3. O ye beloved of God! O ye children of His Kingdom! Verily, verily, the new heaven and the new earth are come. The holy City, new Jerusalem, hath come down from on high in the form of a maid of heaven, veiled, beauteous, and unique, and prepared for reunion with her lovers on earth. The angelic company of the Celestial Concourse hath joined in a call that hath run throughout the universe, all loudly and mightily acclaiming: "This is the City of God and His abode, wherein shall dwell the pure and holy among His servants. He shall live with them, for they are His people and He is their Lord." 3.1

He hath wiped away their tears, kindled their light, rejoiced their hearts and enraptured their souls. Death shall no more overtake them neither shall sorrow, weeping or tribulation afflict them. The Lord God Omnipotent hath been enthroned in His Kingdom and hath made all things new. This is the truth and what truth can be greater 3.2

than that announced by the Revelation of St. John the Divine?

3.3 He is Alpha and Omega. He is the One that will give unto him that is athirst of the fountain of the water of life and bestow upon the sick the remedy of true salvation. He whom such grace aideth is verily he that receiveth the most glorious heritage from the Prophets of God and His holy ones. The Lord will be his God, and he His dearly beloved son.

3.4 Rejoice, then, O ye beloved of the Lord and His chosen ones, and ye the children of God and His people, raise your voices to laud and magnify the Lord, the Most High; for His light hath beamed forth, His signs have appeared and the billows of His rising ocean have scattered on every shore many a precious pearl.

4.1 4. Praise be to Him Who hath made the world of being, and hath fashioned all that is, Him Who hath raised up the sincere to a station of honor* and hath made the invisible world to appear on the plane of the visible—yet still, in their drunken stupor,† do men wander and stray.

---

* Qur'án 17:81
† Qur'án 15:72

He hath laid down the foundations of the lofty 4.2
Citadel, He hath inaugurated the Cycle of Glory,
He hath brought forth a new creation on this day
that is clearly Judgement Day—and still do the
heedless stay fast in their drunken sleep.

The Bugle* hath sounded, the Trumpet† hath 4.3
been blown, the Crier hath raised his call, and all
upon the earth have swooned away—but still do
the dead, in the tombs of their bodies, sleep on.

And the second clarion‡ hath sounded, there 4.4
hath followed the second blast after the first,§ and
the dread woe hath come, and every nursing mother hath forgot the infant at her breast**—yet still
the people, confused and distracted, heed it not.

And the Resurrection hath dawned, and the 4.5
Hour hath struck, and the Path hath been drawn
straight, and the Balance hath been set up, and all
upon the earth have been gathered together††—
but still the people see no sign of the way.

The light hath shone forth, and radiance flood- 4.6
eth Mount Sinai, and a gentle wind bloweth from

---

* Qur'án 39:68; *Epistle to the Son of the Wolf*, p. 133

† Qur'án 74:8

‡ Qur'án 39:68

§ Qur'án 79:6

** Qur'án 22:2

†† Qur'án 34:39

over the gardens of the Ever-Forgiving Lord; the sweet breaths of the spirit are passing by, and those who lay buried in the grave are rising up—and still do the heedless slumber on in their tombs.

4.7 The flames of hell have been made to blaze, and heaven hath been brought nigh; the celestial gardens are in flower, and fresh pools are brimming over, and paradise gleameth in beauty—but the unaware are still mired down in their empty dreams.

4.8 The veil hath fallen away, the curtain is lifted, the clouds have parted, the Lord of Lords is in plain sight—yet all hath passed the sinners by.

4.9 It is He Who hath made for you the new creation,* and brought on the woe† that surpasseth all others, and gathered the holy together in the realm on high. Verily in this are signs for those who have eyes to see.

4.10 And among His signs is the appearance of omens and joyous prophecies, of hints and clues, the spreading of many and various tidings, and the anticipations of the righteous, they who have now attained their goal.

---

* Qur'án 29:19
† Qur'án 79:34

And among His signs are His splendors, rising 4.11
above the horizon of oneness, His lights streaming out from the dayspring of might, and the announcement of the Most Great Glad-Tidings by
His Herald, the One, the Incomparable. Verily in
this is a brilliant proof for the company of those
who know.

Among His signs is His being manifest, being 4.12
seen by all, standing as His own proof, and His
presence among witnesses in every region, among
peoples who fell upon Him even as wolves, and
compassed Him about from every side.

Among His signs is His withstanding power- 4.13
ful nations and all-conquering states, and a host
of enemies thirsting for His blood, intent at every
moment upon His ruin, wheresoever He might
be. Verily this is a matter deserving the scrutiny of
those who ponder the signs and tokens of God.

Another of His signs is the marvel of His dis- 4.14
course, the eloquence of His utterance, the rapid-
ity with which His Writings were revealed, His
words of wisdom, His verses, His epistles, His
communes, His unfolding of the Qur'án, both
the abstruse verses thereof and the clear. By thy
very life! This thing is plain as day to whoever will
regard it with the eye of justice.

4.15   Again among His signs is the dawning sun of His knowledge, and the rising moon of His arts and skills, and His demonstrating perfection in all His ways, as testified by the learned and accomplished of many nations.

4.16   And again among His signs is the fact that His beauty stayed inviolate, and His human temple was protected as He revealed His splendors, despite the massed attacks of all His foes, who came against Him in their thousands with their darting arrows, spears and swords. Herein is verily a wonder and a warning to any fair judge.

4.17   And among His signs is His long-suffering, His tribulations and His woes, His agony in His chains and fetters, and His calling out at every moment: "Come unto Me, come unto Me, ye righteous! Come unto Me, come unto Me, ye lovers of the good! Come unto Me, come unto Me, ye dawning points of light!" Verily the gates of mystery are opened wide—but still do the wicked disport themselves with their vain cavillings!*

4.18   Yet another of His signs is the promulgation of His Book, His decisive Holy Text wherein He reproved the kings, and His dire warning to

---

* Qur'án 6:91; 52:12

that one* whose mighty rule was felt around the world—and whose great throne then toppled down in a matter of brief days—this being a fact clearly established and widely known.

And among His signs is the sublimity of His grandeur, His exalted state, His towering glory, and the shining out of His beauty above the horizon of the Prison: so that heads were bowed before Him and voices lowered, and humble were the faces that turned His way. This is a proof never witnessed in the ages gone before.   4.19

Again among His signs are the extraordinary things He continually did, the miracles He performed, the wonders appearing from Him without interruption like the streaming down of His clouds—and the acknowledgement, even by unbelievers, of His powerful light. By His own life! This was clearly verified, it was demonstrated to those of every persuasion who came into the presence of the living, the self-subsisting Lord.   4.20

And yet another of His signs is the wide-spreading rays of the sun of His era, the rising moon of His times in the heaven of all the ages: His day, which standeth at the summit of all days, for its   4.21

---

* Napoleon III

rank and power, its sciences and its arts, reaching far and wide, that have dazzled the world and astonished the minds of men.

4.22 Verily is this a matter settled and established for all time.

5.1 5. The world's great Light, once resplendent upon all mankind, hath set, to shine everlastingly from the Abhá Horizon, His Kingdom of fadeless glory, shedding splendor upon His loved ones from on high and breathing into their hearts and souls the breath of eternal life.

5.2 Ponder in your hearts that which He hath foretold in His Tablet of the Divine Vision that hath been spread throughout the world. Therein He saith: "Thereupon she wailed and exclaimed: 'May the world and all that is therein be a ransom for Thy woes. O Sovereign of heaven and earth! Wherefore hast Thou left Thyself in the hands of the dwellers of this prison-city of 'Akká? Hasten Thou to other dominions, to Thy retreats above, whereon the eyes of the people of names have never fallen.' We smiled and spake not. Reflect upon these most exalted words, and comprehend the purpose of this hidden and sacred mystery."

5.3 O ye beloved of the Lord! Beware, beware lest ye hesitate and waver. Let not fear fall upon you, neither be troubled nor dismayed. Take ye good heed lest this calamitous day slacken the flames of your ardor, and quench your tender hopes. Today is the day for steadfastness and constancy. Blessed are they that stand firm and immovable as the rock and brave the storm and stress of this tempestuous hour. They, verily, shall be the recipients of God's grace; they, verily, shall receive His divine assistance, and shall be truly victorious. They shall shine amidst mankind with a radiance which the dwellers of the Pavilion of Glory laud and magnify. To them is proclaimed this celestial call, revealed in His Most Holy Book: "Let not your hearts be perturbed, O people, when the glory of My Presence is withdrawn, and the ocean of My utterance is stilled. In My presence amongst you there is a wisdom, and in My absence there is yet another, inscrutable to all but God, the Incomparable, the All-Knowing. Verily, We behold you from Our realm of glory, and shall aid whosoever will arise for the triumph of Our Cause with the hosts of the Concourse on high and a company of Our favored angels."

The Sun of Truth, that Most Great Light, hath 5.4 set upon the horizon of the world to rise with deathless splendor over the Realm of the Limitless. In His Most Holy Book He calleth the firm and steadfast of His friends: "Be not dismayed, O peoples of the world, when the daystar of My beauty is set, and the heaven of My tabernacle is concealed from your eyes. Arise to further My Cause, and to exalt My Word amongst men."

6.1   6. O ye peoples of the Kingdom! How many a soul expended all its span of life in worship, endured the mortification of the flesh, longed to gain an entry into the Kingdom, and yet failed, while ye, with neither toil nor pain nor self-denial, have won the prize and entered in.

6.2   It is even as in the time of the Messiah, when the Pharisees and the pious were left without a portion, while Peter, John and Andrew, given neither to pious worship nor ascetic practice, won the day. Wherefore, thank ye God for setting upon your heads the crown of glory everlasting, for granting unto you this immeasurable grace.

6.3   The time hath come when, as a thank-offering for this bestowal, ye should grow in faith and constancy as day followeth day, and should draw ever nearer to the Lord, your God, becoming magnetized to such a degree, and so aflame, that your holy melodies in praise of the Beloved will reach upward to the Company on high; and that each one of you, even as a nightingale in this rose garden of God, will glorify the Lord of Hosts, and become the teacher of all who dwell on earth.

7. O ye spiritual friends of 'Abdu'l-Bahá! A trusted messenger hath arrived and hath, in the world of the spirit, delivered a message from God's loved ones. This auspicious courier bringeth fragrances of great ardor and wafteth the life-giving breezes of the love of God. He maketh the heart to dance for joy and filleth up the soul with an ecstasy of love and rapture. So intensely hath the glory of Divine Unity penetrated souls and hearts that all are now bound one to another with heavenly ties, and all are even as a single heart, a single soul. Wherefore reflections of the spirit and impressions of the Divine are now mirrored clear and sharp in the deep heart's core. I beg of God to strengthen these spiritual bonds as day followeth day, and make this mystic oneness to shine ever more brightly, until at last all shall be as troops marshaled together beneath the banner of the Covenant within the sheltering shade of the Word of God; that they may strive with all their might until universal fellowship, close and warm, and unalloyed love, and spiritual relationships, will connect all the hearts in the world. Then will all humankind, because of this fresh and dazzling bounty, be gathered in

a single homeland. Then will conflict and dissension vanish from the face of the earth, then will mankind be cradled in love for the beauty of the All-Glorious. Discord will change to accord, dissension to unison. The roots of malevolence will be torn out, the basis of aggression destroyed. The bright rays of union will obliterate the darkness of limitations, and the splendors of heaven will make the human heart to be even as a mine veined richly with the love of God.

7.2   O ye loved ones of the Lord! This is the hour when ye must associate with all the earth's peoples in extreme kindliness and love, and be to them the signs and tokens of God's great mercy. Ye must become the very soul of the world, the living spirit in the body of the children of men. In this wondrous Age, at this time when the Ancient Beauty, the Most Great Name, bearing unnumbered gifts, hath risen above the horizon of the world, the Word of God hath infused such awesome power into the inmost essence of humankind that He hath stripped men's human qualities of all effect, and hath, with His all-conquering might, unified the peoples in a vast sea of oneness.

7.3   Now is the time for the lovers of God to raise high the banners of unity, to intone, in the assemblages of the world, the verses of friendship and love and to demonstrate to all that the grace of God is one. Thus will the tabernacles of holiness be upraised on the summits of the earth, gathering all peoples into the protective shadow of the Word of Oneness. This great bounty will dawn over the world at the time when the lovers of God shall arise to carry out His Teachings, and to scatter far and wide the fresh, sweet scents of universal love.

In every dispensation, there hath been the com- 7.4
mandment of fellowship and love, but it was a commandment limited to the community of those in mutual agreement, not to the dissident foe. In this wondrous age, however, praised be God, the commandments of God are not delimited, not restricted to any one group of people, rather have all the friends been commanded to show forth fellowship and love, consideration and generosity and loving-kindness to every community on earth. Now must the lovers of God arise to carry out these instructions of His: let them be kindly fathers to the children of the human race, and compassionate brothers to the youth, and self-denying offspring to those bent with years. The meaning of this is that ye must show forth tenderness and love to every human being, even to your enemies, and welcome them all with unalloyed friendship, good cheer, and loving-kindness. When ye meet

with cruelty and persecution at another's hands, keep faith with him; when malevolence is directed your way, respond with a friendly heart. To the spears and arrows rained upon you, expose your breasts for a target mirror-bright; and in return for curses, taunts and wounding words, show forth abounding love. Thus will all peoples witness the power of the Most Great Name, and every nation acknowledge the might of the Ancient Beauty, and see how He hath toppled down the walls of discord, and how surely He hath guided all the peoples of the earth to oneness; how He hath lit man's world, and made this earth of dust to send forth streams of light.

7.5   These human creatures are even as children, they are brash and unconcerned. These children must be reared with infinite, loving care, and tenderly fostered in the embraces of mercy, so that they may taste the spiritual honey-sweetness of God's love; that they may become like unto candles shedding their beams across this darksome world, and may clearly perceive what blazing crowns of glory the Most Great Name, the Ancient Beauty, hath set on the brows of His beloved, what bounties He hath bestowed on the hearts of those He holdeth dear, what a love He hath cast into the breasts of humankind, and what treasures of friendship He hath made to appear amongst all men.

O God, my God! Aid Thou Thy trusted servants to have loving and tender hearts. Help them to spread, amongst all the nations of the earth, the light of guidance that cometh from the Company on high. Verily Thou art the Strong, the Powerful, the Mighty, the All-Subduing, the Ever-Giving. Verily Thou art the Generous, the Gentle, the Tender, the Most Bountiful. 7.6

8. O ye beloved of 'Abdu'l-Bahá and ye handmaids of the Merciful! It is early morning, and the reviving winds of the Abhá Paradise are blowing over all creation, but they can stir only the pure of heart, and only the pure sense can detect their fragrance. Only the perceiving eye beholdeth the rays of the sun; only the listening ear can hear the singing of the Concourse on high. Although the plentiful rains of spring, the bestowals of Heaven, pour down upon all things, they can only fructify good soil; they love not brackish ground, where no results of all the bounty can be shown. 8.1

Today the soft and holy breathings of the Abhá Realm are passing over every land, but only the 8.2

pure in heart draw nigh and derive a benefit therefrom. It is the hope of this wronged soul that from the grace of the Self-Subsistent One and by the manifest power of the Word of God, the heads of the unmindful may be cleared, that they may perceive these sweet savors which blow from secret rosebeds of the spirit.

8.3 O ye friends of God! True friends are even as skilled physicians, and the Teachings of God are as healing balm, a medicine for the conscience of man. They clear the head, so that a man can breathe them in and delight in their sweet fragrance. They waken those who sleep. They bring awareness to the unheeding, and a portion to the outcast, and to the hopeless, hope.

8.4 If in this day a soul shall act according to the precepts and the counsels of God, he will serve as a divine physician to mankind, and like the trump of Isráfíl,* he will call the dead of this contingent world to life; for the confirmations of the Abhá Realm are never interrupted, and such a virtuous soul hath, to befriend him, the unfailing help of the Company on high. Thus shall a sorry gnat be-

---

* Believed to be the angel appointed to sound the trumpet on the Day of Resurrection to raise the dead at the bidding of the Lord.

come an eagle in the fullness of his strength, and a feeble sparrow change to a royal falcon in the heights of ancient glory.

Wherefore, look not on the degree of your ca- 8.5 pacity, ask not if you are worthy of the task: rest ye your hopes on the help and loving-kindness, the favors and bestowals of Bahá'u'lláh—may my soul be offered up for His friends! Urge on the steed of high endeavor over the field of sacrifice, and carry away from this wide arena the prize of divine grace.

O ye handmaids of the merciful Lord! How 8.6 many queens of this world laid down their heads on a pillow of dust and disappeared. No fruit was left of them, no trace, no sign, not even their names. For them, no more granting of bestowals; for them, no more living at all. Not so the handmaids who ministered at the Threshold of God; these have shone forth like glittering stars in the skies of ancient glory, shedding their splendors across all the reaches of time. These have fulfilled their dearest hopes in the Abhá Paradise; they have tasted the honey of reunion in the congregation of the Lord. Such souls as these profited from their existence here on earth: they plucked the fruit of life. As for the rest, "There surely came upon them a time when they were a thing not spoken of."

8.7 O ye lovers of this wronged one! Cleanse ye your eyes, so that ye behold no man as different from yourselves. See ye no strangers; rather see all men as friends, for love and unity come hard when ye fix your gaze on otherness. And in this new and wondrous age, the Holy Writings say that we must be at one with every people; that we must see neither harshness nor injustice, neither malevolence, nor hostility, nor hate, but rather turn our eyes toward the heaven of ancient glory. For each of the creatures is a sign of God, and it was by the grace of the Lord and His power that each did step into the world; therefore they are not strangers, but in the family; not aliens, but friends, and to be treated as such.

8.8 Wherefore must the loved ones of God associate in affectionate fellowship with stranger and friend alike, showing forth to all the utmost loving-kindness, disregarding the degree of their capacity, never asking whether they deserve to be loved. In every instance let the friends be considerate and infinitely kind. Let them never be defeated by the malice of the people, by their aggression and their hate, no matter how intense. If others hurl their darts against you, offer them milk and honey in return; if they poison your lives, sweeten their souls; if they injure you, teach them how to be comforted; if they inflict a wound upon you, be a balm to their sores; if they sting you, hold to their lips a refreshing cup.

O God, my God! These are Thy feeble servants; 8.9 they are Thy loyal bondsmen and Thy handmaidens, who have bowed themselves down before Thine exalted Utterance and humbled themselves at Thy Threshold of light, and borne witness to Thy oneness through which the Sun hath been made to shine in midday splendor. They have listened to the summons Thou didst raise from out Thy hidden Realm, and with hearts quivering with love and rapture, they have responded to Thy call.

O Lord, shower upon them all the outpourings 8.10 of Thy mercy, rain down upon them all the waters of Thy grace. Make them to grow as beauteous plants in the garden of heaven, and from the full and brimming clouds of Thy bestowals and out of the deep pools of Thine abounding grace make Thou this garden to flower and keep it ever green and lustrous, ever fresh and shimmering and fair.

Thou art verily the Mighty, the Exalted, the 8.11 Powerful, He Who alone, in the heavens and on the earth, abideth unchanged. There is none other God save Thee, the Lord of manifest tokens and signs.

9.1   9. O thou whose heart overfloweth with love for the Lord! I address thee from this consecrated spot, to gladden thy bosom with mine epistle to thee, for this is such a letter as maketh the heart of him who believeth in God's oneness to wing its flight toward the summits of bliss.

9.2   Thank thou God for having enabled thee to enter into His Kingdom of might. Erelong will thy Lord's bounties descend upon thee, one following the other, and He will make of thee a sign for every seeker after truth.

9.3   Hold thou fast to the Covenant of thy Lord, and as the days go by, increase thy store of love for His beloved ones. Bend thou with tenderness over the servitors of the All-Merciful, that thou mayest hoist the sail of love upon the ark of peace that moveth across the seas of life. Let nothing grieve thee, and be thou angered at none. It behooveth thee to be content with the Will of God, and a true and loving and trusted friend to all the peoples of the earth, without any exceptions whatever. This is the quality of the sincere, the way of the saints, the emblem of those who believe in the unity of God, and the raiment of the people of Bahá.

9.4   Thank thou and bless thou the Lord for He hath allowed thee to offer Him the Right of God.*

---

* Ḥuqúqu'lláh

This is verily a special favor on His part, for thee; praise Him then for this commandment that is set forth in the Scriptures of thy Lord, of Him that is the Ancient of Days.

Verily is He the Loving, the Tender, the Ever-Bestowing. 9.5

10. O thou dear handmaid of God! Thy letter 10.1 hath been received and its contents noted. Thou didst ask for a rule whereby to guide thy life.

Believe thou in God, and keep thine eyes fixed 10.2 upon the exalted Kingdom; be thou enamored of the Abhá Beauty; stand thou firm in the Covenant; yearn thou to ascend into the Heaven of the Universal Light. Be thou severed from this world, and reborn through the sweet scents of holiness that blow from the realm of the All-Highest. Be thou a summoner to love, and be thou kind to all the human race. Love thou the children of men and share in their sorrows. Be thou of those who foster peace. Offer thy friendship, be worthy of trust. Be thou a balm to every sore, be thou a medicine for every ill. Bind thou the souls together. Recite thou the verses of guidance. Be engaged in the worship of thy Lord, and rise up to lead the people aright. Loose thy tongue and teach, and let thy face be bright with the fire of God's love. Rest thou not for a moment, seek thou to draw no easeful breath.

Thus mayest thou become a sign and symbol of God's love, and a banner of His grace.

11.1   11. Service to the friends is service to the Kingdom of God, and consideration shown to the poor is one of the greatest teachings of God.

12.1   12. Know thou of a certainty that Love is the secret of God's holy Dispensation, the manifestation of the All-Merciful, the fountain of spiritual outpourings. Love is heaven's kindly light, the Holy Spirit's eternal breath that vivifieth the human soul. Love is the cause of God's revelation unto man, the vital bond inherent, in accordance with the divine creation, in the realities of things. Love is the one means that ensureth true felicity both in this world and the next. Love is the light that guideth in darkness, the living link that uniteth God with man, that assureth the progress of every illumined soul. Love is the most great law that ruleth this mighty and heavenly cycle, the unique power that bindeth together the divers elements of this material world, the supreme magnetic force that directeth the movements of the spheres in the celestial realms. Love revealeth with unfailing and limitless power the mysteries latent in the universe. Love is the spirit of life unto the adorned body of mankind, the establisher of true civilization in this mortal world, and the shedder of imperishable glory upon every high-aiming race and nation.

Whatsoever people is graciously favored there- 12.2 with by God, its name shall surely be magnified and extolled by the Concourse from on high, by the company of angels, and the denizens of the Abhá Kingdom. And whatsoever people turneth its heart away from this Divine Love—the revelation of the Merciful—shall err grievously, shall fall into despair, and be utterly destroyed. That people shall be denied all refuge, shall become even as the vilest creatures of the earth, victims of degradation and shame.

O ye beloved of the Lord! Strive to become the 12.3 manifestations of the love of God, the lamps of divine guidance shining amongst the kindreds of the earth with the light of love and concord.

All hail to the revealers of this glorious light! 12.4

13. O thou daughter of the Kingdom! Thy let- 13.1 ter dated 5 December 1918 was received. It contained the good news that the friends of God and the maidservants of the Merciful have gathered in summer at Green Acre, have been engaged day and night in the commemoration of God, have served the oneness of the world of humanity, have shown love to all religions, have remained aloof from

every religious prejudice and have been kind to all people. The divine religions must be the cause of oneness among men, and the means of unity and love; they must promulgate universal peace, free man from every prejudice, bestow joy and gladness, exercise kindness to all men and do away with every difference and distinction. Just as Bahá'u'lláh addressing the world of humanity saith: "O people! Ye are the fruits of one tree and the leaves of one branch." At most it is this, that some souls are ignorant, they must be educated; some are sick, they must be healed; some are still of tender age, they must be helped to attain maturity, and the utmost kindness must be shown to them. This is the conduct of the people of Bahá.

13.2   I hope that thy brothers and sisters will all become the well-wishers of the world of mankind.

14.1   14. O ye two blessed souls! Your letters were received. They showed that ye have investigated the truth and have been freed from imitations and superstitions, that ye observe with your own eyes and not with those of others, hearken with your own ears and not with the ears of others, and discover mysteries with the help of your own consciences and not with those of others. For the imitator saith that such a man hath seen, such a man hath heard, and such a conscience hath discovered; in other words he dependeth upon the sight, the hearing and the conscience of others and hath no will of his own.

Now, praise be to God, ye have shown willpower and have turned to the Sun of Truth. The plain of your hearts hath been illumined by the lights of the Lord of the Kingdom and ye have been led to the straight path, have marched along the road that leadeth to the Kingdom, have entered the Abhá Paradise, and have secured a portion and share of the fruit of the Tree of Life. 14.2

Blessed are ye and a goodly home awaiteth you. Upon you be greetings and praise. 14.3

15. O captive of the love of God! The letter which thou didst write at the time of thy departure hath been received. It brought me joy; and it is my hope that thine inner eye may be opened wide, so that unto thee the very core of the divine mysteries may be disclosed. 15.1

Thou didst begin thy letter with a blessed phrase, saying: "I am a Christian." O would that all were truly Christian! It is easy to be a Christian on the tongue, but hard to be a true one. Today some five hundred million souls are Christian, but the real Christian is very rare: he is that soul from whose 15.2

45

comely face there shineth the splendor of Christ, and who showeth forth the perfections of the Kingdom; this is a matter of great moment, for to be a Christian is to embody every excellence there is. I hope that thou, too, shalt become a true Christian. Praise thou God that at last, through the divine teachings, thou hast obtained both sight and insight to the highest degree, and hast become firmly rooted in certitude and faith. It is my hope that others as well will achieve illumined eyes and hearing ears, and attain to everlasting life: that these many rivers, each flowing along in diverse and separated beds, will find their way back to the circumambient sea, and merge together and rise up in a single wave of surging oneness; that the unity of truth, through the power of God, will make these illusory differences to vanish away. This is the one essential: for if unity be gained, all other problems will disappear of themselves.

15.3   O honored lady! In accordance with the divine teachings in this glorious dispensation we should not belittle anyone and call him ignorant, saying: "You know not, but I know." Rather, we should look upon others with respect, and when attempting to explain and demonstrate, we should speak as if we are investigating the truth, saying: "Here these things are before us. Let us investigate to determine where and in what form the truth can be found." The teacher should not consider himself as learned and others ignorant. Such a thought breedeth pride, and pride is not conducive to influence. The teacher should not see in himself any superiority; he should speak with the utmost kindliness, lowliness and humility, for such speech exerteth influence and educateth the souls.

O honored lady! For a single purpose were the Prophets, each and all, sent down to earth; for this was Christ made manifest, for this did Bahá'u'lláh raise up the call of the Lord: that the world of man should become the world of God, this nether realm the Kingdom, this darkness light, this satanic wickedness all the virtues of heaven—and unity, fellowship and love be won for the whole human race, that the organic unity should reappear and the bases of discord be destroyed and life everlasting and grace everlasting become the harvest of mankind. 15.4

O honored lady! Look about thee at the world: here unity, mutual attraction, gathering together, engender life, but disunity and inharmony spell death. When thou dost consider all phenomena, thou wilt see that every created thing hath come into being through the mingling of many elements, and once this collectivity of elements is dissolved, 15.5

and this harmony of components is dissevered, the life form is wiped out.

15.6   O honored lady! In cycles gone by, though harmony was established, yet, owing to the absence of means, the unity of all mankind could not have been achieved. Continents remained widely divided, nay even among the peoples of one and the same continent association and interchange of thought were wellnigh impossible. Consequently intercourse, understanding and unity amongst all the peoples and kindreds of the earth were unattainable. In this day, however, means of communication have multiplied, and the five continents of the earth have virtually merged into one. And for everyone it is now easy to travel to any land, to associate and exchange views with its peoples, and to become familiar, through publications, with the conditions, the religious beliefs and the thoughts of all men. In like manner all the members of the human family, whether peoples or governments, cities or villages, have become increasingly interdependent. For none is self-sufficiency any longer possible, inasmuch as political ties unite all peoples and nations, and the bonds of trade and industry, of agriculture and education, are being strengthened every day. Hence the unity of all mankind can in this day be achieved. Verily this is none other but one of the wonders of this wondrous age, this glorious century. Of this past ages have been deprived, for this century—the century of light—hath been endowed with unique and unprecedented glory, power and illumination. Hence the miraculous unfolding of a fresh marvel every day. Eventually it will be seen how bright its candles will burn in the assemblage of man.

Behold how its light is now dawning upon the world's darkened horizon. The first candle is unity in the political realm, the early glimmerings of which can now be discerned. The second candle is unity of thought in world undertakings, the consummation of which will erelong be witnessed. The third candle is unity in freedom which will surely come to pass. The fourth candle is unity in religion which is the cornerstone of the foundation itself, and which, by the power of God, will be revealed in all its splendor. The fifth candle is the unity of nations—a unity which in this century will be securely established, causing all the peoples of the world to regard themselves as citizens of one common fatherland. The sixth candle is unity of races, making of all that dwell on earth peoples and kindreds of one race. The seventh candle is unity of language, i.e., the choice of a universal tongue in which all peoples will be instructed and converse. 15.7

Each and every one of these will inevitably come to pass, inasmuch as the power of the Kingdom of God will aid and assist in their realization.

16.1   16. O ye illumined loved ones and ye handmaids of the Merciful! At a time when the somber night of ignorance, of neglect of the divine world, of being veiled from God, had overspread the earth, a bright morning dawned and a rising light lit up the eastern sky. Then rose the Sun of Truth and the splendors of the Kingdom were shed over east and west. Those who had eyes to see rejoiced at the glad tidings and cried out: "O blessed, blessed are we!," and they witnessed the inner reality of all things, and uncovered the mysteries of the Kingdom. Delivered then from their fancies and their doubts, they beheld the light of truth, and so exhilarated did they become from draining the chalice of God's love, that they utterly forgot the world and their own selves. Dancing for joy they hastened to the place of their own martyrdom and there, where men die for love, they flung away their heads and hearts.

16.2   But those with unseeing eyes were astonished at this tumult, and they cried, "Where is the light?" and again, "We see no light! We see no rising sun! Here is no truth. This is but fantasy and nothing more." Bat-like they fled into the underground dark, and there, to their way of thinking, they found a measure of security and peace.

This, however, is but the beginning of the 16.3 dawn, and the heat of the rising Orb of Truth is not yet at the fullness of its power. Once the sun hath mounted to high noon, its fires will burn so hot as to stir even the creeping things beneath the earth; and although it is not for them to behold the light, yet will they all be set in frenzied motion by the impact of the heat.

Wherefore, O ye beloved of God, offer up 16.4 thanks that ye have, in the day of the dawning, turned your faces unto the Light of the World and beheld its splendors. Ye have received a share of the light of truth, ye have enjoyed a portion of those blessings that endure forever; and therefore, as a returning of thanks for this bounty, rest ye not for a moment, sit ye not silent, carry to men's ears the glad tidings of the Kingdom, spread far and wide the Word of God.

Act in accordance with the counsels of the 16.5 Lord: that is, rise up in such wise, and with such qualities, as to endow the body of this world with a living soul, and to bring this young child, humanity, to the stage of adulthood. So far as ye are able, ignite a candle of love in every meeting, and with tenderness rejoice and cheer ye every heart. Care for the stranger as for one of your own; show to alien souls the same loving kindness ye bestow upon your faithful friends. Should any come to blows with you, seek to be friends with him; should any stab you to the heart, be ye a healing salve unto his sores; should any taunt and mock at you, meet him with love. Should any heap his blame upon you, praise ye him; should he offer you a deadly poison, give him the choicest honey in exchange; and should he threaten your life, grant him a remedy that will heal him evermore. Should he be pain itself, be ye his medicine; should he be thorns, be ye his roses and sweet herbs. Perchance such ways and words from you will make this darksome world turn bright at last; will make this dusty earth turn heavenly, this devilish prison place become a royal palace of the Lord—so that war and strife will pass and be no more, and love and trust will pitch their tents on the summits of the world. Such is the essence of God's admonitions; such in sum are the teachings for the Dispensation of Bahá.

17.1   17. O ye who are the chosen ones of the Abhá Kingdom! Praise ye the Lord of Hosts for He, riding upon the clouds, hath come down to this world out of the heaven of the invisible realm, so that East and West were lit by the glory of the Sun of Truth, and the call of the Kingdom was raised, and the heralds of the realm above, with melodies of the Concourse on high, sang out the glad tidings of the Coming. Then the whole world of being did quiver for joy, and still the people, even as the Messiah saith, slept on: for the day of the Manifestation, when the Lord of Hosts descended, found them wrapped in the slumber of unknowing. As He saith in the Gospel, My coming is even as when the thief is in the house, and the goodman of the house watcheth not.

From amongst all mankind hath He chosen 17.2 you, and your eyes have been opened to the light of guidance and your ears attuned to the music of the Company above; and blessed by abounding grace, your hearts and souls have been born into new life. Thank ye and praise ye God that the hand of infinite bestowals hath set upon your heads this gem-studded crown, this crown whose lustrous jewels will forever flash and sparkle down all the reaches of time.

To thank Him for this, make ye a mighty 17.3 effort, and choose for yourselves a noble goal. Through the power of faith, obey ye the teachings of God, and let all your actions conform to His laws. Read ye *The Hidden Words*, ponder the inner meanings thereof, act in accord therewith. Read, with close attention, the Tablets of Ṭarázát (Ornaments), Kalimát (Words of Paradise), Tajallíyyát (Effulgences), Ishráqát (Splendors), and Bishárát (Glad Tidings), and rise up as ye are bidden in the heavenly teachings. Thus may each one of you be even as a candle casting its light, the center of attraction wherever people come together; and from you, as from a bed of flowers, may sweet scents be shed.

17.4   Raise ye a clamor like unto a roaring sea; like a prodigal cloud, rain down the grace of heaven. Lift up your voices and sing out the songs of the Abhá Realm. Quench ye the fires of war, lift high the banners of peace, work for the oneness of humankind and remember that religion is the channel of love unto all peoples. Be ye aware that the children of men are sheep of God and He their loving Shepherd, that He careth tenderly for all His sheep and maketh them to feed in His own green pastures of grace and giveth them to drink from the wellspring of life. Such is the way of the Lord. Such are His bestowals. Such, from among His teachings, is His precept of the oneness of mankind.

17.5   The portals of His blessings are opened wide and His signs are published abroad and the glory of truth is blazing forth; inexhaustible are the blessings. Know ye the value of this time. Strive ye with all your hearts, raise up your voices and shout, until this dark world be filled with light, and this narrow place of shadows be widened out, and this dust heap of a fleeting moment be changed into a mirror for the eternal gardens of heaven, and this globe of earth receive its portion of celestial grace.

Then will aggression crumble away, and all that maketh for disunity be destroyed, and the structure of oneness be raised—that the Blessed Tree may cast its shade over east and west, and the Tabernacle of the singleness of man be set up on the high summits, and flags that betoken love and fellowship flutter from their staffs around the world until the sea of truth lift high its waves, and earth bring forth the roses and sweet herbs of blessings without end, and become from pole to pole the Abhá Paradise.

These are the counsels of 'Abdu'l-Bahá. It is my hope that out of the bestowals of the Lord of Hosts ye will become the spiritual essence and the very radiance of humankind, binding the hearts of all with bonds of love; that through the power of the Word of God ye will bring to life the dead now buried in the graves of their sensual desires; that ye will, with the rays of the Sun of Truth, restore the sight of those whose inner eye is blind; that ye will bring spiritual healing to the spiritually sick. These things do I hope for, out of the bounties and the bestowals of the Beloved.

17.8   At all times do I speak of you and call you to mind. I pray unto the Lord, and with tears I implore Him to rain down all these blessings upon you, and gladden your hearts, and make blissful your souls, and grant you exceeding joy and heavenly delights. . . .

17.9   O Thou loving Provider! These souls have hearkened to the summons of the Kingdom, and have gazed upon the glory of the Sun of Truth. They have risen upward to the refreshing skies of love; they are enamored of Thy nature, and they worship Thy beauty. Unto Thee have they turned themselves, speaking together of Thee, seeking out Thy dwelling, and thirsting for the waterbrooks of Thy heavenly realm.

17.10   Thou art the Giver, the Bestower, the Ever-Loving.

18.1   18. O thou possessor of a seeing heart! Although, materially speaking, thou art deprived of physical sight, yet, praise be to God, spiritual insight is thine. Thy heart seeth and thy spirit heareth. Bodily sight is subject to a thousand maladies and assuredly will ultimately be lost. Thus no importance should be attached to it. But the sight of the heart is illumined. It discerneth and discovereth the divine Kingdom. It is everlasting and eternal. Praise God, therefore, that the sight of thy heart is illumined, and the hearing of thy mind responsive.

Each of the meetings ye have organized, wherein 18.2 ye feel heavenly emotions and comprehend realities and significances, is like unto the firmament, and those souls are as resplendent stars shining with the light of guidance.

Happy is the soul that seeketh, in this brilliant 18.3 era, heavenly teachings, and blessed is the heart which is stirred and attracted by the love of God.

19. Praise be to Him through Whose splendors 19.1 the earth and the heavens are aglow, through Whose fragrant breathings the gardens of holiness that adorn the hearts of the chosen are trembling for joy, to Him Who hath shed His light and brightened the face of the firmament. Verily there appeared luminous and sparkling stars, glittering, shining out, and casting forth their rays upon the supreme horizon. They derived their grace and brilliance from the bounties of the Abhá Realm, then, stars of guidance, they poured down their lights upon this earth.

19.2 Praise be to Him Who hath fashioned this new era, this age of majesty, even as an unfolding pageant where the realities of all things can be exposed to view. Now are clouds of bounty raining down and the gifts of the loving Lord are clearly manifest; for both the seen and the unseen worlds have been illumined, and the Promised One hath come to earth and the beauty of the Adored One hath shone forth.

19.3 Salutations, blessings, and welcome to that Universal Reality, that Perfect Word, that Manifest Book, that Splendor which hath dawned in the highest heaven, that Guide of all nations, that Light of the world—the billowing ocean of Whose abounding grace hath flooded all creation, in such wise that the waves thereof have cast upon the sands of this visible world their shining pearls. Now hath the Truth appeared, and falsehood fled away; now hath the day dawned and jubilation taken over, wherefore men's souls are sanctified, their spirits purged, their hearts rejoiced, their minds purified, their secret thoughts made wholesome, their consciences washed clean, their inmost selves made holy: for the Day of Resurrection hath come to pass, and the bestowals of thy Lord, the Forgiving, have encompassed all things. Salutations and praise be unto those luminous, resplendent stars that are shedding down their rays from the highest heaven, those celestial bodies of the girdling zodiac of the Abhá Realm. May glory rest upon them.

And now, O thou honored man who hath hearkened unto the Great Announcement, rise up to serve the Cause of God with the resistless power of the Abhá Kingdom and the breaths that blow from the spirit of the Company on high. Grieve thou not over what the Pharisees, and the purveyors of false rumors among writers for the press, are saying of Bahá. Call thou to mind the days of Christ, and the afflictions heaped upon Him by the people, and all the torments and tribulations inflicted upon His disciples. Since ye are lovers of the Abhá Beauty, ye also must, for His love's sake, incur the peoples' blame, and all that befell those of a former age must likewise befall you. Then will the faces of the chosen be alight with the splendors of the Kingdom of God, and will shine down the ages, yea, down all the cycles of time, while the deniers shall remain in their manifest loss. It will be even as was said by the Lord Christ: they shall persecute you for My name's sake. 19.4

Remind them of these words and say unto them: "Verily did the Pharisees rise up against Messiah, despite the bright beauty of His face and all His comeliness, and they cried out that He 19.5

was not Messiah [Masíḥ] but a monster [Masíkh], because He had claimed to be Almighty God, the sovereign Lord of all, and told them, 'I am God's Son, and verily in the inmost being of His only Son, His mighty Ward, clearly revealed with all His attributes, all His perfections, standeth the Father.' This, they said, was open blasphemy and slander against the Lord according to the clear and irrefutable texts of the Old Testament. Therefore they passed the sentence upon Him, decreeing that His blood be shed, and they hanged Him on the cross, where He cried out, 'O My beloved Lord, how long wilt Thou abandon Me to them? Lift Me up unto Thee, shelter Me close to Thee, make Me a dwelling by Thy throne of glory. Verily art Thou the Answerer of prayers, and Thou art the Clement, the Merciful. O My Lord! Verily this world with all its vastness can no longer contain Me, and I love this cross, out of love for Thy beauty, and yearning for Thy realm on high, and because of this fire, fanned by the gusts of Thy holiness, aflame within My heart. Help me, O Lord, to ascend unto Thee, sustain Me that I may reach unto Thy sacred Threshold, O My loving Lord! Verily Thou art the Merciful, the Possessor of great bounty! Verily Thou art the Generous! Verily Thou art the Compassionate! Verily Thou art the All-Knowing! There is none other God save Thee, the Mighty, the Powerful!'"

Never would the Pharisees have been emboldened to calumniate Him and charge Him with that grievous sin, but for their ignorance of the inner core of mysteries and the fact that they paid no heed to His splendors and regarded not His proofs. Else would they have acknowledged His words, and borne witness to the verses He revealed, confessed the truth of His utterances, sought shelter under the protective shadow of His banner, learned of His signs and tokens, and rejoiced in His blissful tidings. 19.6

Know thou that the Divine Essence, which is called the Invisible of the Invisibles, never to be described, beyond the reach of mind—is sanctified above any mention, any definition or hint or allusion, any acclamation or praise. In the sense that It is that It is, the intellect can never grasp It, and the soul seeking knowledge of It is but a wanderer in the desert, and far astray. "No vision taketh in Him, but He taketh in all vision: He is the Subtile, the All-Informed."* 19.7

When, however, thou dost contemplate the innermost essence of all things, and the indi- 19.8

---

* Qur'án 6:103

viduality of each, thou wilt behold the signs of thy Lord's mercy in every created thing, and see the spreading rays of His Names and Attributes throughout all the realm of being, with evidences which none will deny save the froward and the unaware. Then wilt thou observe that the universe is a scroll that discloseth His hidden secrets, which are preserved in the well-guarded Tablet. And not an atom of all the atoms in existence, not a creature from amongst the creatures but speaketh His praise and telleth of His attributes and names, revealeth the glory of His might and guideth to His oneness and His mercy: and none will gainsay this who hath ears to hear, eyes to see, and a mind that is sound.

19.9 And whensoever thou dost gaze upon creation all entire, and dost observe the very atoms thereof, thou wilt note that the rays of the Sun of Truth are shed upon all things and shining within them, and telling of that Daystar's splendors, Its mysteries, and the spreading of Its lights. Look thou upon the trees, upon the blossoms and fruits, even upon the stones. Here too wilt thou behold the Sun's rays shed upon them, clearly visible within them, and manifested by them.

19.10 Shouldst thou, however, turn thy gaze unto a Mirror, brilliant, stainless, and pure, wherein the divine Beauty is reflected, therein wilt thou find the Sun shining with Its rays, Its heat, Its disc, Its fair form all entire. For each separate entity possesseth its allotted portion of the solar light and telleth of the Sun, but that Universal Reality in all Its splendor, that stainless Mirror Whose qualities are appropriate to the qualities of the Sun revealed within It—expresseth in their entirety the attributes of the Source of Glory. And that Universal Reality is Man, the divine Being, the Essence that abideth forever. "Say, Call upon God, or call upon the All-Merciful; whichsoever ye call upon, most beauteous are His Names."*

This is the meaning of the Messiah's words, that the Father is in the Son.† Dost thou not see that should a stainless mirror proclaim, "Verily is the sun ashine within me, together with all its qualities, tokens and signs," such an utterance by such a mirror would be neither deceptive nor false? No, by the One Who created It, shaped It, fashioned It, and made It to be an entity conformable to the attributes of the glory within It! Praised be He Who created It! Praised be He Who fashioned It! Praised be He Who made It manifest!

19.11

---

* Qur'án 17:110
† John 14:11

19.12   Such were the words uttered by Christ. On account of these words they cavilled at and assailed Him when He said unto them, "Verily the Son is in the Father, and the Father is in the Son."* Be thou informed of this, and learn thou the secrets of thy Lord. As for the deniers, they are veiled from God: they see not, they hear not, neither do they understand. "Leave them to entertain themselves with their cavillings."† Abandon them to their wanderings along river beds where no stream flows. Like grazing beasts they cannot tell paste from pearl. Are they not shut away from the mysteries of thy Lord, the Clement, the Merciful?

19.13   For thy part, rejoice at this best of all glad tidings, and rise up to exalt the Word of God and to spread abroad His sweet savors in all that vast and mighty land. Know thou of a certainty that thy Lord will come to thine aid with a company of the Concourse on high and hosts of the Abhá Kingdom. These will mount the attack, and will furiously assail the forces of the ignorant, the blind. Erelong wilt thou behold the flush of daybreak spreading from out the Most Exalted Realm, and the morn encompassing all regions. It will put the dark to flight, and the gloom

---

* John 14:10
† Qur'án 6:91

of night will fade and pass, and the bright brow of the Faith shine forth, and the Daystar rise and overspread the world. On that day will the faithful rejoice, and the steadfast be blissful; then will the slanderers take themselves off, and the waverers be blotted out, even as deepest shadows fall away at the first light of the breaking dawn.

Greetings be unto thee, and praise.   19.14

O God, my God! This is Thy radiant servant,   19.15
Thy spiritual thrall, who hath drawn nigh unto Thee and approached Thy presence. He hath turned his face unto Thine, acknowledging Thy oneness, confessing Thy singleness, and he hath called out in Thy name among the nations, and led the people to the streaming waters of Thy mercy, O Thou Most generous Lord! To those who asked he hath given to drink from the cup of guidance that brimmeth over with the wine of Thy measureless grace.

O Lord, assist him under all conditions,   19.16
cause him to learn Thy well-guarded mysteries, and shower down upon him Thy hidden pearls. Make of him a banner rippling from castle summits in the winds of Thy heavenly aid, make of him a wellspring of crystal waters.

O my forgiving Lord! Light up the hearts   19.17
with the rays of a lamp that sheddeth abroad its

beams, disclosing to those among Thy people whom Thou hast bounteously favored, the realities of all things.

19.18 Verily, Thou art the Mighty, the Powerful, the Protector, the Strong, the Beneficent! Verily, Thou art the Lord of all mercies!

20.1 20.* When Christ appeared, twenty centuries ago, although the Jews were eagerly awaiting His Coming, and prayed every day, with tears, saying: "O God, hasten the Revelation of the Messiah," yet when the Sun of Truth dawned, they denied Him and rose against Him with the greatest enmity, and eventually crucified that divine Spirit, the Word of God, and named Him Beelzebub, the evil one, as is recorded in the Gospel. The reason for this was that they said: "The Revelation of Christ, according to the clear text of the Torah, will be attested by certain signs, and so long as these signs have not appeared, whoso layeth claim to be a Messiah is an impostor. Among these signs is this, that the Messiah should come from an unknown place, yet we all know this man's house in Nazareth, and can any good thing come out of Nazareth? The second

---

* Written especially for Dr. Esslemont's immortal work *Bahá'u'lláh and the New Era*.

sign is that He shall rule with a rod of iron, that is, He must act with the sword, but this Messiah has not even a wooden staff. Another of the conditions and signs is this: He must sit upon the throne of David and establish David's sovereignty. Now, far from being enthroned, this man has not even a mat to sit on. Another of the conditions is this: the promulgation of all the laws of the Torah; yet this man has abrogated these laws, and has even broken the sabbath day, although it is the clear text of the Torah that whosoever layeth claim to prophethood and revealeth miracles and breaketh the sabbath day, must be put to death. Another of the signs is this, that in His reign justice will be so advanced that righteousness and well-doing will extend from the human even to the animal world—the snake and the mouse will share one hole, and the eagle and the partridge one nest, the lion and the gazelle shall dwell in one pasture, and the wolf and the kid shall drink from one fountain. Yet now, injustice and tyranny have waxed so great in His time that they have crucified Him! Another of the conditions is this, that in the days of the Messiah the Jews will prosper and triumph over all the peoples of the world, but now they are living in the utmost abasement and servitude in the empire of the Romans. Then how can this be the Messiah promised in the Torah?"

20.2   In this wise did they object to that Sun of Truth, although that Spirit of God was indeed the One promised in the Torah. But as they did not understand the meaning of these signs, they crucified the Word of God. Now the Bahá'ís hold that the recorded signs did come to pass in the Manifestation of Christ, although not in the sense which the Jews understood, the description in the Torah being allegorical. For instance, among the signs is that of sovereignty. For Bahá'ís say that the sovereignty of Christ was a heavenly, divine, everlasting sovereignty, not a Napoleonic sovereignty that vanisheth in a short time. For well nigh two thousand years this sovereignty of Christ hath been established, and until now it endureth, and to all eternity that Holy Being will be exalted upon an everlasting throne.

20.3   In like manner all the other signs have been made manifest, but the Jews did not understand. Although nearly twenty centuries have elapsed since Christ appeared with divine splendor, yet the Jews are still awaiting the coming of the Messiah and regard themselves as true and Christ as false.

21.1   21. O thou distinguished personage, thou seeker after truth! Thy letter of 4 April 1921 hath been read with love.

The existence of the Divine Being hath been 21.2
clearly established, on the basis of logical proofs,
but the reality of the Godhead is beyond the grasp
of the mind. When thou dost carefully consider
this matter, thou wilt see that a lower plane can
never comprehend a higher. The mineral kingdom, for example, which is lower, is precluded
from comprehending the vegetable kingdom; for
the mineral, any such understanding would be
utterly impossible. In the same way, no matter
how far the vegetable kingdom may develop, it
will achieve no conception of the animal kingdom, and any such comprehension at its level
would be unthinkable, for the animal occupieth
a plane higher than that of the vegetable: this
tree cannot conceive of hearing and sight. And
the animal kingdom, no matter how far it may
evolve, can never become aware of the reality of
the intellect, which discovereth the inner essence
of all things, and comprehendeth those realities
which cannot be seen; for the human plane as
compared with that of the animal is very high.
And although these beings all coexist in the contingent world, in each case the difference in their
stations precludeth their grasp of the whole; for
no lower degree can understand a higher, such
comprehension being impossible.

21.3   The higher plane, however, understandeth the lower. The animal, for instance, comprehendeth the mineral and vegetable, the human understandeth the planes of the animal, vegetable and mineral. But the mineral cannot possibly understand the realms of man. And notwithstanding the fact that all these entities coexist in the phenomenal world, even so, no lower degree can ever comprehend a higher.

21.4   Then how could it be possible for a contingent reality, that is, man, to understand the nature of that preexistent Essence, the Divine Being? The difference in station between man and the Divine Reality is thousands upon thousands of times greater than the difference between vegetable and animal. And that which a human being would conjure up in his mind is but the fanciful image of his human condition, it doth not encompass God's reality but rather is encompassed by it. That is, man graspeth his own illusory conceptions, but the Reality of Divinity can never be grasped: It, Itself, encompasseth all created things, and all created things are in Its grasp. That Divinity which man doth imagine for himself existeth only in his mind, not in truth. Man, however, existeth both in his mind and in truth; thus man is greater than that fanciful reality which he is able to imagine.

The furthermost limits of this bird of clay are 21.5
these: he can flutter along for some short distance,
into the endless vast; but he can never soar upward
to the Sun in the high heavens. We must, nevertheless, set forth reasoned or inspired proofs as to
the existence of the Divine Being, that is, proofs
commensurate with the understanding of man.

It is obvious that all created things are con- 21.6
nected one to another by a linkage complete and
perfect, even, for example, as are the members of
the human body. Note how all the members and
component parts of the human body are connected one to another. In the same way, all the
members of this endless universe are linked one
to another. The foot and the step, for example,
are connected to the ear and the eye; the eye must
look ahead before the step is taken. The ear must
hear before the eye will carefully observe. And
whatever member of the human body is deficient,
produceth a deficiency in the other members. The
brain is connected with the heart and stomach,
the lungs are connected with all the members. So
is it with the other members of the body.

And each one of these members hath its own 21.7
special function. The mind force—whether we
call it preexistent or contingent—doth direct and
coordinate all the members of the human body,

seeing to it that each part or member duly performeth its own special function. If, however, there be some interruption in the power of the mind, all the members will fail to carry out their essential functions, deficiencies will appear in the body and the functioning of its members, and the power will prove ineffective.

21.8 Likewise, look into this endless universe: a universal power inevitably existeth, which encompasseth all, directing and regulating all the parts of this infinite creation; and were it not for this Director, this Coordinator, the universe would be flawed and deficient. It would be even as a madman; whereas ye can see that this endless creation carrieth out its functions in perfect order, every separate part of it performing its own task with complete reliability, nor is there any flaw to be found in all its workings. Thus it is clear that a Universal Power existeth, directing and regulating this infinite universe. Every rational mind can grasp this fact.

21.9 Furthermore, although all created things grow and develop, yet are they subjected to influences from without. For instance, the sun giveth heat, the rain nourisheth, the wind bringeth life, so that man can develop and grow. Thus it is clear that the human body is under influences from the outside, and that without those influences man could not grow. And likewise, those outside influences are subjected to other influences in their turn. For example, the growth and development of a human being is dependent upon the existence of water, and water is dependent upon the existence of rain, and rain is dependent upon the existence of clouds, and clouds are dependent upon the existence of the sun, which causeth land and sea to produce vapor, the condensation of vapor forming the clouds. Thus each one of these entities exerteth its influence and is likewise influenced in its turn. Inescapably then, the process leadeth to One Who influenceth all, and yet is influenced by none, thus severing the chain. The inner reality of that Being, however, is not known, although His effects are clear and evident.

And further, all created beings are limited, and this very limitation of all beings proveth the reality of the Limitless; for the existence of a limited being denoteth the existence of a Limitless One.

21.10

To sum it up, there are many such proofs, establishing the existence of that Universal Reality. And since that Reality is preexistent, It is untouched by the conditions that govern phenomena; for whatever entity is subject to circumstances and the play

21.11

of events is contingent, not preexistent. Know then: that divinity which other communions and peoples have conjured up, falleth within the scope of their imagination, and not beyond it, whereas the reality of the Godhead is beyond all conceiving.

21.12   As to the Holy Manifestations of God, They are the focal points where the signs, tokens and perfections of that sacred, preexistent Reality appear in all their splendor. They are an eternal grace, a heavenly glory, and on Them dependeth the everlasting life of humankind. To illustrate: the Sun of Truth dwelleth in a sky to which no soul hath any access, and which no mind can reach, and He is far beyond the comprehension of all creatures. Yet the Holy Manifestations of God are even as a looking glass, burnished and without stain, which gathereth streams of light out of that Sun, and then scattereth the glory over the rest of creation. In that polished surface, the Sun with all Its majesty standeth clearly revealed. Thus, should the mirrored Sun proclaim, "I am the Sun!" this is but truth; and should It cry, "I am not the Sun!" this is the truth as well. And although the Daystar, with all Its glory, Its beauty, Its perfections, be clearly visible in that mirror without stain, still It hath not come down from Its own lofty station in the realms above, It hath not made Its way into the mirror; rather doth It continue to abide, as It will forever, in the supernal heights of Its own holiness.

And further, all the earth's creatures require 21.13 the bounty of the sun, for their very existence is dependent upon solar light and heat. Should they be deprived of the sun, they would be wiped out. This is the being with God, as referred to in the Holy Books: man must be with his Lord.

It is clear, then, that the essential reality of God 21.14 is revealed in His perfections; and the sun, with its perfections, reflected in a mirror, is a visible thing, an entity clearly expressing the bounty of God.

My hope is that thou wilt acquire a percep- 21.15 tive eye, a hearing ear, and that the veils will be removed from thy sight.

22. O thou who art turning thy face towards 22.1 God! Close thine eyes to all things else, and open them to the realm of the All-Glorious. Ask whatsoever thou wishest of Him alone; seek whatsoever thou seekest from Him alone. With a look He granteth a hundred thousand hopes, with a glance He healeth a hundred thousand incurable ills, with a nod He layeth balm on every wound, with a glimpse He freeth the hearts from the shackles

of grief. He doeth as He doeth, and what recourse have we? He carrieth out His Will, He ordaineth what He pleaseth. Then better for thee to bow down thy head in submission, and put thy trust in the All-Merciful Lord.

23.1 23. O thou who dost search after truth! Thy letter of 13 December 1920 hath come.

23.2 From the days of Adam until today, the religions of God have been made manifest, one following the other, and each one of them fulfilled its due function, revived mankind, and provided education and enlightenment. They freed the people from the darkness of the world of nature and ushered them into the brightness of the Kingdom. As each succeeding Faith and Law became revealed it remained for some centuries a richly fruitful tree and to it was committed the happiness of humankind. However, as the centuries rolled by, it aged, it flourished no more and put forth no fruit, wherefore was it then made young again.

23.3 The religion of God is one religion, but it must ever be renewed. Moses, for example, was sent forth to man and He established a Law, and the Children of Israel, through that Mosaic Law, were delivered out of their ignorance and came into the light; they were lifted up from their abjectness and attained to a glory that fadeth not. Still, as the long years wore on, that radiance passed by, that splendor set, that bright day turned to night; and once that night grew triply dark, the star of the Messiah dawned, so that again a glory lit the world.

23.4 Our meaning is this: the religion of God is one, and it is the educator of humankind, but still, it needs must be made new. When thou dost plant a tree, its height increaseth day by day. It putteth forth blossoms and leaves and luscious fruits. But after a long time, it doth grow old, yielding no fruitage any more. Then doth the Husbandman of Truth take up the seed from that same tree, and plant it in a pure soil; and lo, there standeth the first tree, even as it was before.

23.5 Note thou carefully that in this world of being, all things must ever be made new. Look at the material world about thee, see how it hath now been renewed. The thoughts have changed, the ways of life have been revised, the sciences and arts show a new vigor, discoveries and inventions are new, perceptions are new. How then could such a vital power as religion—the guarantor of mankind's great advances, the very means of attaining everlasting life, the fosterer of infinite excellence, the light of both worlds—not be made new?

This would be incompatible with the grace and loving-kindness of the Lord.

23.6   Religion, moreover, is not a series of beliefs, a set of customs; religion is the teachings of the Lord God, teachings which constitute the very life of humankind, which urge high thoughts upon the mind, refine the character, and lay the groundwork for man's everlasting honor.

23.7   Note thou: could these fevers in the world of the mind, these fires of war and hate, of resentment and malice among the nations, this aggression of peoples against peoples, which have destroyed the tranquillity of the whole world ever be made to abate, except through the living waters of the teachings of God? No, never!

23.8   And this is clear: a power above and beyond the powers of nature must needs be brought to bear, to change this black darkness into light, and these hatreds and resentments, grudges and spites, these endless wrangles and wars, into fellowship and love amongst all the peoples of the earth. This power is none other than the breathings of the Holy Spirit and the mighty inflow of the Word of God.

24.1   24. O spiritual youth! Praise thou God that thou hast found thy way into the Kingdom of Splendors, and hast rent asunder the veil of vain imaginings, and that the core of the inner mystery hath been made known unto thee.

This people, all of them, have pictured a god 24.2 in the realm of the mind, and worship that image which they have made for themselves. And yet that image is comprehended, the human mind being the comprehender thereof, and certainly the comprehender is greater than that which lieth within its grasp; for imagination is but the branch, while mind is the root; and certainly the root is greater than the branch. Consider then, how all the peoples of the world are bowing the knee to a fancy of their own contriving, how they have created a creator within their own minds, and they call it the Fashioner of all that is—whereas in truth it is but an illusion. Thus are the people worshipping only an error of perception.

But that Essence of Essences, that Invisible of 24.3 Invisibles, is sanctified above all human speculation, and never to be overtaken by the mind of man. Never shall that immemorial Reality lodge within the compass of a contingent being. His is another realm, and of that realm no understanding can be won. No access can be gained thereto; all entry is forbidden there. The utmost one can say is that Its existence can be proved, but the conditions of Its existence are unknown.

24.4   That such an Essence doth exist, the philosophers and learned doctors one and all have understood; but whenever they tried to learn something of Its being, they were left bewildered and dismayed, and at the end, despairing, their hopes in ruins, they went their way, out of this life. For to comprehend the state and the inner mystery of that Essence of Essences, that Most Secret of Secrets, one needs must have another power and other faculties; and such a power, such faculties would be more than humankind can bear, wherefore no word of Him can come to them.

24.5   If, for example, one be endowed with the senses of hearing, of taste, of smell, of touch—but be deprived of the sense of sight, it will not be possible for one to gaze about; for sight cannot be realized through hearing or tasting, or the sense of smell or touch. In the same way, with the faculties at man's disposal it is beyond the realm of possibility for him to grasp that unseeable Reality, holy and sanctified above all the skeptics' doubts. For this, other faculties are required, other senses; should such powers become available to him, then could a human being receive some knowledge of that world; otherwise, never.

25.1   25. O thou handmaid of God! It is recorded in eastern histories that Socrates journeyed to Palestine and Syria and there, from men learned in the things of God, acquired certain spiritual truths; that when he returned to Greece, he promulgated two beliefs: one, the unity of God, and the other, the immortality of the soul after its separation from the body; that these concepts, so foreign to their thought, raised a great commotion among the Greeks, until in the end they gave him poison and killed him.

And this is authentic; for the Greeks believed in 25.2 many gods, and Socrates established the fact that God is one, which obviously was in conflict with Greek beliefs.

The Founder of monotheism was Abraham; it 25.3 is to Him that this concept can be traced, and the belief was current among the Children of Israel, even in the days of Socrates.

The above, however, cannot be found in the 25.4 Jewish histories; there are many facts which are not included in Jewish history. Not all the events of the life of Christ are set forth in the history of Josephus, a Jew, although it was he who wrote the history of the times of Christ. One may not, therefore, refuse to believe in events of Christ's day on the grounds that they are not to be found in the history of Josephus.

Eastern histories also state that Hippocrates so- 25.5 journed for a long time in the town of Tyre, and this is a city in Syria.

26.1   26. O thou who seekest the Kingdom of Heaven! Thy letter hath been received and its contents noted.

26.2   The Holy Manifestations of God possess two stations: one is the physical station, and one the spiritual. In other words, one station is that of a human being, and one, of the Divine Reality. If the Manifestations are subjected to tests, it is in Their human station only, not in the splendor of Their Divine Reality.

26.3   And further, these tests are such only from the viewpoint of mankind. That is, to outward seeming, the human condition of the Holy Manifestations is subjected to tests, and when Their strength and endurance have by this means been revealed in the plenitude of power, other men receive instruction therefrom, and are made aware of how great must be their own steadfastness and endurance under tests and trials. For the Divine Educator must teach by word and also by deed, thus revealing to all the straight pathway of truth.

26.4   As to my station, it is that of the servant of Bahá; 'Abdu'l-Bahá, the visible expression of servitude to the Threshold of the Abhá Beauty.

27.1   27. In cycles gone by, each one of the Manifestations of God hath had His own rank in the world of existence, and each hath represented a stage in the development of humanity. But the Manifestation of the Most Great Name—may my life be a sacrifice for His loved ones—was an expression of the coming of age, the maturing of man's inmost reality in this world of being. For the sun is the source and wellspring of light and heat, the focal point of splendors, and it compriseth all the perfections that are made manifest by the other stars which have dawned upon the world. Make thou an effort that thou mayest take thy place under the sun and receive an abundant share of its dazzling light. In truth do I tell thee, once thou hast attained this station, thou shalt behold the saints bowing down their heads in all humility before Him. Haste thou to life before death cometh; haste thou to the spring season before autumn draweth in; and before illness striketh, haste thou to healing—that thou mayest become a physician of the spirit who, with the breaths of the Holy Spirit, healeth all manner of sickness in this famed and glorious age.

28. O leaf upon the Tree of Life! The Tree of Life, of which mention is made in the Bible, is Bahá'u'lláh, and the daughters of the Kingdom are the leaves upon that blessed Tree. Then thank thou   28.1

God that thou hast become related to that Tree, and that thou art flourishing, tender and fresh.

28.2 The gates of the Kingdom are opened wide, and every favored soul is seated at the banquet table of the Lord, receiving his portion of that heavenly feast. Praised be God, thou too art present at this table, taking thy share of the bountiful food of heaven. Thou art serving the Kingdom, and art well acquainted with the sweet savors of the Abhá Paradise.

28.3 Then strive thou with all thy might to guide the people, and eat thou of the bread that hath come down from heaven. For this is the meaning of Christ's words: "I am the living bread which came down from heaven . . . he that eateth of this bread shall live forever."*

29.1 29. O thou who art captivated by the truth and magnetized by the Heavenly Kingdom! Thy long letter hath come and it brought great joy, as it clearly betokened thy strenuous efforts and high purposes. Praised be God, thou wishest well to men, and yearnest after the Kingdom of Bahá, and art longing to see the human race press forward. It is my hope that because of these high ideals, these

---

* John 6:51, 58

noble intimations of the heart, and these tidings of heaven, thou shalt become so luminous that down all the ages the light of thy love for God will shed its glory.

Thou hast described thyself as a student in the school of spiritual progress. Fortunate art thou! If these schools of progress lead to the university of heaven, then branches of knowledge will be developed whereby humanity will look upon the tablet of existence as a scroll endlessly unfolding; and all created things will be seen upon that scroll as letters and words. Then will the different planes of meaning be learned, and then within every atom of the universe will be witnessed the signs of the oneness of God. Then will man hear the cry of the Lord of the Kingdom, and behold the confirmations of the Holy Spirit coming to succor him. Then will he feel such bliss, such ecstasy, that the wide world with its vastness will no longer contain him, and he will set out for the Kingdom of God, and hurry along to the realm of the spirit. For once a bird hath grown its wings, it remaineth on the ground no more, but soareth upward into high heaven— except for those birds that are tied by the leg, or those whose wings are broken, or mired down. 29.2

O thou seeker after truth! The world of the Kingdom is one world. The only difference is that 29.3

spring returneth over and over again, and setteth up a great new commotion throughout all created things. Then plain and hillside come alive, and trees turn delicately green, and leaves, blossoms and fruits come forth in beauty, infinite and tender. Wherefore the dispensations of past ages are intimately connected with those that follow them: indeed, they are one and the same, but as the world groweth, so doth the light, so doth the downpour of heavenly grace, and then the Daystar shineth out in noonday splendor.

29.4 O thou seeker after the Kingdom! Every divine Manifestation is the very life of the world, and the skilled physician of each ailing soul. The world of man is sick, and that competent Physician knoweth the cure, arising as He doth with teachings, counsels and admonishments that are the remedy for every pain, the healing balm to every wound. It is certain that the wise physician can diagnose his patient's needs at any season, and apply the cure. Wherefore, relate thou the Teachings of the Abhá Beauty to the urgent needs of this present day, and thou wilt see that they provide an instant remedy for the ailing body of the world. Indeed, they are the elixir that bringeth eternal health.

29.5 The treatment ordered by wise physicians of the past, and by those that follow after, is not one and the same, rather doth it depend on what aileth the patient; and although the remedy may change, the aim is always to bring the patient back to health. In the dispensations gone before, the feeble body of the world could not withstand a rigorous or powerful cure. For this reason did Christ say: "I have yet many things to say unto you, matters needing to be told, but ye cannot bear to hear them now. Howbeit when that Comforting Spirit, Whom the Father will send, shall come, He will make plain unto you the truth."*

Therefore, in this age of splendors, teachings once limited to the few are made available to all, that the mercy of the Lord may embrace both east and west, that the oneness of the world of humanity may appear in its full beauty, and that the dazzling rays of reality may flood the realm of the mind with light.   29.6

The descent of the New Jerusalem denoteth a heavenly Law, that Law which is the guarantor of human happiness and the effulgence of the world of God.   29.7

Emmanuel† was indeed the Herald of the Second Coming of Christ, and a Summoner to the   29.8

---

* cf. John 15:26; 16:12–13

† Regarding this Tablet Shoghi Effendi's secretary wrote on his behalf, 9 May 1938, ". . . this obviously refers to the Báb, as the text shows clearly, and is in no way a reference to Swedenborg."

pathway of the Kingdom. It is evident that the Letter is a member of the Word, and this membership in the Word signifieth that the Letter is dependent for its value on the Word, that is, it deriveth its grace from the Word; it has a spiritual kinship with the Word, and is accounted an integral part of the Word. The Apostles were even as Letters, and Christ was the essence of the Word Itself; and the meaning of the Word, which is grace everlasting, cast a splendor on those Letters. Again, since the Letter is a member of the Word, it therefore, in its inner meaning, is consonant with the Word.

29.9 It is our hope that thou wilt in this day arise to promote that which Emmanuel foretold. Know thou for a certainty that thou wilt succeed in this, for the confirmations of the Holy Spirit are continually descending, and the power of the Word will exert such an influence that the Letter shall become the mirror in which the splendid Sun—the Word Itself—will be reflected, and the grace and glory of the Word will illumine the whole earth.

29.10 As for the heavenly Jerusalem that hath come to rest on the summits of the world, and God's Holy of Holies, Whose banner is now lifted high, this comprehendeth within itself all the perfections, all the knowledge of the dispensations gone before. Beyond this, it heraldeth the oneness of the children of men. It is the flag of universal peace, the spirit of eternal life; it is the glory of the perfections of God, the circumambient grace of all existence, the ornament bedecking all created things, the source of inner quietude for all humankind.

Direct thine attention to the holy Tablets; 29.11 read thou the Ishráqát, Tajallíyyát, the Words of Paradise, the Glad Tidings, the Ṭarázát, the Most Holy Book. Then wilt thou see that today these heavenly Teachings are the remedy for a sick and suffering world, and a healing balm for the sores on the body of mankind. They are the spirit of life, the ark of salvation, the magnet to draw down eternal glory, the dynamic power to motivate the inner self of man.

30. Existence is of two kinds: one is the exis- 30.1 tence of God which is beyond the comprehension of man. He, the invisible, the lofty and the incomprehensible, is preceded by no cause but rather is the Originator of the cause of causes. He, the Ancient, hath had no beginning and is the all-independent. The second kind of existence is the human existence. It is a common existence, comprehensible to the human mind, is not ancient, is dependent and hath a cause to it. The mortal substance does not become eternal and vice

versa; the human kind does not become a Creator and vice versa. The transformation of the innate substance is impossible.

30.2 In the world of existence—that which is comprehensible—there are stages of mortality: the first stage is the mineral world, next is the vegetable world. In the latter world the mineral doth exist but with a distinctive feature which is the vegetable characteristic. Likewise in the animal world, the mineral and vegetable characteristics are present and in addition the characteristics of the animal world are to be found, which are the faculties of hearing and of sight. In the human world the characteristics of the mineral, vegetable and animal worlds are found and in addition that of the human kind, namely the intellectual characteristic, which discovereth the realities of things and comprehendeth universal principles.

30.3 Man, therefore, on the plane of the contingent world is the most perfect being. By man is meant the perfect individual, who is like unto a mirror in which the divine perfections are manifested and reflected. But the sun doth not descend from the height of its sanctity to enter into the mirror, but when the latter is purified and turned towards the Sun of Truth, the perfections of this Sun, consisting of light and heat, are reflected and manifested in that mirror. These souls are the Divine Manifestations of God.

31. O thou who art dear, and wise! Thy letter 31.1
dated 27 May 1906 hath been received and its contents are most pleasing and have brought great joy.

Thou didst ask whether this Cause, this new 31.2
and living Cause, could take the place of the dead
religious rites and ceremonials of England; whether it would be possible, now that various groups
have appeared, whose members are highly placed
divines and theologians, far superior in their attainments to those of the past, for this new Cause so to
impress the members of such groups as to gather
them and the rest into its all-protecting shade.

O thou dear friend! Know thou that the distin- 31.3
guished Individual of every age is endowed according to the perfections of His age. That Individual
who in past ages was set above His fellows was gifted
according to the virtues of His time. But in this age
of splendors, this era of God, the preeminent Personage, the luminous Orb, the chosen Individual
will shine out with such perfections and such power
as ultimately to dazzle the minds of every community and group. And since such a Personage is superior
to all others in spiritual perfections and heavenly attainments, and is indeed the focal center of divine

blessings and the pivot of the circle of light, He will encompass all others, and there is no doubt whatsoever that He will shine out with such power as to gather every soul into His sheltering shade.

31.4   When ye consider this matter with care, it will become apparent that this is according to a universal law, which one can find at work in all things: the whole attracteth the part, and in the circle, the center is the pivot of the compasses. Ponder thou upon the Spirit*: because He was the focal center of spiritual power, the wellspring of divine bounties, although at the beginning He gathered unto Himself only a very few souls, later on He was able, because of that all-subduing power that He had, to unite within the sheltering Tabernacle of Christendom all the differing sects. Compare the present with the past, and see how great is the difference; thus canst thou arrive at truth and certitude.

31.5   The differences among the religions of the world are due to the varying types of minds. So long as the powers of the mind are various, it is certain that men's judgments and opinions will differ one from another. If, however, one single, universal perceptive power be introduced—a power encompassing all the rest—those differing opinions will

* Jesus

merge, and a spiritual harmony and oneness will become apparent. For example, when the Christ was made manifest, the minds of the various contemporary peoples, their views, their emotional attitudes, whether they were Romans, Greeks, Syrians, Israelites, or others, were at variance with one another. But once His universal power was brought to bear, it gradually succeeded, after the lapse of three hundred years, in gathering together all those divergent minds under the protection, and within the governance, of one central Point, all sharing the same spiritual emotions in their hearts.

To use a metaphor, when an army is placed under various commanders, each with his own strategy, they will obviously differ as to battle lines and movements of the troops; but once the Supreme Commander, who is thoroughly versed in the arts of war, taketh over, those other plans will disappear, for the supremely gifted general will bring the whole army under his control. This is intended only as a metaphor, not an exact comparison. Now if you should say that each and every one of those other generals is highly skilled in the military art, is thoroughly proficient and experienced, and therefore will not subject himself to the rule of one individual, no matter how indescribably great, your statement is untenable, for the above situation is 31.6

demonstrably what cometh to pass, and there is no doubt thereof whatever.

31.7 Such is the case with the holy Manifestations of God. Such in particular is the case with the divine reality of the Most Great Name, the Abhá Beauty. When once He standeth revealed unto the assembled peoples of the world and appeareth with such comeliness, such enchantments—alluring as a Joseph in the Egypt of the spirit—He enslaveth all the lovers on earth.

31.8 As to those souls who are born into this life as ethereal and radiant entities and yet, on account of their handicaps and trials, are deprived of great and real advantages, and leave the world without having lived to the full—certainly this is a cause for grieving. This is the reason why the universal Manifestations of God unveil Their countenances to man, and endure every calamity and sore affliction, and lay down Their lives as a ransom; it is to make these very people, the ready ones, the ones who have capacity, to become dawning points of light, and to bestow upon them the life that fadeth never. This is the true sacrifice: the offering of oneself, even as did Christ, as a ransom for the life of the world.

31.9 As to the influence of holy Beings and the continuance of Their grace to mankind after They have put away Their human form, this is, to Bahá'ís, an indisputable fact. Indeed, the flooding grace, the streaming splendors of the holy Manifestations appear after Their ascension from this world. The exaltation of the Word, the revelation of the power of God, the conversion of God-fearing souls, the bestowal of everlasting life—it was following the Messiah's martyrdom that all these were increased and intensified. In the same way, ever since the ascension of the Blessed Beauty, the bestowals have been more abundant, the spreading light is brighter, the tokens of the Lord's might are more powerful, the influence of the Word is much stronger, and it will not be long before the motion, the heat, the brilliance, the blessings of the Sun of His reality will encompass all the earth.

Grieve thou not over the slow advance of the 31.10 Bahá'í Cause in that land. This is but the early dawn. Consider how, with the Cause of Christ, three hundred years had to go by, before its great influence was made manifest. Today, not sixty years from its birth, the light of this Faith hath been shed around the planet.

Regarding the health society of which thou art 31.11 a member, once it cometh under the shelter of this Faith its influence shall increase a hundredfold.

Thou dost observe that love among the Bahá'ís 31.12 is very great, and that love is the main thing. Just as love's power hath been developed to such a high degree among the Bahá'ís, and is far greater than among the people of other religions, so is it with all else as well; for love is the ground of all things.

31.13 Regarding the translation of the Books and Tablets of the Blessed Beauty, erelong will translations be made into every tongue, with power, clarity and grace. At such time as they are translated, conformably to the originals, and with power and grace of style, the splendors of their inner meanings will be shed abroad, and will illumine the eyes of all mankind. Do thy very best to ensure that the translation is in conformity with the original.

31.14 The Blessed Beauty proceeded to Haifa on many occasions. Thou beheldest Him there, but thou didst not know Him at that time. It is my hope that thou wilt attain unto the true meeting with Him, which is to behold Him with the inner, not the outer eye.

31.15 The essence of Bahá'u'lláh's Teaching is all-embracing love, for love includeth every excellence of humankind. It causeth every soul to go forward. It bestoweth on each one, for a heritage, immortal life. Erelong shalt thou bear witness that His celestial Teachings, the very glory of reality itself, shall light up the skies of the world.

31.16 The brief prayer which thou didst write at the close of thy letter was indeed original, touching and beautiful. Recite thou this prayer at all times.

32. O ye handmaids of the Lord! In this century—the century of the Almighty Lord—the Daystar of the Realms above, the Light of Truth, shineth in its meridian splendor and its rays illuminate all regions. For this is the age of the Ancient Beauty, the day of the revelation of the might and power of the Most Great Name—may my life be offered up as a sacrifice for His loved ones. 32.1

In the ages to come, though the Cause of God may rise and grow a hundredfold and the shade of the Sadratu'l-Muntahá shelter all mankind, yet this present century shall stand unrivalled, for it hath witnessed the breaking of that Morn and the rising of that Sun. This century is, verily, the source of His Light and the dayspring of His Revelation. Future ages and generations shall behold the diffusion of its radiance and the manifestations of its signs. 32.2

Wherefore, exert yourselves, haply ye may obtain your full share and portion of His bestowals. 32.3

33. O servant of God! We have noted what thou didst write to Jináb-i-Ibn-Abhar, and thy question regarding the verse: "Whoso layeth claim to a Revelation direct from God, ere the expiration of a full thousand years, such a man is assuredly a lying impostor." 33.1

The meaning of this is that any individual who, before the expiry of a full thousand years—years 33.2

known and clearly established by common usage and requiring no interpretation—should lay claim to a Revelation direct from God, even though he should reveal certain signs, that man is assuredly false and an impostor.

33.3 This is not a reference to the Universal Manifestation, for it is clearly set forth in the Holy Writings that centuries, nay thousands of years, must pass on to completion, before a Manifestation like unto this Manifestation shall appear again.

33.4 It is possible, however, that after the completion of a full thousand years, certain Holy Beings will be empowered to deliver a Revelation: this, however, will not be through a Universal Manifestation. Wherefore every day of the cycle of the Blessed Beauty is in reality equal to one year, and every year of it is equal to a thousand years.

33.5 Consider, for example, the sun: its transit from one zodiacal sign to the next occurreth within a short period of time, yet only after a long period doth it attain the plenitude of its resplendency, its heat and glory, in the sign of Leo. It must first complete one full revolution through the other constellations before it will enter the sign of Leo again, to blaze out in its full splendor. In its other stations, it revealeth not the fullness of its heat and light.

The substance is, that prior to the completion 33.6
of a thousand years, no individual may presume to
breathe a word. All must consider themselves to be
of the order of subjects, submissive and obedient
to the commandments of God and the laws of the
House of Justice. Should any deviate by so much
as a needle's point from the decrees of the Universal House of Justice, or falter in his compliance
therewith, then is he of the outcast and rejected.

As to the cycle of the Blessed Beauty—the 33.7
times of the Greatest Name—this is not limited
to a thousand or two thousand years. . . .

When it is said that the period of a thousand 33.8
years beginneth with the Manifestation of the
Blessed Beauty and every day thereof is a thousand
years, the intent is a reference to the cycle of the
Blessed Beauty, which in this context will extend
over many ages into the unborn reaches of time.

34. O thou who art serving the world of hu- 34.1
manity! Thy letter was received and from its
contents we felt exceedingly glad. It was a decisive
proof and a brilliant evidence. It is appropriate
and befitting that in this illumined age—the age
of the progress of the world of humanity—we
should be self-sacrificing and should serve the
human race. Every universal cause is divine and

every particular one is temporal. The principles of the divine Manifestations of God were, therefore, all-universal and all-inclusive.

34.2 Every imperfect soul is self-centered and thinketh only of his own good. But as his thoughts expand a little he will begin to think of the welfare and comfort of his family. If his ideas still more widen, his concern will be the felicity of his fellow citizens; and if still they widen, he will be thinking of the glory of his land and of his race. But when ideas and views reach the utmost degree of expansion and attain the stage of perfection, then will he be interested in the exaltation of humankind. He will then be the well-wisher of all men and the seeker of the weal and prosperity of all lands. This is indicative of perfection.

34.3 Thus, the divine Manifestations of God had a universal and all-inclusive conception. They endeavored for the sake of everyone's life and engaged in the service of universal education. The area of their aims was not limited—nay, rather, it was wide and all-inclusive.

34.4 Therefore, ye must also be thinking of everyone, so that mankind may be educated, character moderated and this world may turn into a Garden of Eden.

34.5 Love ye all religions and all races with a love that is true and sincere and show that love through deeds and not through the tongue; for the latter hath no importance, as the majority of men are, in speech, well-wishers, while action is the best.

35. O army of God! A letter signed jointly by all of you hath been received. It was most eloquent and full of flavor, and reading it was a delight. 35.1

Ye had written of the fasting month. Fortunate are ye to have obeyed the commandment of God, and kept this fast during the holy season. For this material fast is an outer token of the spiritual fast; it is a symbol of self-restraint, the withholding of oneself from all appetites of the self, taking on the characteristics of the spirit, being carried away by the breathings of heaven and catching fire from the love of God. 35.2

Your letter also betokened your unity and the closeness of your hearts. It is my hope that the west, through the boundless grace that God is pouring down in this new era, will become the east, the dawning-point of the Sun of Truth, and western believers the daysprings of light, and manifestors of the signs of God; that they will be guarded from the doubts of the heedless and will stay firm and unmovable in the Covenant and Testament; that they will toil by day and by night until they awaken those who sleep, and make mindful those who are 35.3

unaware, and bring in the outcast to be intimates of the inner circle, and bestow upon the destitute their portion of eternal grace. Let them be heralds of the Kingdom, and call out to the denizens of this nether world, and summon them to enter the realm on high.

35.4 O army of God! Today, in this world, every people is wandering astray in its own desert, moving here and there according to the dictates of its fancies and whims, pursuing its own particular caprice. Amongst all the teeming masses of the earth, only this community of the Most Great Name is free and clear of human schemes and hath no selfish purpose to promote. Alone amongst them all, this people hath arisen with aims purified of self, following the Teachings of God, most eagerly toiling and striving toward a single goal: to turn this nether dust into high heaven, to make of this world a mirror for the Kingdom, to change this world into a different world, and cause all humankind to adopt the ways of righteousness and a new manner of life.

35.5 O army of God! Through the protection and help vouchsafed by the Blessed Beauty—may my life be a sacrifice to His loved ones—ye must conduct yourselves in such a manner that ye may stand out distinguished and brilliant as the sun among other souls. Should any one of you enter a city, he should become a center of attraction by reason of his sincerity, his faithfulness and love, his honesty and fidelity, his truthfulness and loving-kindness towards all the peoples of the world, so that the people of that city may cry out and say: "This man is unquestionably a Bahá'í, for his manners, his behavior, his conduct, his morals, his nature, and disposition reflect the attributes of the Bahá'ís." Not until ye attain this station can ye be said to have been faithful to the Covenant and Testament of God. For He hath, through irrefutable Texts, entered into a binding Covenant with us all, requiring us to act in accordance with His sacred instructions and counsels.

O army of God! The time hath come for the 35.6 effects and perfections of the Most Great Name to be made manifest in this excellent age, so as to establish, beyond any doubt, that this era is the era of Bahá'u'lláh, and this age is distinguished above all other ages.

O army of God! Whensoever ye behold a per- 35.7 son whose entire attention is directed toward the Cause of God; whose only aim is this, to make the Word of God to take effect; who, day and night, with pure intent, is rendering service to the Cause; from whose behavior not the slightest trace of egotism or private motives is discerned—who, rather, wandereth distracted in the wilderness of the love of God, and drinketh only from the cup of the knowledge of God, and is utterly engrossed in spreading the sweet savors of God, and is enamored of the holy verses of the Kingdom of God—know ye for a certainty that this individual will be supported and reinforced by heaven; that like unto the morning star, he will forever gleam brightly out of the skies of eternal grace. But if he show the slightest taint of selfish desires and self love, his efforts will lead to nothing and he will be destroyed and left hopeless at the last.

35.8   O army of God! Praise be to God, Bahá'u'lláh hath lifted the chains from off the necks of humankind, and hath set man free from all that trammeled him, and told him: Ye are the fruits of one tree and the leaves of one branch; be ye compassionate and kind to all the human race. Deal ye with strangers the same as with friends, cherish ye others just as ye would your own. See foes as friends; see demons as angels; give to the tyrant the same great love ye show the loyal and true, and even as gazelles from the scented cities of Khatá and Khutan* offer up sweet musk to the ravening

---

* Cities in China celebrated for their musk-producing animals.

wolf. Be ye a refuge to the fearful; bring ye rest and peace to the disturbed; make ye a provision for the destitute; be a treasury of riches for the poor; be a healing medicine for those who suffer pain; be ye doctor and nurse to the ailing; promote ye friendship, and honor, and conciliation, and devotion to God, in this world of nonexistence.

O army of God! Make ye a mighty effort: per- 35.9 chance ye can flood this earth with light, that this mud hut, the world, may become the Abhá Paradise. The dark hath taken over, and the brute traits prevail. This world of man is now an arena for wild beasts, a field where the ignorant, the heedless, seize their chance. The souls of men are ravening wolves and animals with blinded eyes, they are either deadly poison or useless weeds—all except for a very few who indeed do nurture altruistic aims and plans for the well-being of their fellow men: but ye must in this matter—that is, the serving of humankind—lay down your very lives, and as ye yield yourselves, rejoice.

O army of God! The Exalted One, the Báb, gave 35.10 up His life. The Blessed Perfection gave up a hundred lives at every breath. He bore calamities. He suffered anguish. He was imprisoned. He was chained. He was made homeless and was banished to distant lands. Finally, then, He lived out His days in the

Most Great Prison. Likewise, a great multitude of the lovers of God who followed this path have tasted the honey of martyrdom and they gave up everything—life, possessions, kindred—all they had. How many homes were reduced to rubble; how many dwellings were broken into and pillaged; how many a noble building went to the ground; how many a palace was battered into a tomb. And all this came about that humankind might be illumined, that ignorance might yield to knowledge, that men of earth might become men of heaven, that discord and dissension might be torn out by the roots, and the Kingdom of Peace become established over all the world. Strive ye now that this bounty become manifest, and this best-beloved of all hopes be realized in splendor throughout the community of man.

35.11   O army of God! Beware lest ye harm any soul, or make any heart to sorrow; lest ye wound any man with your words, be he known to you or a stranger, be he friend or foe. Pray ye for all; ask ye that all be blessed, all be forgiven. Beware, beware, lest any of you seek vengeance, even against one who is thirsting for your blood. Beware, beware, lest ye offend the feelings of another, even though he be an evildoer, and he wish you ill. Look ye not upon the creatures, turn ye to their Creator.

See ye not the never-yielding people, see but the Lord of Hosts. Gaze ye not down upon the dust, gaze upward at the shining sun, which hath caused every patch of darksome earth to glow with light.

O army of God! When calamity striketh, 35.12 be ye patient and composed. However afflictive your sufferings may be, stay ye undisturbed, and with perfect confidence in the abounding grace of God, brave ye the tempest of tribulations and fiery ordeals.

Last year a number of the unfaithful, both from 35.13 within and from without, both known to us and strangers, took before the Sulṭán of Turkey slanderous charges against these homeless exiles, bringing against us grave accusations with no basis in fact. The Government, conformably with prudence, determined to look into these charges, and dispatched a Commission of Investigation to this city. It is obvious what an opportunity this afforded our ill-wishers, and what a storm they unleashed, all this beyond description by tongue or pen. Only one who witnessed it could know what a turmoil they created and what an earthquake of anguish was the result. And notwithstanding this, the response was to depend utterly upon God, and to remain composed, confident, long-suffering, undisturbed, to such a degree that a person knowing nothing of the situation would have thought us easy of heart and mind, perfectly happy, thriving and at peace.

35.14 Then it came about that the accusers themselves, those who had made the defamatory charges against us, joined with the members of the Commission to investigate the accusations, so that plaintiffs, witnesses and judge were all one and the same, and the conclusion was foregone. Nevertheless, to be fair, it must be stated that up to now His Majesty the Sulṭán of Turkey hath paid no heed to these false charges, this defamation, these fables and traducements, and hath acted with justice. . . .

35.15 O Thou Provider! Thou hast breathed over the friends in the West the sweet fragrance of the Holy Spirit, and with the light of divine guidance Thou hast lit up the western sky. Thou hast made those who were once remote to draw near unto Thyself; Thou hast turned strangers into loving friends; Thou hast awakened those who slept; Thou hast made the heedless mindful.

35.16 O Thou Provider! Assist Thou these noble friends to win Thy good pleasure, and make them well-wishers of stranger and friend alike. Bring them into the world that abideth forever; grant them a portion of heavenly grace; cause them to be true Bahá'ís, sincerely of God; save them from outward semblances, and establish them firmly in the truth. Make them signs and tokens of the Kingdom, luminous stars above the horizons of this nether life. Make them to be a comfort and a solace to humankind and servants to the peace of the world. Exhilarate them with the wine of Thy counsel, and grant that all of them may tread the path of Thy commandments.

O Thou Provider! The dearest wish of this 35.17 servant of Thy Threshold is to behold the friends of east and west in close embrace; to see all the members of human society gathered with love in a single great assemblage, even as individual drops of water collected in one mighty sea; to behold them all as birds in one garden of roses, as pearls of one ocean, as leaves of one tree, as rays of one sun.

Thou art the Mighty, the Powerful, and Thou art 35.18 the God of strength, the Omnipotent, the All-Seeing.

36. O ye two favored handmaids of the Lord! 36.1 The letter from Mother Beecher hath been received, and truly it spoke for you both, wherefore I address the two of you together. This seemeth very good to me, for ye two pure beings are even as a single precious gem, ye are two boughs branched from a single tree; ye both adore the same Beloved, ye both are longing for the same resplendent Sun.

36.2 My hope is that all the handmaids of God in that region will unite like unto the waves of one unending sea; for although blown about as the wind listeth, these are separate in themselves, yet in truth are they all at one with the boundless deep.

36.3 How good it is if the friends be as close as sheaves of light, if they stand together side by side in a firm unbroken line. For now have the rays of reality from the Sun of the world of existence, united in adoration all the worshippers of this light; and these rays have, through infinite grace, gathered all peoples together within this wide-spreading shelter; therefore must all souls become as one soul, and all hearts as one heart. Let all be set free from the multiple identities that were born of passion and desire, and in the oneness of their love for God find a new way of life.

36.4 O ye two handmaids of God! Now is the time for you to become as bounteous cups that are filled to overflowing, and even as the reviving gusts that blow from the Abhá Paradise, to scatter the fragrance of musk across that land. Release yourselves from this world's life, and at every stage long ye for nonexistence; for when the ray returneth to the sun, it is wiped out, and when the drop cometh to the sea, it vanisheth, and when the true lover findeth his Beloved, he yieldeth up his soul.

Until a being setteth his foot in the plane of 36.5
sacrifice, he is bereft of every favor and grace; and
this plane of sacrifice is the realm of dying to the
self, that the radiance of the living God may then
shine forth. The martyr's field is the place of detachment from self, that the anthems of eternity
may be upraised. Do all ye can to become wholly
weary of self, and bind yourselves to that Countenance of Splendors; and once ye have reached such
heights of servitude, ye will find, gathered within
your shadow, all created things. This is boundless
grace; this is the highest sovereignty; this is the life
that dieth not. All else save this is at the last but
manifest perdition and great loss.

Praise be to God, the gate of boundless grace is 36.6
opened wide, the heavenly table is set, the servants
of the Merciful and His handmaids are present at
the feast. Strive ye to receive your share of this eternal food, so that ye shall be loved and cherished in
this world and the next.

37. O ye dear friends of 'Abdu'l-Bahá! A blessed 37.1
letter hath been received from you, telling of the
election of a Spiritual Assembly. It hath rejoiced
my heart to know that, God be praised, the friends
in that area, with absolute unity, fellowship and
love, have held this new election and were suc-

cessful in voting for souls who are sanctified, are favored at the Holy Threshold and are well known amongst the friends to be staunch and firm in the Covenant.

37.2 Now must those elected representatives arise to serve with spirituality and joy, with purity of intent, with strong attraction to the fragrances of the Almighty, and well supported by the Holy Spirit. Let them raise up the banner of guidance, and as soldiers of the Company on high, let them exalt God's Word, spread abroad His sweet savors, educate the souls of men, and promote the Most Great Peace.

37.3 Truly, blessed souls have been elected. The moment I read their names, I felt a thrill of spiritual joy to know that, praised be God, persons have been raised up in that country who are servants of the Kingdom, and ready to lay down their lives for Him Who hath neither likeness nor peer.

37.4 O ye dear friends of mine! Light up this Assembly with the splendor of God's love. Make it ring out with the joyous music of the hallowed spheres, make it thrive on those foods that are served at the Lord's Supper, at the heavenly banquet table of God. Come ye together in gladness unalloyed, and at the beginning of the meeting, recite ye this prayer:

O Thou Lord of the Kingdom! Though our 37.5 bodies be gathered here together, yet our spell-bound hearts are carried away by Thy love, and yet are we transported by the rays of Thy resplendent face. Weak though we be, we await the revelations of Thy might and power. Poor though we be, with neither goods nor means, still take we riches from the treasures of Thy Kingdom. Drops though we be, still do we draw from out Thy ocean deeps. Motes though we be, still do we gleam in the glory of Thy splendid Sun.

O Thou our Provider! Send down Thine 37.6 aid, that each one gathered here may become a lighted candle, each one a center of attraction, each one a summoner to Thy heavenly realms, till at last we make this nether world the mirror image of Thy Paradise.

O ye dear friends of mine! It is incumbent upon 37.7 the assemblies of those regions to be connected one with another and to correspond with one another, and also to communicate with the assemblies of the east, thus to become agencies for union throughout the world.

O ye spiritual friends! Such must be your constancy 37.8 that should the evil-wishers put every believer to death and only one remain, that one, singly and alone, will withstand all the peoples of the earth, and will go on scattering far and wide the sweet and holy fragrances of God. Wherefore, should any fearsome news, any word of terrifying events, reach you from the Holy Land, see to it that ye waver not, be ye not stricken by grief, be ye not shaken. Rather, rise ye up instantly, with iron resolve, and serve ye the Kingdom of God.

37.9 This Servant of the Lord's Threshold hath been in peril at all times. He is in peril now. At no time have I had any hope of safety, and my dearest wish is this: to drink of the martyr's bounteous and brimful cup, and die on the field of sacrifice, delighting in that wine which is the most precious of God's gifts. This is my highest hope, this my most vehement desire.

37.10 We hear that the Tablets of Ishráqát (Splendors), Ṭarázát (Ornaments), Bishárát (Glad Tidings), Tajallíyyát (Effulgences), and Kalimát (Words of Paradise) have been translated and published in those regions. In these Tablets will ye have a model of how to be and how to live.

38.1 38. O handmaid of God, who tremblest even as a fresh and tender branch in the winds of the love of God! I have read thy letter, which telleth of thine abundant love, thine intense devotion, and of thy being occupied with the remembrance of thy Lord.

Depend thou upon God. Forsake thine own   38.2
will and cling to His, set aside thine own desires
and lay hold of His, that thou mayest become
an example, holy, spiritual, and of the Kingdom,
unto His handmaids.

Know thou, O handmaid, that in the sight of   38.3
Bahá, women are accounted the same as men, and
God hath created all humankind in His own image, and after His own likeness. That is, men and
women alike are the revealers of His names and attributes, and from the spiritual viewpoint there is
no difference between them. Whosoever draweth
nearer to God, that one is the most favored,
whether man or woman. How many a handmaid,
ardent and devoted, hath, within the sheltering
shade of Bahá, proved superior to the men, and
surpassed the famous of the earth.

The House of Justice, however, according to   38.4
the explicit text of the Law of God, is confined to
men; this for a wisdom of the Lord God's, which
will erelong be made manifest as clearly as the sun
at high noon.

As to you, O ye other handmaids who are en-   38.5
amored of the heavenly fragrances, arrange ye holy
gatherings, and found ye Spiritual Assemblies, for
these are the basis for spreading the sweet savors of
God, exalting His Word, uplifting the lamp of His
grace, promulgating His religion and promoting

His Teachings, and what bounty is there greater than this? These Spiritual Assemblies are aided by the Spirit of God. Their defender is 'Abdu'l-Bahá. Over them He spreadeth His wings. What bounty is there greater than this? These Spiritual Assemblies are shining lamps and heavenly gardens, from which the fragrances of holiness are diffused over all regions, and the lights of knowledge are shed abroad over all created things. From them the spirit of life streameth in every direction. They, indeed, are the potent sources of the progress of man, at all times and under all conditions. What bounty is there greater than this?

39.1   39. O handmaid of God! Thy letter hath been received, bringing its news that an Assembly hath been established in that city.

39.2   Look ye not upon the fewness of thy numbers, rather, seek ye out hearts that are pure. One consecrated soul is preferable to a thousand other souls. If a small number of people gather lovingly together, with absolute purity and sanctity, with their hearts free of the world, experiencing the emotions of the Kingdom and the powerful magnetic forces of the Divine, and being at one in their happy fellowship, that gathering will exert its influence over all the earth. The nature of that band of people, the words they speak, the deeds they do, will unleash the bestowals of Heaven, and provide a foretaste of eternal bliss. The hosts of the Company on high will defend them, and the angels of the Abhá Paradise, in continuous succession, will come down to their aid.

The meaning of "angels" is the confirmations of God and His celestial powers. Likewise angels are blessed beings who have severed all ties with this nether world, have been released from the chains of self and the desires of the flesh, and anchored their hearts to the heavenly realms of the Lord. These are of the Kingdom, heavenly; these are of God, spiritual; these are revealers of God's abounding grace; these are dawning-points of His spiritual bestowals. 39.3

O handmaid of God! Praise be to Him, thy dear husband hath perceived the sweet scents that blow from the gardens of heaven. Now, as day followeth day, must thou, through the love of God, and thine own good actions, draw him ever closer to the Faith. 39.4

Those were indeed dire events in San Francisco.* Disasters of this kind should serve to awaken the people, and diminish the love of their hearts for 39.5

---

* The earthquake of 1906

this inconstant world. It is in this nether world that such tragic things take place: this is the cup that yieldeth bitter wine.

40.1   40. O ye whom 'Abdu'l-Bahá loveth! I have read your reports with great joy; they are of a nature to cheer and refresh the heart and gladden the soul. If this Assembly, through the holy breathings of the All-Merciful and His divine confirmations, endure and remain fixed and firm, it shall produce notable results and it shall succeed in enterprises of great moment.

40.2   The Spiritual Assemblies to be established in this Age of God, this holy century, have, it is indisputable, had neither peer nor likeness in the cycles gone before. For those assemblages that wielded power were based on the support of mighty leaders of men, while these Assemblies are based on the support of the Beauty of Abhá. The defenders and patrons of those other assemblages were either a prince, or a king, or a chief priest, or the mass of the people. But these Spiritual Assemblies have for their defender, their supporter, their helper, their inspirer, the omnipotent Lord.

40.3   Look ye not upon the present, fix your gaze upon the times to come. In the beginning, how small is the seed, yet in the end it is a mighty tree. Look ye not upon the seed, look ye upon the tree, and its blossoms, and its leaves and its fruits. Consider the days of Christ, when none but a small band followed Him; then observe what a mighty tree that seed became, behold ye its fruitage. And now shall come to pass even greater things than these, for this is the summons of the Lord of Hosts, this is the trumpet-call of the living Lord, this is the anthem of world peace, this is the standard of righteousness and trust and understanding raised up among all the variegated peoples of the globe; this is the splendor of the Sun of Truth, this is the holiness of the spirit of God Himself. This most powerful of dispensations will encompass all the earth, and beneath its banner will all peoples gather and be sheltered together. Know then the vital import of this tiny seed that the true Husbandman hath, with the hands of His mercy, sown in the ploughed fields of the Lord, and watered with the rain of bestowals and bounties and is now nurturing in the heat and light of the Daystar of Truth.

Wherefore, O ye loved ones of God, offer up 40.4 thanks unto Him, since He hath made you the object of such bounties, and the recipients of such gifts. Blessed are ye, glad tidings to you, for this abounding grace.

41.1   41. O thou who art steadfast in the Covenant, and staunch! The letter which thou didst write . . . hath been shown to me, and the opinions expressed therein were most commendable. It is incumbent upon the Spiritual Consultative Assembly of New York to be in complete agreement with that of Chicago, and for these two assemblies of consultation jointly to approve whatever they consider suitable for publication and distribution. Following that, let them send one copy to 'Akká, so that it may also be approved from here, after which the material will be returned to be published and circulated.

41.2   The question of coordinating and unifying the two Spiritual Assemblies, that of Chicago and of New York, is of the utmost importance, and once a Spiritual Assembly is duly formed in Washington, these two Assemblies should also establish ties of unity with that Assembly. To sum it up, it is the desire of the Lord God that the loved ones of God and the handmaids of the Merciful in the West should come closer together in harmony and unity as day followeth day, and until this is accomplished, the work will never go forward. The Spiritual Assemblies are collectively the most effective of all instruments for establishing unity and harmony. This matter is of the utmost importance; this is the magnet that draweth down the confirmations of God. If once the beauty of the unity of the friends—this Divine Beloved—be decked in the adornments of the Abhá Kingdom, it is certain that within a very short time those countries will become the Paradise of the All-Glorious, and that out of the west the splendors of unity will cast their bright rays over all the earth.

We are striving with heart and soul, resting neither day nor night, seeking not a moment's ease, to make this world of man the mirror of the unity of God. Then how much more must the beloved of the Lord reflect that unity? And this cherished hope, this yearning wish of ours will be visibly fulfilled only on the day when the true friends of God arise to carry out the Teachings of the Abhá Beauty—may my life be a ransom for His lovers! One amongst His Teachings is this, that love and good faith must so dominate the human heart that men will regard the stranger as a familiar friend, the malefactor as one of their own, the alien even as a loved one, the enemy as a companion dear and close. Who killeth them, him will they call a bestower of life; who turneth away from them, him will they regard as turning towards them; who denieth their message, him will they consider as one acknowledging its truth. The meaning is that they must treat all humankind even as they treat their sympathizers, their fellow-believers, their loved ones and familiar friends.

41.4   Should such a torch light up the world community, ye will find that the whole earth is sending forth a fragrance, that it hath become a delightsome paradise, and the face of it the image of high heaven. Then will the whole world be one native land, its diverse peoples one single kind, the nations of both east and west one household.

41.5   It is my hope that such a day will come, that such a splendor will shine forth, that such a vision will be unveiled in its full beauty.

42.1   42. O ye coworkers who are supported by armies from the realm of the All-Glorious! Blessed are ye, for ye have come together in the sheltering shade of the Word of God, and have found a refuge in the cave of His Covenant; ye have brought peace to your hearts by making your home in the Abhá Paradise, and are lulled by the gentle winds that blow from their source in His loving-kindness; ye have arisen to serve the Cause of God and to spread His religion far and wide, to promote His Word and to raise high the banners of holiness throughout all those regions.

42.2   By the life of Bahá! Verily will the consummate power of the Divine Reality breathe into you the bounties of the Holy Spirit, and aid you to perform an exploit whose like the eye of creation hath never looked upon.

O ye League of the Covenant! Verily the Abhá 42.3 Beauty made a promise to the beloved who are steadfast in the Covenant, that He would reinforce their strivings with the strongest of supports, and succor them with His triumphant might. Erelong shall ye see that your illumined assemblage hath left conspicuous signs and tokens in the hearts and souls of men. Hold ye fast to the hem of God's garment, and direct all your efforts toward furthering His Covenant, and burning ever more brightly with the fire of His love, that your hearts may leap for joy in the breathings of servitude which well out from the breast of 'Abdu'l-Bahá. Rally your hearts, make firm your steps, trust in the everlasting bounties that will be shed upon you, one following another from the Kingdom of Abhá. Whensoever ye gather in that radiant assemblage, know ye that the splendors of Bahá are shining over you. It behooveth you to seek agreement and to be united; it behooveth you to be in close communion one with the other, at one both in body and soul, till ye match the Pleiades or a string of lustrous pearls. Thus will ye be solidly established; thus will your words prevail, your star shine out, and your hearts be comforted. . . .

42.4   Whenever ye enter the council-chamber, recite this prayer with a heart throbbing with the love of God and a tongue purified from all but His remembrance, that the All-Powerful may graciously aid you to achieve supreme victory:

42.5   O God, my God! We are servants of Thine that have turned with devotion to Thy Holy Face, that have detached ourselves from all besides Thee in this glorious Day. We have gathered in this Spiritual Assembly, united in our views and thoughts, with our purposes harmonized to exalt Thy Word amidst mankind. O Lord, our God! Make us the signs of Thy Divine Guidance, the Standards of Thine exalted Faith amongst men, servants to Thy mighty Covenant, O Thou our Lord Most High, manifestations of Thy Divine Unity in Thine Abhá Kingdom, and resplendent stars shining upon all regions. Lord! Aid us to become seas surging with the billows of Thy wondrous Grace, streams flowing from Thine all-glorious Heights, goodly fruits upon the Tree of Thy heavenly Cause, trees waving through the breezes of Thy Bounty in Thy celestial Vineyard. O God! Make our souls dependent upon the Verses of Thy Divine Unity, our hearts cheered with the outpourings of Thy Grace, that we may unite even as the waves of one sea and become merged together as the rays of Thine effulgent Light; that our thoughts, our views, our feelings may become as one reality, manifesting the spirit of union throughout the world. Thou art the Gracious, the Bountiful, the Bestower, the Almighty, the Merciful, the Compassionate.

43. The prime requisites for them that take counsel together are purity of motive, radiance of spirit, detachment from all else save God, attraction to His Divine Fragrances, humility and lowliness amongst His loved ones, patience and long-suffering in difficulties and servitude to His exalted Threshold. Should they be graciously aided to acquire these attributes, victory from the unseen Kingdom of Bahá shall be vouchsafed to them. 43.1

44. The members thereof* must take counsel together in such wise that no occasion for ill-feeling or discord may arise. This can be attained when every member expresseth with absolute freedom his own opinion and setteth forth his argument. Should anyone oppose, he must on no account feel hurt for not until matters are fully discussed 44.1

_____

* Of a Spiritual Assembly

can the right way be revealed. The shining spark of truth cometh forth only after the clash of differing opinions. If after discussion, a decision be carried unanimously well and good; but if, the Lord forbid, differences of opinion should arise, a majority of voices must prevail.

45.1   45. The first condition is absolute love and harmony amongst the members of the assembly. They must be wholly free from estrangement and must manifest in themselves the Unity of God, for they are the waves of one sea, the drops of one river, the stars of one heaven, the rays of one sun, the trees of one orchard, the flowers of one garden. Should harmony of thought and absolute unity be nonexistent, that gathering shall be dispersed and that assembly be brought to naught. The second condition is that the members of the assembly should unitedly elect a chairman and lay down guidelines and bylaws for their meetings and discussions. The chairman should have charge of such rules and regulations and protect and enforce them; the other members should be submissive, and refrain from conversing on superfluous and extraneous matters. They must, when coming together, turn their faces to the Kingdom on high and ask aid from the Realm of Glory. They must then proceed with the utmost devotion, courtesy, dignity, care and moderation to express their views. They must in every matter search out the truth and not insist upon their own opinion, for stubbornness and persistence in one's views will lead ultimately to discord and wrangling and the truth will remain hidden. The honored members must with all freedom express their own thoughts, and it is in no wise permissible for one to belittle the thought of another, nay, he must with moderation set forth the truth, and should differences of opinion arise a majority of voices must prevail, and all must obey and submit to the majority. It is again not permitted that any one of the honored members object to or censure, whether in or out of the meeting, any decision arrived at previously, though that decision be not right, for such criticism would prevent any decision from being enforced. In short, whatsoever thing is arranged in harmony and with love and purity of motive, its result is light, and should the least trace of estrangement prevail the result shall be darkness upon darkness. . . . If this be so regarded, that assembly shall be of God, but otherwise it shall lead to coolness and alienation that proceed from the Evil One. . . . Should they endeavor to fulfill these conditions the Grace of the Holy Spirit shall be vouchsafed unto them, and that assembly shall become the center of the Divine blessings, the hosts of Divine confirmation shall come to their aid, and they shall day by day receive a new effusion of Spirit.

46.1   46. O ye who are firm in the Covenant! 'Abdu'l-Bahá is constantly engaged in ideal communication with any Spiritual Assembly which is instituted through the divine bounty, and the members of which, in the utmost devotion, turn to the divine Kingdom and are firm in the Covenant. To them he is wholeheartedly attached and with them he is linked by everlasting ties. Thus correspondence with that gathering is sincere, constant and uninterrupted.

46.2   At every instant, I beg for you assistance, bounty, and a fresh favor and blessing, so that the confirmations of Bahá'u'lláh may, like unto the sea, be constantly surging, the lights of the Sun of Truth may shine upon you all and that ye may be confirmed in service, may become the manifestations of bounty and that each one of you may, at dawn, turn unto the Holy Land and may experience spiritual emotions with all intensity.

47.1   47. O ye true friends! Your letter hath been received and it brought great joy. God be praised, ye had made ready an entertainment and established the feast which is to be held every nineteen days.

Whatsoever gathering is arranged with the utmost love, and where those who attend are turning their faces toward the Kingdom of God, and where the discourse is of the Teachings of God, and the effect of which is to cause those present to advance— that gathering is the Lord's, and that festive table hath come down from heaven.

It is my hope that this feast will be given on one day out of every nineteen, for it bringeth you closer together; it is the very wellspring of unity and loving-kindness.   47.2

Ye observe to what a degree the world is in continual turmoil and conflict, and to what a pass its nations have now come. Perchance will the lovers of God succeed in upraising the banner of human unity, so that the one-colored tabernacle of the Kingdom of Heaven will cast its sheltering shadow over all the earth; that misunderstandings among the world's peoples will vanish away; that all nations will mingle one with another, dealing with one another even as the lover with his beloved.   47.3

It is your duty to be exceedingly kind to every human being, and to wish him well; to work for the upliftment of society; to blow the breath of life into the dead; to act in accordance with the instructions of Bahá'u'lláh and walk His path— until ye change the world of man into the world of God.   47.4

48.1   48. O ye loyal servants of the Ancient Beauty! In every cycle and dispensation, the feast hath been favored and loved, and the spreading of a table for the lovers of God hath been considered a praise-worthy act. This is especially the case today, in this dispensation beyond compare, this most generous of ages, when it is highly acclaimed, for it is truly accounted among such gatherings as are held to worship and glorify God. Here the holy verses, the heavenly odes and laudations are intoned, and the heart is quickened, and carried away from itself.

48.2   The primary intent is to kindle these stirrings of the spirit, but at the same time it follows quite naturally that those present should partake of food, so that the world of the body may mirror the spirit's world, and flesh take on the qualities of soul; and just as the spiritual delights are here in profusion, so too the material delights.

48.3   Happy are ye to be observing this rule with all its mystic meanings, thus keeping the friends of God alert and heedful, and bringing them peace of mind, and joy.

49.1   49. Thy letter hath been received. Thou didst write of the Nineteen Day festivity, and this re-joiced my heart. These gatherings cause the divine table to descend from heaven, and draw down the confirmations of the All-Merciful. My hope is that the breathings of the Holy Spirit will be wafted over them, and that each one present shall, in great assemblies, with an eloquent tongue and a heart flooded with the love of God, set himself to acclaiming the rise of the Sun of Truth, the dawn of the Daystar that lighteth all the world.

50. You have asked as to the feast in every Bahá'í month. This feast is held to foster comradeship and love, to call God to mind and supplicate Him with contrite hearts, and to encourage benevolent pursuits. 50.1

That is, the friends should there dwell upon God and glorify Him, read the prayers and holy verses, and treat one another with the utmost affection and love. 50.2

51. As to the Nineteen Day Feast, it rejoiceth mind and heart. If this feast be held in the proper fashion, the friends will, once in nineteen days, find themselves spiritually restored, and endued with a power that is not of this world. 51.1

52. O servant of the One true God! The Lord be praised, the loved ones of God are found in every land, and are, one and all, neath the shadow 52.1

of the Tree of Life and under the protection of His good providence. His care and loving-kindness surge even as the eternal billows of the sea, and His blessings are continually showered from His eternal Kingdom.

52.2 Ours should be the prayer that His blessings may be vouchsafed in still greater abundance, and ours to hold fast to such means as shall ensure a fuller outpouring of His grace and a greater measure of His divine assistance.

52.3 One of the greatest of these means is the spirit of true fellowship and loving communion amongst the friends. Remember the saying: "Of all pilgrimages the greatest is to relieve the sorrow-laden heart."

53.1 53. Verily, 'Abdu'l-Bahá inhaleth the fragrance of the love of God from every meeting place where the Word of God is uttered and proofs and arguments set forth that shed their rays across the world, and where they recount the tribulations of 'Abdu'l-Bahá at the evil hands of those who have violated the Covenant of God.

53.2 O handmaid of the Lord! Speak thou no word of politics; thy task concerneth the life of the soul, for this verily leadeth to man's joy in the world of God. Except to speak well of them, make thou no mention of the earth's kings, and the worldly governments thereof. Rather, confine thine utterance to spreading the blissful tidings of the Kingdom of God, and demonstrating the influence of the Word of God, and the holiness of the Cause of God. Tell thou of abiding joy and spiritual delights, and godlike qualities, and of how the Sun of Truth hath risen above the earth's horizons: tell of the blowing of the spirit of life into the body of the world.

54. Ye have written as to the meetings of the friends, and how filled they are with peace and joy. Of course this is so; for wherever the spiritually minded are gathered together, there in His beauty reigneth Bahá'u'lláh. Thus it is certain that such reunions will yield boundless happiness and peace. 54.1

Today it behooveth one and all to forgo the mention of all else, and to disregard all things. Let their speaking, let their inner state be summed up thus: "Keep all my words of prayer and praise confined to one refrain; make all my life but servitude to Thee." That is, let them concentrate all their thoughts, all their words, on teaching the Cause of God and spreading the Faith of God, and inspiring all to characterize themselves with the characteristics of God; on loving mankind; on being pure and holy in all things, and spotless in their public and private life; on being upright and 54.2

detached, and fervent, and afire. All is to be yielded up, save only the remembrance of God; all is to be dispraised, except His praise. Today, to this melody of the Company on high, the world will leap and dance: "Glory be to my Lord, the All-Glorious!" But know ye this: save for this song of God, no song will stir the world, and save for this nightingale-cry of truth from the Garden of God, no melody will lure away the heart. "Whence cometh this Singer Who speaketh the Beloved's name?"

55.1   55. It befitteth the friends to hold a gathering, a meeting, where they shall glorify God and fix their hearts upon Him, and read and recite the Holy Writings of the Blessed Beauty—may my soul be the ransom of His lovers! The lights of the All-Glorious Realm, the rays of the Supreme Horizon, will be cast upon such bright assemblages, for these are none other than the Mashriqu'l-Adhkárs, the Dawning-Points of God's Remembrance, which must, at the direction of the Most Exalted Pen, be established in every hamlet and city . . . These spiritual gatherings must be held with the utmost purity and consecration, so that from the site itself, and its earth and the air about it, one will inhale the fragrant breathings of the Holy Spirit.

56. Whensoever a company of people shall gather in a meeting place, shall engage in glorifying God, and shall speak with one another of the mysteries of God, beyond any doubt the breathings of the Holy Spirit will blow gently over them, and each shall receive a share thereof. _{56.1}

57. We hear that thou hast in mind to embellish thy house from time to time with a meeting of Bahá'ís, where some among them will engage in glorifying the All-Glorious Lord . . . Know that shouldst thou bring this about, that house of earth will become a house of heaven, and that fabric of stone a congress of the spirit. _{57.1}

58. Thou hast asked about places of worship and the underlying reason therefor. The wisdom in raising up such buildings is that at a given hour, the people should know it is time to meet, and all should gather together, and, harmoniously attuned one to another, engage in prayer; with the result that out of this coming together, unity and affection shall grow and flourish in the human heart. _{58.1}

59. 'Abdu'l-Bahá hath long cherished the desire that a Mashriqu'l-Adhkár be upraised in that _{59.1}

region. Praised be God, thanks to the strenuous efforts of the friends, in recent days the joyful news of this hath been announced. This service is highly acceptable at the Threshold of God, for the Mashriqu'l-Adhkár inspiriteth the lovers of God and delighteth their hearts, and causeth them to become steadfast and firm.

59.2 This is a matter of the utmost significance. If the erection of the House of Worship in a public place would arouse the hostility of evildoers, then the meeting must, in every locality, be held in some hidden place. Even in every hamlet, a place must be set aside as the Mashriqu'l-Adhkár, and even though it be underground.

59.3 Now, praised be God, ye have succeeded in this. Engage ye in the remembrance of God at dawn; rise ye up to praise and glorify Him. Blessed are ye, and joy be yours, O ye the righteous, for having established the Dawning-Point of the Praises of God. Verily I ask of the Lord that He make you standards of salvation and banners of redemption, rippling high over the valleys and hills.

60.1 60. Although to outward seeming the Mashriqu'l-Adhkár is a material structure, yet it hath a spiritual effect. It forgeth bonds of unity from heart to heart; it is a collective center for men's souls. Every city in which, during the days of the Manifestation, a temple was raised up, hath created security and constancy and peace, for such buildings were given over to the perpetual glorification of God, and only in the remembrance of God can the heart find rest. Gracious God! The edifice of the House of Worship hath a powerful influence on every phase of life. Experience hath, in the east, clearly shown this to be a fact. Even if, in some small village, a house was designated as the Ma_sh_riqu'l-A_dh_kár, it produced a marked effect; how much greater would be the impact of one especially raised up.

61. O Lord, O Thou Who dost bless all those who stand firm in the Covenant by enabling them, out of their love for the Light of the World, to expend what they have as an offering to the Ma_sh_riqu'l-A_dh_kár, the dayspring of Thy widespread rays and the proclaimer of Thine evidences, help Thou, both in this world and the world to come, these righteous, these upright and pious ones to draw ever nearer to Thy sacred Threshold, and make bright their faces with Thy dazzling splendors. 61.1

Verily art Thou the Generous, the Ever-Bestowing. 61.2

62.1   62. O my well-beloved daughter of the Kingdom! The letter thou hadst written to Dr. Esslemont
was forwarded by him to the Land of Desire [The
Holy Land]. I read it all through with the greatest
attention. On the one hand, I was deeply touched,
for thou hadst sheared off those fair tresses of thine
with the shears of detachment from this world
and of self-sacrifice in the path of the Kingdom of
God. And on the other, I was greatly pleased, for
that dearly beloved daughter hath evinced so great a
spirit of self-sacrifice as to offer up so precious a part
of her body in the pathway of the Cause of God.
Hadst thou sought my opinion, I would in no wise
have consented that thou shouldst shear off even a
single thread of thy comely and wavy locks; nay,
I myself would have contributed in thy name for
the Mashriqu'l-Adhkár. This deed of thine is, however, an eloquent testimony to thy noble spirit of
self-sacrifice. Thou hast, verily, sacrificed thy life and
great will be the spiritual results thou shalt obtain.
Rest thou confident that day by day thou shalt progress and wax greater in firmness and in constancy.
The bounties of Bahá'u'lláh shall compass thee
about and the joyful tidings from on high shall time
and again be imparted unto thee. And though it be
thine hair that thou hast sacrificed, yet thou shalt be
filled with the Spirit, and though it be this perishable

member of thy body which thou hast laid down in the path of God, yet thou shalt find the Divine Gift, shalt behold the Celestial Beauty, obtain imperishable glory and attain unto everlasting life.

63. O ye blessed souls!* The letter ye had written to Raḥmatu'lláh hath been perused. Many and various were the joyful tidings it conveyed, namely, that through the power of faith and constancy in the Covenant, numerous gatherings have been convened, and the loved ones are everywhere astir and active.

63.1

'Abdu'l-Bahá's ardent desire hath ever been that the soil of that hallowed spot, which in the earliest days of the Cause hath been refreshed and made verdant with the spring showers of grace, may so bloom and blossom as to fill every heart with joy.

63.2

Praised be the Lord, the Cause of God hath been proclaimed and promoted throughout the East and the West in such wise that no mind had ever conceived that the sweet savors of the Lord would so rapidly perfume all regions. This, verily, is only through the consummate bounties of the ever-blessed Beauty, Whose grace and Whose triumphing power are time and again abundantly received.

63.3

* The Bahá'ís of Najaf-Ábád

63.4 One of the wondrous events that has of late come to pass is this, that the edifice of the Ma<u>sh</u>riqu'l-A<u>dh</u>kár is being raised in the very heart of the American continent, and numerous souls from the surrounding regions are contributing for the erection of this holy Temple. Among these is a highly esteemed lady of the city of Manchester, who hath been moved to offer her share.

63.5 Having no portion of goods and earthly riches, she sheared off with her own hands the fine, long and precious tresses that adorned her head so gracefully, and offered them for sale, that the price thereof might promote the cause of the Ma<u>sh</u>riqu'l-A<u>dh</u>kár.

63.6 Consider ye, that though in the eyes of women nothing is more precious than rich and flowing locks, yet notwithstanding this, that highly honored lady hath evinced so rare and beautiful a spirit of self-sacrifice.

63.7 And though this was uncalled for, and 'Abdu'l-Bahá would not have consented to such a deed, yet as it doth reveal so high and noble a spirit of devotion, He was deeply touched thereby. Precious though the hair be in the sight of western women, nay, more precious than life itself, yet she offered it up as a sacrifice for the cause of the Ma<u>sh</u>riqu'l-A<u>dh</u>kár!

It is related that once in the days of the Apostle 63.8
of God* He signified His desire that an army should
advance in a certain direction, and leave was granted
unto the faithful to raise contributions for the holy
war. Among many was one man who gave a thousand camels, each laden with corn, another who gave
half his substance, and still another who offered all
that he had. But a woman stricken in years, whose
sole possession was a handful of dates, came to the
Apostle and laid at His feet her humble contribution. Thereupon the Prophet of God—may my life
be offered up as a sacrifice unto Him—bade that
this handful of dates be placed over and above all
the contributions that had been gathered, thus as-
serting the merit and superiority thereof over all the
rest. This was done because that elderly woman had
no other earthly possessions but these.

And in like manner this esteemed lady had 63.9
nothing else to contribute but her precious locks,
and these she gloriously sacrificed in the cause of
the Mashriqu'l-Adhkár.

Ponder and reflect how mighty and potent hath 63.10
the Cause of God become! A woman of the west hath
given her hair for the glory of the Mashriqu'l-Adhkár.

Nay, this is but a lesson unto them that perceive. 63.11

---

* Muḥammad

63.12 In conclusion I am greatly pleased with the loved ones in Najaf-Ábád for, from the very early dawn of the Cause unto this day they have one and all under all conditions evinced a great spirit of self-sacrifice.

63.13 Zaynu'l-Muqarrabín hath throughout his lifetime prayed with all the sincerity of his stainless soul on behalf of the believers in Najaf-Ábád and implored for them the grace of God and His divine confirmation.

63.14 The Lord be praised that the prayers of this gracious soul have been answered, for the effects thereof are everywhere manifest.

64.1 64. The Mashriqu'l-Adhkár is one of the most vital institutions in the world, and it hath many subsidiary branches. Although it is a House of Worship, it is also connected with a hospital, a drug dispensary, a traveler's hospice, a school for orphans, and a university for advanced studies. Every Mashriqu'l-Adhkár is connected with these five things. My hope is that the Mashriqu'l-Adhkár will now be established in America, and that gradually the hospital, the school, the university, the dispensary and the hospice, all functioning according to the most efficient and orderly procedures, will follow. Make these matters known to the beloved of the Lord, so that they will understand how very great is the importance of this "Dawning-Point of the Remembrance of God." The Temple is not only a place for worship; rather, in every respect is it complete and whole.

O thou dear handmaid of God! If only thou 64.2 couldst know what a high station is destined for those souls who are severed from the world, are powerfully attracted to the Faith, and are teaching, under the sheltering shadow of Bahá'u'lláh! How thou wouldst rejoice, how thou wouldst, in exultation and rapture, spread thy wings and soar heavenward—for being a follower of such a way, and a traveler toward such a Kingdom.

As to the terminology I used in my letter, bid- 64.3 ding thee to consecrate thyself to service in the Cause of God, the meaning of it is this: limit thy thoughts to teaching the Faith. Act by day and night according to the teachings and counsels and admonitions of Bahá'u'lláh. This doth not preclude marriage. Thou canst take unto thyself a husband and at the same time serve the Cause of God; the one doth not preclude the other. Know thou the value of these days; let not this chance escape thee. Beg thou God to make thee a lighted candle, so that thou mayest guide a great multitude through this darksome world.

65.1   65. O thou favored handmaid of the heavenly Kingdom! Thy letter hath been received. It conveyeth high aspirations and noble goals, saying that thou hast in mind to make a journey to the Far East, and that thou art ready to endure extreme hardships, in order to guide the souls, and to spread far and wide the glad tidings of God's Kingdom. This purpose of thine betokeneth that thou, dear handmaid of God, dost cherish the very noblest of all aims.

65.2   When delivering the glad tidings, speak out and say: the Promised One of all the world's peoples hath now been made manifest. For each and every people, and every religion, await a Promised One, and Bahá'u'lláh is that One Who is awaited by all; and therefore the Cause of Bahá'u'lláh will bring about the oneness of mankind, and the tabernacle of unity will be upraised on the heights of the world, and the banners of the universality of all humankind will be unfurled on the peaks of the earth. When thou dost loose thy tongue to deliver this great good news, this will become the means of teaching the people.

65.3   Thy projected journey, however, is to a very far-away land, and unless a group of persons be available, the glad tidings will not take much effect in that place. If ye think best, travel instead to

Persia, and on the way back, go through Japan and China. This would appear to be much better, and far more enjoyable. In any case, do whatever seemeth feasible, and it will be approved.

66. O thou who hast sought illumination from the light of guidance! Praise thou God that He hath directed thee to the light of truth and hath invited thee to enter the Kingdom of Abhá. Thy sight hath been illumined and thy heart hath been turned into a rose garden. I pray for thee that thou mayest ever grow in faith and assurance, shine like unto a torch in the assemblies and bestow upon them the light of guidance. 66.1

Whenever an illumined assembly of the friends of God is gathered, 'Abdu'l-Bahá, although bodily absent, is yet present in spirit and in soul. I am always a traveler to America and am assuredly associating with spiritual and illumined friends. Distance is annihilated and prevents not the close and intimate association of two souls that are closely attached in heart even though they may be in two different countries. I am therefore thy close companion, attuned and in harmony with thy soul. 66.2

67. O thou lady of the Kingdom! Thy letter sent from New York hath been received. Its con- 67.1

tents imparted joy and gladness for they indicated that with a firm resolve and a pure intention thou hast determined to travel to Paris, that thou mayest in that silent city enkindle the fire of the love of God and in the midst of that darkness of nature shine like unto a resplendent candle. This journey is highly praiseworthy and suitable. When thou reachest Paris, thou must strive, no matter how small the number of the friends may be, to institute the assembly of the Covenant and to vivify the souls through the power of the Covenant.

67.2 Paris is exceedingly dispirited and is in a state of torpor and so far it hath not burst into flames although the French nation is an active and lively one. But the world of nature hath fully stretched its pavilion over Paris and hath done away with religious sentiments. But this power of the Covenant shall heat every freezing soul, shall bestow light upon everything that is dark and shall secure for the captive in the hand of nature the true freedom of the Kingdom.

67.3 Arise thou at present in Paris with the power of the Kingdom, with a divine confirmation, with a genuine zeal and ardor and with a flame of the love of God. Roar like unto a lion and exhibit such ecstasy and love among these few souls that praise and glorification may continuously reach thee from the divine Kingdom and mighty confirmations may descend upon thee. Rest thou assured. If thou dost act accordingly and hoist the standard of the Covenant, Paris shall burst into flame. Be constantly attached to and seek always the confirmations of Bahá'u'lláh for these turn the drop into a sea and convert the gnat into an eagle.

68. O ye who are firm in the Covenant and the Testament! Your letter was received and your blessed names were one by one perused. The contents of the letter were divine inspirations and manifest bounties because they were indicative of the union of the friends and the harmony of all hearts. 68.1

Today the most remarkable favor of God centereth around union and harmony among the friends; so that this unity and concord may be the cause of the promulgation of the oneness of the world of humanity, may emancipate the world from this intense darkness of enmity and rancor, and that the Sun of Truth may shine in full and perfect effulgence. 68.2

Today, all the peoples of the world are indulging in self-interest and exert the utmost effort and endeavor to promote their own material interests. They are worshipping themselves and not the di- 68.3

vine reality, nor the world of mankind. They seek diligently their own benefit and not the common weal. This is because they are captives of the world of nature and unaware of the divine teachings, of the bounty of the Kingdom and of the Sun of Truth. But ye, praise be to God, are at present especially favored with this bounty, have become of the chosen, have been informed of the heavenly instructions, have gained admittance into the Kingdom of God, have become the recipients of unbounded blessings and have been baptized with the Water of Life, with the fire of the love of God and with the Holy Spirit.

68.4   Strive, therefore, with heart and soul that ye become ignited candles in the assemblage of the world, glittering stars on the horizon of Truth and may become the cause of the propagation of the light of the Kingdom; in order that the world of humanity may be converted into a divine realm, the nether world may become the world on high, the love of God and the mercy of the Lord may raise their canopy upon the apex of the world, human souls may become the waves of the ocean of truth, the world of humanity may grow into one blessed tree, the verses of oneness may be chanted and the melodies of sanctity may reach the Supreme Concourse.

Day and night I entreat and supplicate to the 68.5
Kingdom of God and beg for you infinite assistance and confirmation. Do not take into consideration your own aptitudes and capacities, but fix your gaze on the consummate bounty, the divine bestowal and the power of the Holy Spirit—the power that converteth the drop into a sea and the star into a sun.

Praise be to God, the hosts of the Supreme 68.6
Concourse secure the victory and the power of the Kingdom is ready to assist and to support. Should ye at every instant unloosen the tongue in thanksgiving and gratitude, ye would not be able to discharge yourselves of the obligation of gratitude for these bestowals.

Consider: eminent personages whose fame hath 68.7
spread all over the world shall, erelong, fade into utter nothingness as the result of their deprivation of this heavenly bounty; no name and no fame shall they leave behind, and of them no fruit and trace shall survive. But as the effulgences of the Sun of Truth have dawned forth upon you and ye have attained everlasting life, ye shall shine and sparkle forevermore from the horizon of existence.

Peter was a fisherman and Mary Magdalene a 68.8
peasant, but as they were specially favored with the blessings of Christ, the horizon of their faith be-

came illumined, and down to the present day they are shining from the horizon of everlasting glory. In this station, merit and capacity are not to be considered; nay rather, the resplendent rays of the Sun of Truth, which have illumined these mirrors, must be taken into account.

68.9 Ye are inviting me to America. I am likewise longing to gaze upon those illumined faces and converse and associate with those true friends. But the magnetic power which shall draw me to those shores is the union and harmony of the friends, their behavior and conduct in accordance with the teachings of God and the firmness of all in the Covenant and the Testament.

68.10 O Divine Providence! This assemblage is composed of Thy friends who are attracted to Thy beauty and are set ablaze by the fire of Thy love. Turn these souls into heavenly angels, resuscitate them through the breath of Thy Holy Spirit, grant them eloquent tongues and resolute hearts, bestow on them heavenly power and merciful susceptibilities, cause them to become the promulgators of the oneness of mankind and the cause of love and concord in the world of humanity, so that the perilous darkness of ignorant prejudice may vanish through the light of the Sun of Truth, this dreary world may become illumined, this material realm may absorb the rays of the world of spirit, these different colors may merge into one color and the melody of praise may rise to the kingdom of Thy sanctity.

Verily, Thou art the Omnipotent and the Almighty! 68.11

69. Thou hast written concerning organization. 69.1 The divine teachings and the admonitions and exhortations of Bahá'u'lláh are manifestly evident. These constitute the organization of the Kingdom and their enforcement is obligatory. The least deviation from them is absolute error.

Thou hast written concerning my travel to 69.2 America. If thou couldst see how the waves of constant occupation are surging, thou wouldst have considered that time for travel is absolutely lacking; in times of fixed residence partial rest is even impossible. God willing, I trust, through the bounty of Bahá'u'lláh, that as soon as means for the composure of mind and of heart are provided, I shall determine to journey and shall inform thee about it.

70. O thou ignited candle! Thy letter was re- 70.1 ceived. Its contents imparted spiritual gladness, for they were pervaded by spiritual sentiments and indicated the attraction of thy heart, attachment to the Kingdom of God and love for His divine teachings.

70.2   Verily, thou showest a high endeavor, hast a pure and sanctified purpose, wishest naught save the good pleasure of God, seekest nothing but the attainment of limitless bounties, and art engaged in the promulgation of divine teachings and the explanation of abstruse metaphysical problems. It is my hope that, by the favor of Bahá'u'lláh, thou and thy respected wife may daily increase in firmness and steadfastness, so that in that exalted land ye may become two upraised standards and two resplendent lights.

70.3   Extensive travel in October, to the north, south, east and west, accompanied by that candle of the love of God, Mrs. Maxwell, would be highly acceptable. My hope is that she may entirely recover; this beloved handmaid of God is like a flame of fire and thinks day and night of nothing save service to God. For the present, travel throughout the northern states, and in the winter season hasten to the states in the south. Your service should consist of eloquent speeches delivered in gatherings wherein ye may promulgate the divine teachings. If possible, undertake at some time a voyage to the Hawaiian Islands.

70.4   The events which have transpired were all recorded fifty years ago in the Tablets of Bahá'u'lláh—Tablets which have been printed, published and spread throughout the world. The teachings of Bahá'u'lláh are the light of this age and the spirit of this century. Expound each of them at every gathering.

The first is investigation of truth,

The second, the oneness of mankind,

The third, universal peace,

The fourth, conformity between science and divine revelation,

The fifth, abandonment of racial, religious, worldly and political prejudices, prejudices which destroy the foundation of mankind.

The sixth is righteousness and justice,

The seventh, the betterment of morals and heavenly education,

The eighth, the equality of the two sexes,

The ninth, the diffusion of knowledge and education,

The tenth, economic questions,

and so on and so forth. Strive that souls may attain unto the light of guidance and hold fast unto the hem of Bahá'u'lláh.

The letter thou hast enclosed was perused. When 70.5 man's soul is rarified and cleansed, spiritual links are established, and from these bonds sensations felt by the heart are produced. The human heart resembleth a mirror. When this is purified human hearts are attuned and reflect one another, and thus spiritual emotions are generated. This is like the world of dreams when man is detached from things which are tangible and experienceth those of the spirit. What amazing laws operate, and what remarkable discoveries are made! And it may even be that detailed communications are registered . . .

70.6 Finally, I hope that in Chicago the friends may become united and may illumine that city, for therein the dawn of the Cause appeared, and in this lieth its preference over other cities. Therefore it must be held in respect; perchance it may, God willing, be freed from all spiritual afflictions, and may attain unto perfect health and become a center of the Covenant and Testament.

71.1 71. O thou beloved maidservant of God! Thy letter was received and its contents revealed the fact that the friends, in perfect energy and vitality, are engaged in the propagation of the heavenly teachings. This news hath caused intense joy and gladness. For every era hath a spirit; the spirit of this illumined era lieth in the teachings of Bahá'u'lláh. For these lay the foundation of the oneness of the world of humanity and promulgate universal brotherhood. They are founded upon the unity of science and religion and upon investigation of truth. They uphold the principle that religion must be the cause of amity, union and harmony among men. They establish the equality of both sexes and propound economic principles which are for the happiness of individuals. They diffuse universal education, that every soul may as much as possible have a share of knowledge. They abrogate and nullify religious, racial, political, patriotic and economic prejudices and the like. Those teachings that are scattered throughout the Epistles and Tablets are the cause of the illumination and the life of the world of humanity. Whoever promulgateth them will verily be assisted by the Kingdom of God.

The President of the Republic, Dr. Wilson, is 71.2 indeed serving the Kingdom of God for he is restless and strives day and night that the rights of all men may be preserved safe and secure, that even small nations, like greater ones, may dwell in peace and comfort, under the protection of Righteousness and Justice. This purpose is indeed a lofty one. I trust that the incomparable Providence will assist and confirm such souls under all conditions.

72. O thou true friend! Read, in the school of 72.1 God, the lessons of the spirit, and learn from love's Teacher the innermost truths. Seek out the secrets

of Heaven, and tell of the overflowing grace and favor of God.

72.2   Although to acquire the sciences and arts is the greatest glory of mankind, this is so only on condition that man's river flow into the mighty sea, and draw from God's ancient source His inspiration. When this cometh to pass, then every teacher is as a shoreless ocean, every pupil a prodigal fountain of knowledge. If, then, the pursuit of knowledge lead to the beauty of Him Who is the Object of all Knowledge, how excellent that goal; but if not, a mere drop will perhaps shut a man off from flooding grace, for with learning cometh arrogance and pride, and it bringeth on error and indifference to God.

72.3   The sciences of today are bridges to reality; if then they lead not to reality, naught remains but fruitless illusion. By the one true God! If learning be not a means of access to Him, the Most Manifest, it is nothing but evident loss.

72.4   It is incumbent upon thee to acquire the various branches of knowledge, and to turn thy face toward the beauty of the Manifest Beauty, that thou mayest be a sign of saving guidance amongst the peoples of the world, and a focal center of understanding in this sphere from which the wise and their wisdom are shut out, except for those who set foot in the Kingdom of lights and become informed of the veiled and hidden mystery, the well-guarded secret.

73. O daughter of the Kingdom! Thy letter hath come and its contents make clear the fact that thou hast directed all thy thoughts toward acquiring light from the realms of mystery. So long as the thoughts of an individual are scattered he will achieve no results, but if his thinking be concentrated on a single point wonderful will be the fruits thereof. 73.1

One cannot obtain the full force of the sunlight when it is cast on a flat mirror, but once the sun shineth upon a concave mirror, or on a lens that is convex, all its heat will be concentrated on a single point, and that one point will burn the hottest. Thus is it necessary to focus one's thinking on a single point so that it will become an effective force. 73.2

Thou didst wish to celebrate the Day of Riḍván with a feast, and to have those present on that day engage in reciting Tablets with delight and joy, and thou didst request me to send thee a letter to be read on that day. My letter is this: 73.3

O ye beloved, and ye handmaids of the Merciful! This is the day when the Daystar of Truth rose over the horizon of life, and its glory spread, and its brightness shone out with such power that it clove 73.4

the dense and high-piled clouds and mounted the skies of the world in all its splendor. Hence do ye witness a new stirring throughout all created things.

73.5 See how, in this day, the scope of sciences and arts hath widened out, and what wondrous technical advances have been made, and to what a high degree the mind's powers have increased, and what stupendous inventions have appeared.

73.6 This age is indeed as a hundred other ages: should ye gather the yield of a hundred ages, and set that against the accumulated product of our times, the yield of this one era will prove greater than that of a hundred gone before. Take ye, for an example, the sum total of all the books that were ever written in ages past, and compare that with the books and treatises that our era hath produced: these books, written in our day alone, far and away exceed the total number of volumes that have been written down the ages. See how powerful is the influence exerted by the Daystar of the world upon the inner essence of all created things!

73.7 But alas, a thousand times alas! The eyes see it not, the ears are deaf, and the hearts and minds are oblivious of this supreme bestowal. Strive ye then, with all your hearts and souls, to awaken those who slumber, to cause the blind to see, and the dead to rise.

74. O bird that singeth sweetly of the Abhá   74.1
Beauty! In this new and wondrous dispensation
the veils of superstition have been torn asunder
and the prejudices of eastern peoples stand condemned. Among certain nations of the East, music was considered reprehensible, but in this new
age the Manifest Light hath, in His holy Tablets,
specifically proclaimed that music, sung or played,
is spiritual food for soul and heart.

The musician's art is among those arts worthy   74.2
of the highest praise, and it moveth the hearts of
all who grieve. Wherefore, O thou <u>Sh</u>ahnáz,* play
and sing out the holy words of God with wondrous tones in the gatherings of the friends, that
the listener may be freed from chains of care and
sorrow, and his soul may leap for joy and humble
itself in prayer to the realm of Glory.

75. Strive with heart and soul in order to bring   75.1
about union and harmony among the white and
the black and prove thereby the unity of the Bahá'í
world wherein distinction of color findeth no
place, but where hearts only are considered. Praise
be to God, the hearts of the friends are united and

---

* <u>Sh</u>ahnáz, the name given to the recipient of this Tablet,
is also the name of a musical mode.

linked together, whether they be from the east or the west, from north or from south, whether they be German, French, Japanese, American, and whether they pertain to the white, the black, the red, the yellow or the brown race. Variations of color, of land and of race are of no importance in the Bahá'í Faith; on the contrary, Bahá'í unity overcometh them all and doeth away with all these fancies and imaginations.

76.1   76. O thou who hast an illumined heart! Thou art even as the pupil of the eye, the very wellspring of the light, for God's love hath cast its rays upon thine inmost being and thou hast turned thy face toward the Kingdom of thy Lord.

76.2   Intense is the hatred, in America, between black and white, but my hope is that the power of the Kingdom will bind these two in friendship, and serve them as a healing balm.

76.3   Let them look not upon a man's color but upon his heart. If the heart be filled with light, that man is nigh unto the threshold of his Lord; but if not, that man is careless of his Lord, be he white or be he black.

77.1   77. O thou revered maidservant of God! Thy letter from Los Angeles was received. Thank divine Providence that thou hast been assisted in service and hast been the cause of the promulgation of the oneness of the world of humanity, so that the darkness of differences among men may be dissipated, and the pavilion of the unity of nations may cast its shadow over all regions. Without such unity, rest and comfort, peace and universal reconciliation are unachievable. This illumined century needeth and calleth for its fulfillment. In every century a particular and central theme is, in accordance with the requirements of that century, confirmed by God. In this illumined age that which is confirmed is the oneness of the world of humanity. Every soul who serveth this oneness will undoubtedly be assisted and confirmed.

I hope that in the assemblies thou mayest sing 77.2 praises with a sweet melody and thus become the cause of joy and gladness to all.

78. O thou who art pure in heart, sanctified 78.1 in spirit, peerless in character, beauteous in face! Thy photograph hath been received revealing thy physical frame in the utmost grace and the best appearance. Thou art dark in countenance and bright in character. Thou art like unto the pupil of the eye which is dark in color, yet it is the fount of light and the revealer of the contingent world.

I have not forgotten nor will I forget thee. I be- 78.2 seech God that He may graciously make thee the sign of His bounty amidst mankind, illumine thy face with the light of such blessings as are vouch-safed by the merciful Lord, single thee out for His love in this age which is distinguished among all the past ages and centuries.

79.1   79. O respected personage! I have read your work, *The Gospel of Wealth*,* and noted therein truly apposite and sound recommendations for easing the lot of humankind.

79.2   To state the matter briefly, the Teachings of Bahá'u'lláh advocate voluntary sharing, and this is a greater thing than the equalization of wealth. For equalization must be imposed from without, while sharing is a matter of free choice.

79.3   Man reacheth perfection through good deeds, voluntarily performed, not through good deeds the doing of which was forced upon him. And sharing is a personally chosen righteous act: that is, the rich should extend assistance to the poor, they should expend their substance for the poor, but of their own free will, and not because the poor have gained this end by force. For the harvest of force is turmoil and the ruin of the social order. On the

---

* An article from Andrew Carnegie's book *The Gospel of Wealth* was published in England in the *Pall Mall Budget* and called *The Gospel of Wealth,* cf. Andrew Carnegie's *Autobiography,* 255n.

other hand voluntary sharing, the freely chosen expending of one's substance, leadeth to society's comfort and peace. It lighteth up the world; it bestoweth honor upon humankind.

I have seen the good effects of your own philan- 79.4
thropy in America, in various universities, peace gatherings, and associations for the promotion of learning, as I travelled from city to city. Wherefore do I pray on your behalf that you shall ever be encompassed by the bounties and blessings of heaven, and shall perform many philanthropic deeds in East and West. Thus may you gleam as a lighted taper in the Kingdom of God, may attain honor and everlasting life, and shine out as a bright star on the horizon of eternity.

80. O thou who art turning thy face to God! 80.1
Thy letter was received. From its contents it became known that thy wish is to serve the poor. What wish better than this! Those souls who are of the Kingdom eagerly wish to be of service to the poor, to sympathize with them, to show kindness to the miserable and to make their lives fruitful. Happy art thou that thou hast such a wish.

Convey on my behalf to thy two children the 80.2
utmost kindness and love. Their letters have been received but, as I have no time, separate letters

cannot be written at present. Show them on my behalf the utmost kindness.

81.1   81. Those souls who during the war have served the poor and have been in the Red Cross Mission work, their services are accepted at the Kingdom of God and are the cause of their everlasting life. Convey to them these glad tidings.

82.1   82. O thou who art firm in the Covenant, thy letter was received. Thou hast exerted a great effort for that prisoner, perchance it may prove to be fruitful. Tell him, however: "The denizens of the world are confined in the prison of nature—a prison that is continuous and eternal. If thou art at present restrained within the limits of a temporary prison, be not grieved at this; my hope is that thou mayest be emancipated from the prison of nature and may attain unto the court of everlasting life. Pray to God day and night and beg forgiveness and pardon. The omnipotence of God shall solve every difficulty."

83.1   83. Convey on behalf of 'Abdu'l-Bahá to thy respected wife my Abhá greetings, and say: "Kindness, training and education extended to prisoners is exceedingly important. Therefore as thou hast exerted an effort in this, hast awakened some of them, and hast been the cause of the turning of their faces to the divine Kingdom, this praiseworthy deed is highly acceptable. Assuredly persevere. Convey on my behalf to the two prisoners in San Quentin the utmost kindness, and tell them: 'That prison in the sight of wise souls is a school of training and development. Ye must strive with heart and soul that ye may become renowned in character and knowledge.'"

84. O thou dear handmaid of God! Thy letter hath been received, and its contents were noted.   84.1

Marriage, among the mass of the people, is a physical bond, and this union can only be temporary, since it is foredoomed to a physical separation at the close.   84.2

Among the people of Bahá, however, marriage must be a union of the body and of the spirit as well, for here both husband and wife are aglow with the same wine, both are enamored of the same matchless Face, both live and move through the same spirit, both are illumined by the same glory. This connection between them is a spiritual one, hence it is a bond that will abide forever. Likewise do they enjoy strong and lasting ties in the physical world as well, for if the marriage is based   84.3

both on the spirit and the body, that union is a true one, hence it will endure. If, however, the bond is physical and nothing more, it is sure to be only temporary, and must inexorably end in separation.

84.4 When, therefore, the people of Bahá undertake to marry, the union must be a true relationship, a spiritual coming together as well as a physical one, so that throughout every phase of life, and in all the worlds of God, their union will endure; for this real oneness is a gleaming out of the love of God.

84.5 In the same way, when any souls grow to be true believers, they will attain a spiritual relationship with one another, and show forth a tenderness which is not of this world. They will, all of them, become elated from a draught of divine love, and that union of theirs, that connection, will also abide forever. Souls, that is, who will consign their own selves to oblivion, strip from themselves the defects of humankind, and unchain themselves from human bondage, will beyond any doubt be illumined with the heavenly splendors of oneness, and will all attain unto real union in the world that dieth not.

85.1 85. As for the question regarding marriage under the Law of God: first thou must choose one who is pleasing to thee, and then the matter is subject to the consent of father and mother. Before thou makest thy choice, they have no right to interfere.

86. Bahá'í marriage is the commitment of the 86.1 two parties one to the other, and their mutual attachment of mind and heart. Each must, however, exercise the utmost care to become thoroughly acquainted with the character of the other, that the binding covenant between them may be a tie that will endure forever. Their purpose must be this: to become loving companions and comrades and at one with each other for time and eternity. . . .

The true marriage of Bahá'ís is this, that hus- 86.2 band and wife should be united both physically and spiritually, that they may ever improve the spiritual life of each other, and may enjoy everlasting unity throughout all the worlds of God. This is Bahá'í marriage.

87. O thou memento of him who died for the 87.1 Blessed Beauty! In recent days, the joyful news of thy marriage to that luminous leaf hath been received, and hath infinitely gladdened the hearts of the people of God. With all humility, prayers of supplication have been offered at the Holy Threshold, that this marriage may be a harbinger of joy

to the friends, that it may be a loving bond for all eternity, and yield everlasting benefits and fruits.

87.2 From separation doth every kind of hurt and harm proceed, but the union of created things doth ever yield most laudable results. From the pairing of even the smallest particles in the world of being are the grace and bounty of God made manifest; and the higher the degree, the more momentous is the union. "Glory be to Him Who hath created all the pairs, of such things as earth produceth, and out of men themselves, and of things beyond their ken."* And above all other unions is that between human beings, especially when it cometh to pass in the love of God. Thus is the primal oneness made to appear; thus is laid the foundation of love in the spirit. It is certain that such a marriage as yours will cause the bestowals of God to be revealed. Wherefore do we offer you felicitations and call down blessings upon you and beg of the Blessed Beauty, through His aid and favor, to make that wedding feast a joy to all and adorn it with the harmony of Heaven.

87.3 O my Lord, O my Lord! These two bright orbs are wedded in Thy love, conjoined in ser-

---

* Qur'án 36:36, and cf. 51:49

vitude to Thy Holy Threshold, united in ministering to Thy Cause. Make Thou this marriage to be as threading lights of Thine abounding grace, O my Lord, the All-Merciful, and luminous rays of Thy bestowals, O Thou the Beneficent, the Ever-Giving, that there may branch out from this great tree boughs that will grow green and flourishing through the gifts that rain down from Thy clouds of grace.

Verily Thou art the Generous, verily Thou art the Almighty, verily Thou art the Compassionate, the All-Merciful. 87.4

88. O ye my two beloved children! The news of your union, as soon as it reached me, imparted infinite joy and gratitude. Praise be to God, those two faithful birds have sought shelter in one nest. I beseech God that He may enable them to raise an honored family, for the importance of marriage lieth in the bringing up of a richly blessed family, so that with entire gladness they may, even as candles, illuminate the world. For the enlightenment of the world dependeth upon the existence of man. If man did not exist in this world, it would have been like a tree without fruit. My hope is that you both may become even as one tree, and may, through the outpourings of the cloud of 88.1

loving-kindness, acquire freshness and charm, and may blossom and yield fruit, so that your line may eternally endure.

88.2 Upon ye be the Glory of the Most Glorious.

89.1 89. O thou who art firm in the Covenant! The letter thou hadst written on 2 May 1919 was received. Praise thou God that in tests thou art firm and steadfast and art holding fast to the Abhá Kingdom. Thou art not shaken by any affliction or disturbed by any calamity. Not until man is tried doth the pure gold distinctly separate from the dross. Torment is the fire of test wherein the pure gold shineth resplendently and the impurity is burned and blackened. At present thou art, praise be to God, firm and steadfast in tests and trials and art not shaken by them.

89.2 Thy wife is not in harmony with thee, but praise be to God, the Blessed Beauty is pleased with thee and is conferring upon thee the utmost bounty and blessings. But still try to be patient with thy wife, perchance she may be transformed and her heart may be illumined. The contribution thou hast made for teaching is highly acceptable and it shall be eternally mentioned in the divine Kingdom for it is the cause of the diffusion of fragrances and the exaltation of the Word of God.

90. O God, my God! This Thy handmaid is 90.1
calling upon Thee, trusting in Thee, turning her
face unto Thee, imploring Thee to shed Thy heavenly bounties upon her, and to disclose unto her
Thy spiritual mysteries, and to cast upon her the
lights of Thy Godhead.

O my Lord! Make the eyes of my husband to 90.2
see. Rejoice Thou his heart with the light of the
knowledge of Thee, draw Thou his mind unto Thy
luminous beauty, cheer Thou his spirit by revealing
unto him Thy manifest splendors.

O my Lord! Lift Thou the veil from before his 90.3
sight. Rain down Thy plenteous bounties upon
him, intoxicate him with the wine of love for
Thee, make him one of Thy angels whose feet
walk upon this earth even as their souls are soaring
through the high heavens. Cause him to become
a brilliant lamp, shining out with the light of Thy
wisdom in the midst of Thy people.

Verily Thou art the Precious, the Ever-Bestow- 90.4
ing, the Open of Hand.

91. O thou who hast bowed thyself down in 91.1
prayer before the Kingdom of God! Blessed art thou,
for the beauty of the divine Countenance hath enraptured thy heart, and the light of inner wisdom
hath filled it full, and within it shineth the bright-

ness of the Kingdom. Know thou that God is with thee under all conditions, and that He guardeth thee from the changes and chances of this world and hath made thee a handmaid in His mighty vineyard. . . .

91.2   As to thy respected husband: it is incumbent upon thee to treat him with great kindness, to consider his wishes and be conciliatory with him at all times, till he seeth that because thou hast directed thyself toward the Kingdom of God, thy tenderness for him and thy love for God have but increased, as well as thy concern for his wishes under all conditions.

91.3   I beg of the Almighty to keep thee firmly established in His love, and ever shedding abroad the sweet breaths of holiness in all those regions.

92.1   92. O ye two believers in God! The Lord, peerless is He, hath made woman and man to abide with each other in the closest companionship, and to be even as a single soul. They are two helpmates, two intimate friends, who should be concerned about the welfare of each other.

92.2   If they live thus, they will pass through this world with perfect contentment, bliss, and peace of heart, and become the object of divine grace and favor in the Kingdom of heaven. But if they do other than this, they will live out their lives in great bitterness, longing at every moment for death, and will be shamefaced in the heavenly realm.

Strive, then, to abide, heart and soul, with each other as two doves in the nest, for this is to be blessed in both worlds. 92.3

93. O thou maidservant of God! Every woman who becometh the maidservant of God outshineth in glory the empresses of the world, for she is related to God, and her sovereignty is everlasting, whereas a handful of dust will obliterate the name and fame of those empresses. In other words, as soon as they go down to the grave they are reduced to naught. The maidservants of God's Kingdom, on the other hand, enjoy eternal sovereignty unaffected by the passing of ages and generations. 93.1

Consider how many empresses have come and gone since the time of Christ. Each was the ruler of a country but now all trace and name of them is lost, while Mary Magdalene, who was only a peasant and a maidservant of God, still shineth from the horizon of everlasting glory. Strive thou, therefore, to remain the maidservant of God. 93.2

Thou hast praised the Convention. This Convention shall acquire great importance in future, for it is serving the divine Kingdom and the world of mankind. It promulgateth universal peace and 93.3

layeth the basis of the oneness of mankind; it freeth the souls from religious, racial and worldly prejudices and gathereth them under the shade of the one-colored pavilion of God. Praise thou God, therefore, that thou hast attended such a Convention and hast listened to the divine Teachings.

94.1   94. O handmaids of the beauty of Abhá! Your letter hath come, and its perusal brought great joy. Praised be God, the women believers have organized meetings where they will learn how to teach the Faith, will spread the sweet savors of the Teachings and make plans for training the children.

94.2   This gathering must be completely spiritual. That is, the discussions must be confined to marshalling clear and conclusive proofs that the Sun of Truth hath indeed arisen. And further, those present should concern themselves with every means of training the girl children; with teaching the various branches of knowledge, good behavior, a proper way of life, the cultivation of a good character, chastity and constancy, perseverance, strength, determination, firmness of purpose; with household management, the education of children, and whatever especially applieth to the needs of girls—to the end that these girls, reared in the stronghold of all perfections, and with the protection of a goodly character, will, when they themselves become mothers, bring up their children from earliest infancy to have a good character and conduct themselves well.

Let them also study whatever will nurture the health of the body and its physical soundness, and how to guard their children from disease. 94.3

When matters are thus well arranged, every child will become a peerless plant in the gardens of the Abhá Paradise. 94.4

95. O handmaids of the Lord! The spiritual assemblage that ye established in that illumined city is most propitious. Ye have made great strides; ye have surpassed the others, have arisen to serve the Holy Threshold, and have won heavenly bestowals. Now with all spiritual zeal must ye gather in that enlightened assemblage and recite the Holy Writings and engage in remembering the Lord. Set ye forth His arguments and proofs. Work ye for the guidance of the women in that land, teach the young girls and the children, so that the mothers may educate their little ones from their earliest days, thoroughly train them, rear them to have a goodly character and good morals, guide them to all the virtues of humankind, prevent the development of any behavior that would be worthy of 95.1

blame, and foster them in the embrace of Bahá'í education. Thus shall these tender infants be nurtured at the breast of the knowledge of God and His love. Thus shall they grow and flourish, and be taught righteousness and the dignity of humankind, resolution and the will to strive and to endure. Thus shall they learn perseverance in all things, the will to advance, high-mindedness and high resolve, chastity and purity of life. Thus shall they be enabled to carry to a successful conclusion whatsoever they undertake.

95.2 Let the mothers consider that whatever concerneth the education of children is of the first importance. Let them put forth every effort in this regard, for when the bough is green and tender it will grow in whatever way ye train it. Therefore is it incumbent upon the mothers to rear their little ones even as a gardener tendeth his young plants. Let them strive by day and by night to establish within their children faith and certitude, the fear of God, the love of the Beloved of the worlds, and all good qualities and traits. Whensoever a mother seeth that her child hath done well, let her praise and applaud him and cheer his heart; and if the slightest undesirable trait should manifest itself, let her counsel the child and punish him, and use means based on reason, even a slight verbal chas-

tisement should this be necessary. It is not, however, permissible to strike a child, or vilify him, for
the child's character will be totally perverted if he
be subjected to blows or verbal abuse.

96. O handmaids of the Merciful! Render ye   96.1
thanks unto the Ancient Beauty that ye have been
raised up and gathered together in this mightiest of
centuries, this most illumined of ages. As befitting
thanks for such a bounty, stand ye staunch and
strong in the Covenant and, following the precepts
of God and the holy Law, suckle your children
from their infancy with the milk of a universal
education, and rear them so that from their earliest
days, within their inmost heart, their very nature, a
way of life will be firmly established that will conform to the divine Teachings in all things.

For mothers are the first educators, the first   96.2
mentors; and truly it is the mothers who determine
the happiness, the future greatness, the courteous
ways and learning and judgment, the understanding and the faith of their little ones.

97. There are certain pillars which have been   97.1
established as the unshakable supports of the Faith
of God. The mightiest of these is learning and the
use of the mind, the expansion of consciousness,

and insight into the realities of the universe and the hidden mysteries of Almighty God.

97.2 To promote knowledge is thus an inescapable duty imposed on every one of the friends of God. It is incumbent upon that Spiritual Assembly, that assemblage of God, to exert every effort to educate the children, so that from infancy they will be trained in Bahá'í conduct and the ways of God, and will, even as young plants, thrive and flourish in the soft-flowing waters that are the counsels and admonitions of the Blessed Beauty.

98.1 98. Were there no educator, all souls would remain savage, and were it not for the teacher, the children would be ignorant creatures.

98.2 It is for this reason that, in this new cycle, education and training are recorded in the Book of God as obligatory and not voluntary. That is, it is enjoined upon the father and mother, as a duty, to strive with all effort to train the daughter and the son, to nurse them from the breast of knowledge and to rear them in the bosom of sciences and arts. Should they neglect this matter, they shall be held responsible and worthy of reproach in the presence of the stern Lord.

99.1 99. Thou didst write as to the children: from the very beginning, the children must receive divine education and must continually be reminded to remember their God. Let the love of God pervade their inmost being, commingled with their mother's milk.

100. My wish is that these children should receive a Bahá'í education, so that they may progress both here and in the Kingdom, and rejoice thy heart. 100.1

In a time to come, morals will degenerate to an extreme degree. It is essential that children be reared in the Bahá'í way, that they may find happiness both in this world and the next. If not, they shall be beset by sorrows and troubles, for human happiness is founded upon spiritual behavior. 100.2

101. O ye who have peace of soul! Among the divine Texts as set forth in the Most Holy Book and also in other Tablets is this: it is incumbent upon the father and mother to train their children both in good conduct and the study of books; study, that is, to the degree required, so that no child, whether girl or boy, will remain illiterate. Should the father fail in his duty he must be compelled to discharge his responsibility, and should he be unable to comply, let the House of Justice take over the education of the children; in no case is a child to be left without an education. This is one of the stringent and inescapable commandments 101.1

to neglect which would draw down the wrathful indignation of Almighty God.

102.1   102. O true companions! All humankind are as children in a school, and the Dawning-Points of Light, the Sources of divine revelation, are the teachers, wondrous and without peer. In the school of realities they educate these sons and daughters, according to teachings from God, and foster them in the bosom of grace, so that they may develop along every line, show forth the excellent gifts and blessings of the Lord, and combine human perfections; that they may advance in all aspects of human endeavor, whether outward or inward, hidden or visible, material or spiritual, until they make of this mortal world a widespread mirror, to reflect that other world which dieth not.

102.2   O ye friends of God! Because, in this most momentous of ages, the Sun of Truth hath risen at the highest point of the spring equinox, and cast its rays on every clime, it shall kindle such tremulous excitement, it shall release such vibrations in the world of being, it shall stimulate such growth and development, it shall stream out with such a glory of light, and clouds of grace shall pour down such plentiful waters, and fields and plains shall teem with such a galaxy of sweet-smelling plants and blooms, that this lowly earth will become the Abhá Kingdom, and this nether world the world above. Then will this fleck of dust be as the vast circle of the skies, this human place the palace-court of God, this spot of clay the dayspring of the endless favors of the Lord of Lords.

Wherefore, O loved ones of God! Make ye a 102.3 mighty effort till you yourselves betoken this advancement and all these confirmations, and become focal centers of God's blessings, daysprings of the light of His unity, promoters of the gifts and graces of civilized life. Be ye in that land vanguards of the perfections of humankind; carry forward the various branches of knowledge, be active and progressive in the field of inventions and the arts. Endeavor to rectify the conduct of men, and seek to excel the whole world in moral character. While the children are yet in their infancy feed them from the breast of heavenly grace, foster them in the cradle of all excellence, rear them in the embrace of bounty. Give them the advantage of every useful kind of knowledge. Let them share in every new and rare and wondrous craft and art. Bring them up to work and strive, and accustom them to hardship. Teach them to dedicate their lives to matters of great import, and inspire them to undertake studies that will benefit mankind.

103.1   103. The education and training of children is among the most meritorious acts of humankind and draweth down the grace and favor of the All-Merciful, for education is the indispensable foundation of all human excellence and alloweth man to work his way to the heights of abiding glory. If a child be trained from his infancy, he will, through the loving care of the Holy Gardener, drink in the crystal waters of the spirit and of knowledge, like a young tree amid the rilling brooks. And certainly he will gather to himself the bright rays of the Sun of Truth, and through its light and heat will grow ever fresh and fair in the garden of life.

103.2   Therefore must the mentor be a doctor as well: that is, he must, in instructing the child, remedy its faults; must give him learning, and at the same time rear him to have a spiritual nature. Let the teacher be a doctor to the character of the child, thus will he heal the spiritual ailments of the children of men.

103.3   If, in this momentous task, a mighty effort be exerted, the world of humanity will shine out with other adornings, and shed the fairest light. Then will this darksome place grow luminous, and this abode of earth turn into Heaven. The very demons will change to angels then, and wolves to shepherds of the flock, and the wild-dog pack to gazelles that pasture on the plains of oneness, and ravening beasts to peaceful herds, and birds of prey, with talons sharp as knives, to songsters warbling their sweet native notes.

For the inner reality of man is a demarcation line between the shadow and the light, a place where the two seas meet;* it is the lowest point on the arc of descent,† and therefore is it capable of gaining all the grades above. With education it can achieve all excellence; devoid of education it will stay on, at the lowest point of imperfection. 103.4

Every child is potentially the light of the world— and at the same time its darkness; wherefore must the question of education be accounted as of primary importance. From his infancy, the child must be nursed at the breast of God's love, and nurtured in the embrace of His knowledge, that he may radiate light, grow in spirituality, be filled with wisdom and learning, and take on the characteristics of the angelic host. 103.5

Since ye have been assigned to this holy task, ye must therefore exert every effort to make that school 103.6

---

* Qur'án 25:55, 35:13, 55:19–25. See also Marriage Prayer revealed by 'Abdu'l-Bahá beginning "He is God! O peerless Lord! In Thine almighty wisdom Thou hast enjoined marriage upon the peoples . . ."

† See *Some Answered Questions*, pp. 328–9 for 'Abdu'l-Bahá's comments on the arc of descent and ascent.

famed in all respects throughout the world; to make it the cause of exalting the Word of the Lord.

104.1   104. O loved ones of God and handmaids of the Merciful! A large body of scholars is of the opinion that variations among minds and differing degrees of perception are due to differences in education, training and culture. That is, they believe that minds are equal to begin with, but that training and education will result in mental variations and differing levels of intelligence, and that such variations are not an inherent component of the individuality but are the result of education: that no one hath any inborn superiority over another. . . .

104.2   The Manifestations of God are likewise in agreement with the view that education exerteth the strongest possible influence on humankind. They affirm, however, that differences in the level of intelligence are innate; and this fact is obvious, and not worth debating. For we see that children of the same age, the same country, the same race, indeed of the same family, and trained by the same individual, still are different as to the degree of their comprehension and intelligence. One will make rapid progress, one will receive instruction only gradually, one will remain at the lowest stage of all. For no matter how much you may polish a shell, it will not turn into a gleaming pearl, nor can you change a dull pebble into a gem whose pure rays will light the world. Never, through training and cultivation, will the colocynth and the bitter tree* change into the Tree of Blessedness.† That is to say, education cannot alter the inner essence of a man, but it doth exert tremendous influence, and with this power it can bring forth from the individual whatever perfections and capacities are deposited within him. A grain of wheat, when cultivated by the farmer, will yield a whole harvest, and a seed, through the gardener's care, will grow into a great tree. Thanks to a teacher's loving efforts, the children of the primary school may reach the highest levels of achievement; indeed, his benefactions may lift some child of small account to an exalted throne. Thus is it clearly demonstrated that by their essential nature, minds vary as to their capacity, while education also playeth a great role and exerteth a powerful effect on their development.

105. As to the difference between that material civilization now prevailing, and the divine civilization which will be one of the benefits to derive from

---

* cf. Qur'án 37:60 (The Tree of Zaqqúm)
† cf. Qur'án 24:35

the House of Justice, it is this: material civilization, through the power of punitive and retaliatory laws, restraineth the people from criminal acts; and notwithstanding this, while laws to retaliate against and punish a man are continually proliferating, as ye can see, no laws exist to reward him. In all the cities of Europe and America, vast buildings have been erected to serve as jails for the criminals.

105.2 Divine civilization, however, so traineth every member of society that no one, with the exception of a negligible few, will undertake to commit a crime. There is thus a great difference between the prevention of crime through measures that are violent and retaliatory, and so training the people, and enlightening them, and spiritualizing them, that without any fear of punishment or vengeance to come, they will shun all criminal acts. They will, indeed, look upon the very commission of a crime as a great disgrace and in itself the harshest of punishments. They will become enamored of human perfections, and will consecrate their lives to whatever will bring light to the world and will further those qualities which are acceptable at the Holy Threshold of God.

105.3 See then how wide is the difference between material civilization and divine. With force and punishments, material civilization seeketh to restrain the people from mischief, from inflicting harm on society and committing crimes. But in a divine civilization, the individual is so conditioned that with no fear of punishment, he shunneth the perpetration of crimes, seeth the crime itself as the severest of torments, and with alacrity and joy, setteth himself to acquiring the virtues of humankind, to furthering human progress, and to spreading light across the world.

106. Among the greatest of all services that can possibly be rendered by man to Almighty God is the education and training of children, young plants of the Abhá Paradise, so that these children, fostered by grace in the way of salvation, growing like pearls of divine bounty in the shell of education, will one day bejewel the crown of abiding glory. _{106.1}

It is, however, very difficult to undertake this service, even harder to succeed in it. I hope that thou wilt acquit thyself well in this most important of tasks, and successfully carry the day, and become an ensign of God's abounding grace; that these children, reared one and all in the holy Teachings, will develop natures like unto the sweet airs that blow across the gardens of the All-Glorious, and will waft their fragrance around the world. _{106.2}

107.1   107. It is the hope of 'Abdu'l-Bahá that those youthful souls in the schoolroom of the deeper knowledge will be tended by one who traineth them to love. May they all, throughout the reaches of the spirit, learn well of the hidden mysteries; so well that in the Kingdom of the All-Glorious, each one of them, even as a nightingale endowed with speech, will cry out the secrets of the Heavenly Realm, and like unto a longing lover pour forth his sore need and utter want of the Beloved.

108.1   108. Ye should consider the question of goodly character as of the first importance. It is incumbent upon every father and mother to counsel their children over a long period, and guide them unto those things which lead to everlasting honor.

108.2   Encourage ye the school children, from their earliest years, to deliver speeches of high quality, so that in their leisure time they will engage in giving cogent and effective talks, expressing themselves with clarity and eloquence.

109.1   109. O ye recipients of the favors of God! In this new and wondrous Age, the unshakable foundation is the teaching of sciences and arts. According to explicit Holy Texts, every child must be taught crafts and arts, to the degree that is needful. Wherefore, in every city and village, schools must be established and every child in that city or village is to engage in study to the necessary degree.

It followeth that whatever soul shall offer his aid 109.2 to bring this about will assuredly be accepted at the heavenly Threshold, and extolled by the Company on high.

Since ye have striven hard toward this all-important end, it is my hope that ye will reap your 109.3 reward from the Lord of clear tokens and signs, and that the glances of heavenly grace will turn your way.

110. As to the organization of the schools: if 110.1 possible the children should all wear the same kind of clothing, even if the fabric is varied. It is preferable that the fabric as well should be uniform; if, however, this is not possible, there is no harm done. The more cleanly the pupils are, the better; they should be immaculate. The school must be located in a place where the air is delicate and pure. The children must be carefully trained to be most courteous and well-behaved. They must be constantly encouraged and made eager to gain all the summits of human accomplishment, so that from their earliest years they will be taught to have high aims, to conduct themselves well, to be chaste, pure,

and undefiled, and will learn to be of powerful resolve and firm of purpose in all things. Let them not jest and trifle, but earnestly advance unto their goals, so that in every situation they will be found resolute and firm.

110.2   Training in morals and good conduct is far more important than book learning. A child that is cleanly, agreeable, of good character, well-behaved—even though he be ignorant—is preferable to a child that is rude, unwashed, ill-natured, and yet becoming deeply versed in all the sciences and arts. The reason for this is that the child who conducts himself well, even though he be ignorant, is of benefit to others, while an ill-natured, ill-behaved child is corrupted and harmful to others, even though he be learned. If, however, the child be trained to be both learned and good, the result is light upon light.

110.3   Children are even as a branch that is fresh and green; they will grow up in whatever way ye train them. Take the utmost care to give them high ideals and goals, so that once they come of age, they will cast their beams like brilliant candles on the world, and will not be defiled by lusts and passions in the way of animals, heedless and unaware, but instead will set their hearts on achieving everlasting honor and acquiring all the excellences of humankind.

111. The root cause of wrongdoing is ignorance, 111.1
and we must therefore hold fast to the tools of perception and knowledge. Good character must be
taught. Light must be spread afar, so that, in the
school of humanity, all may acquire the heavenly
characteristics of the spirit, and see for themselves
beyond any doubt that there is no fiercer hell, no
more fiery abyss, than to possess a character that
is evil and unsound; no more darksome pit nor
loathsome torment than to show forth qualities
which deserve to be condemned.

The individual must be educated to such a 111.2
high degree that he would rather have his throat
cut than tell a lie, and would think it easier to be
slashed with a sword or pierced with a spear than
to utter calumny or be carried away by wrath.

Thus will be kindled the sense of human dignity 111.3
and pride, to burn away the reapings of lustful appetites. Then will each one of God's beloved shine
out as a bright moon with qualities of the spirit,
and the relationship of each to the Sacred Threshold of his Lord will be not illusory but sound and
real, will be as the very foundation of the building,
not some embellishment on its façade.

It followeth that the children's school must be a 111.4
place of utmost discipline and order, that instruction must be thorough, and provision must be

made for the rectification and refinement of character; so that, in his earliest years, within the very essence of the child, the divine foundation will be laid and the structure of holiness raised up.

111.5 Know that this matter of instruction, of character rectification and refinement, of heartening and encouraging the child, is of the utmost importance, for such are basic principles of God.

111.6 Thus, if God will, out of these spiritual schools illumined children will arise, adorned with all the fairest virtues of humankind, and will shed their light not only across Persia, but around the world.

111.7 It is extremely difficult to teach the individual and refine his character once puberty is passed. By then, as experience hath shown, even if every effort be exerted to modify some tendency of his, it all availeth nothing. He may, perhaps, improve somewhat today; but let a few days pass and he forgetteth, and turneth backward to his habitual condition and accustomed ways. Therefore it is in early childhood that a firm foundation must be laid. While the branch is green and tender it can easily be made straight.

111.8 Our meaning is that qualities of the spirit are the basic and divine foundation, and adorn the true essence of man; and knowledge is the cause of human progress. The beloved of God must attach great importance to this matter, and carry it forward with enthusiasm and zeal.

112. In this holy Cause the question of orphans hath the utmost importance. The greatest consideration must be shown towards orphans; they must be taught, trained and educated. The Teachings of Bahá'u'lláh, especially, must by all means be given to them as far as is possible. 112.1

I supplicate God that thou mayest become a kind parent to orphaned children, quickening them with the fragrances of the Holy Spirit, so that they will attain the age of maturity as true servants of the world of humanity and as bright candles in the assemblage of mankind. 112.2

113. O handmaid of God! . . . To the mothers must be given the divine Teachings and effective counsel, and they must be encouraged and made eager to train their children, for the mother is the first educator of the child. It is she who must, at the very beginning, suckle the newborn at the breast of God's Faith and God's Law, that divine love may enter into him even with his mother's milk, and be with him till his final breath. 113.1

So long as the mother faileth to train her children, and start them on a proper way of life, the training 113.2

which they receive later on will not take its full effect. It is incumbent upon the Spiritual Assemblies to provide the mothers with a well-planned program for the education of children, showing how, from infancy, the child must be watched over and taught. These instructions must be given to every mother to serve her as a guide, so that each will train and nurture her children in accordance with the Teachings.

113.3 Thus will these young plants in the garden of God's love grow and flourish under the warmth of the Sun of Truth, the gentle spring winds of Heaven, and their mother's guiding hand. Thus, in the Abhá Paradise, will each become a tree, bearing his clustered fruit, and each one, in this new and wondrous season, out of the bounties of the spring, will become possessed of all beauty and grace.

114.1 114. O ye loving mothers, know ye that in God's sight, the best of all ways to worship Him is to educate the children and train them in all the perfections of humankind; and no nobler deed than this can be imagined.

115.1 115. O ye two well-loved handmaids of God! Whatever a man's tongue speaketh, that let him prove by his deeds. If he claimeth to be a believer, then let him act in accordance with the precepts of the Abhá Kingdom.

Praised be God, ye two have demonstrated the 115.2
truth of your words by your deeds, and have won
the confirmations of the Lord God. Every day at
first light, ye gather the Bahá'í children together
and teach them the communes and prayers. This
is a most praiseworthy act, and bringeth joy to the
children's hearts: that they should, at every morn,
turn their faces toward the Kingdom and make
mention of the Lord and praise His Name, and in
the sweetest of voices, chant and recite.

These children are even as young plants, and 115.3
teaching them the prayers is as letting the rain
pour down upon them, that they may wax tender
and fresh, and the soft breezes of the love of God
may blow over them, making them to tremble
with joy.

Blessedness awaiteth you, and a fair haven. 115.4

116. O thou daughter of the Kingdom! Thy 116.1
letters were received. Their contents indicated that
thy mother hath ascended to the invisible realm and
that thou hast been left alone. Thy wish is to serve
thy father, who is dear to thee, and also to serve
the Kingdom of God, and thou art perplexed as to
which of the two thou shouldst do. Assuredly engage in service to thy father, and as well, whenever
thou findest time, diffuse the divine fragrances.

117.1 117. O dear one of 'Abdu'l-Bahá! Be the son of thy father and be the fruit of that tree. Be a son that hath been born of his soul and heart and not only of water and clay. A real son is such a one as hath branched from the spiritual part of man. I ask God that thou mayest be at all times confirmed and strengthened.

118.1 118. O ye young Bahá'í children, ye seekers after true understanding and knowledge! A human being is distinguished from an animal in a number of ways. First of all, he is made in the image of God, in the likeness of the Supernal Light, even as the Torah saith, "Let us make man in our image, after our likeness."* This divine image betokeneth all the qualities of perfection whose lights, emanating from the Sun of Truth, illumine the realities of man. And among the greatest of these attributes of perfection are wisdom and knowledge. Ye must therefore put forth a mighty effort, striving by night and day and resting not for a moment, to acquire an abundant share of all the sciences and arts, that the Divine Image, which shineth out from the Sun of Truth, may illumine the mirror of the hearts of men.

118.2 It is the longing desire of 'Abdu'l-Bahá to see each one of you accounted as the foremost professor in the

---

* Genesis 1:26

academies, and in the school of inner significances, each one becoming a leader in wisdom.

119. It is incumbent upon Bahá'í children to surpass other children in the acquisition of sciences and arts, for they have been cradled in the grace of God. 119.1

Whatever other children learn in a year, let Bahá'í children learn in a month. The heart of 'Abdu'l-Bahá longeth, in its love, to find that Bahá'í young people, each and all, are known throughout the world for their intellectual attainments. There is no question but that they will exert all their efforts, their energies, their sense of pride, to acquire the sciences and arts. 119.2

120. O my dear children! Your letter was received. A degree of joy was attained that is beyond words or writing that, praise be to God, the power of the Kingdom of God hath trained such children who, from their early childhood, eagerly wish to acquire Bahá'í education that they may, from the period of their childhood, engage in service to the world of humanity. 120.1

My highest wish and desire is that ye who are my children may be educated according to the teachings of Bahá'u'lláh and may receive a Bahá'í training; that ye may each become a lighted candle 120.2

in the world of humanity, may be devoted to the service of all mankind, may give up your rest and comfort, so that ye may become the cause of the tranquillity of the world of creation.

120.3 Such is my hope for you and I trust that ye may become the cause of my joy and gladness in the Kingdom of God.

121.1 121. O thou whose years are few, yet whose mental gifts are many! How many a child, though young in years, is yet mature and sound in judgment! How many an aged person is ignorant and confused! For growth and development depend on one's powers of intellect and reason, not on one's age or length of days.

121.2 Although still in the season of childhood, yet hast thou recognized thy Lord, while myriads of women are oblivious of Him and are shut away from His heavenly Kingdom and deprived of His bestowals. Render thou thanks unto thy Lord for this wondrous gift.

121.3 I beg of God to heal thy mother, who is honored in the Kingdom of heaven.

122.1 122. As to thy question regarding the education of children: it behooveth thee to nurture them at the breast of the love of God, and urge them onward to the things of the spirit, that they may turn their faces unto God; that their ways may conform to the rules of good conduct and their character be second to none; that they make their own all the graces and praiseworthy qualities of humankind; acquire a sound knowledge of the various branches of learning, so that from the very beginning of life they may become spiritual beings, dwellers in the Kingdom, enamored of the sweet breaths of holiness, and may receive an education religious, spiritual, and of the Heavenly Realm. Verily will I call upon God to grant them a happy outcome in this.

123. O thou who gazest upon the Kingdom of God! Thy letter was received and we note that thou art engaged in teaching the children of the believers, that these tender little ones have been learning *The Hidden Words* and the prayers and what it meaneth to be a Bahá'í. 123.1

The instruction of these children is even as the work of a loving gardener who tendeth his young plants in the flowering fields of the All-Glorious. There is no doubt that it will yield the desired results; especially is this true of instruction as to Bahá'í obligations and Bahá'í conduct, for the little children must needs be made aware in their very heart and soul that "Bahá'í" is not just a name but 123.2

a truth. Every child must be trained in the things of the spirit, so that he may embody all the virtues and become a source of glory to the Cause of God. Otherwise, the mere word "Bahá'í," if it yield no fruit, will come to nothing.

123.3 Strive then to the best of thine ability to let these children know that a Bahá'í is one who embodieth all the perfections, that he must shine out like a lighted taper—not be darkness upon darkness and yet bear the name "Bahá'í."

123.4 Name thou this school the Bahá'í Sunday School.*

124.1 124. The Sunday school for the children in which the Tablets and Teachings of Bahá'u'lláh are read, and the Word of God is recited for the children is indeed a blessed thing. Thou must certainly continue this organized activity without cessation, and attach importance to it, so that day by day it may grow and be quickened with the breaths of the Holy Spirit. If this activity is well organized, rest thou assured that it will yield great results. Firmness and steadfastness, however, are necessary, otherwise it will continue for some time, but later be gradually forgotten. Perseverance is an essential condition. In every project firmness

---

* A Bahá'í children's class in Kenosha, Wisconsin.

and steadfastness will undoubtedly lead to good results; otherwise it will exist for some days, and then be discontinued.

125. The changing of teachers should be nei- 125.1
ther too frequent nor too much delayed; moderation is preferable. Holding your meetings when it
is the time of prayer in other churches is not advisable; it would lead to alienation, since the Bahá'í
children who have their own Sunday school would
be deprived of it if they tried to attend other Sunday schools. Moreover, the admission of children
of non-Bahá'í parents to the school for Bahá'í
children is permissible. And if, in this school, an
outline of the fundamental principles underlying
all religions be set forth for the information of the
children, it can do no harm.

As the children are few in number, it is not pos- 125.2
sible to have different classes and naturally only one
is necessary. Concerning the last question regarding
differences among children, act as ye deem advisable.

126. Thy letter was received. Praise be to God 126.1
it imparted the good news of thy health and safety
and indicated that thou art ready to enter an ag-
ricultural school. This is highly suitable. Strive
as much as possible to become proficient in the

science of agriculture, for in accordance with the divine teachings the acquisition of sciences and the perfection of arts are considered acts of worship. If a man engageth with all his power in the acquisition of a science or in the perfection of an art, it is as if he has been worshipping God in churches and temples. Thus as thou enterest a school of agriculture and strivest in the acquisition of that science thou art day and night engaged in acts of worship—acts that are accepted at the threshold of the Almighty. What bounty greater than this that science should be considered as an act of worship and art as service to the Kingdom of God.

127.1   127. O thou servant of the One true God! In this universal dispensation man's wondrous craftsmanship is reckoned as worship of the Resplendent Beauty. Consider what a bounty and blessing it is that craftsmanship is regarded as worship. In former times, it was believed that such skills were tantamount to ignorance, if not a misfortune, hindering man from drawing nigh unto God. Now consider how His infinite bestowals and abundant favors have changed hellfire into blissful paradise, and a heap of dark dust into a luminous garden.

127.2   It behooveth the craftsmen of the world at each moment to offer a thousand tokens of gratitude at the Sacred Threshold, and to exert their highest endeavor and diligently pursue their professions so that their efforts may produce that which will manifest the greatest beauty and perfection before the eyes of all men.

128. Thy letter was received. I hope that thou 128.1 mayest be protected and assisted under the providence of the True One, be occupied always in mentioning the Lord and display effort to complete thy profession. Thou must endeavor greatly so that thou mayest become unique in thy profession and famous in those parts, because attaining perfection in one's profession in this merciful period is considered to be worship of God. And whilst thou art occupied with thy profession, thou canst remember the True One.

129. O Friends of the Pure and Omnipotent 129.1 God! To be pure and holy in all things is an attribute of the consecrated soul and a necessary characteristic of the unenslaved mind. The best of perfections is immaculacy and the freeing of oneself from every defect. Once the individual is, in every respect, cleansed and purified, then will he become a focal center reflecting the Manifest Light.

129.2 First in a human being's way of life must be purity, then freshness, cleanliness, and independence of spirit. First must the stream bed be cleansed, then may the sweet river waters be led into it. Chaste eyes enjoy the beatific vision of the Lord and know what this encounter meaneth; a pure sense inhaleth the fragrances that blow from the rose gardens of His grace; a burnished heart will mirror forth the comely face of truth.

129.3 This is why, in Holy Scriptures, the counsels of heaven are likened to water, even as the Qur'án saith: "And pure water send We down from Heaven,"* and the Gospel: "Except a man be baptized of water and of the spirit, he cannot enter into the Kingdom of God."† Thus is it clear that the Teachings which come from God are heavenly outpourings of grace; they are rain-showers of divine mercy, and they cleanse the human heart.

129.4 My meaning is this, that in every aspect of life, purity and holiness, cleanliness and refinement, exalt the human condition and further the development of man's inner reality. Even in the physical realm, cleanliness will conduce to spirituality, as the Holy Writings clearly state. And although

* Qur'án 25:50
† cf. John 3:5

bodily cleanliness is a physical thing, it hath, nevertheless, a powerful influence on the life of the spirit. It is even as a voice wondrously sweet, or a melody played: although sounds are but vibrations in the air which affect the ear's auditory nerve, and these vibrations are but chance phenomena carried along through the air, even so, see how they move the heart. A wondrous melody is wings for the spirit, and maketh the soul to tremble for joy. The purport is that physical cleanliness doth also exert its effect upon the human soul.

Observe how pleasing is cleanliness in the sight 129.5 of God, and how specifically it is emphasized in the Holy Books of the Prophets; for the Scriptures forbid the eating or the use of any unclean thing. Some of these prohibitions were absolute, and binding upon all, and whoso transgressed the given law was abhorred of God and anathematized by the believers. Such, for example, were things categorically forbidden, the perpetration of which was accounted a most grievous sin, among them actions so loathsome that it is shameful even to speak their name.

But there are other forbidden things which do 129.6 not cause immediate harm, and the injurious effects of which are only gradually produced: such acts are also repugnant to the Lord, and blameworthy in His sight, and repellent. The absolute unlawfulness of these, however, hath not been expressly set forth in the Text, but their avoidance is necessary to purity, cleanliness, the preservation of health, and freedom from addiction.

129.7 Among these latter is smoking tobacco, which is dirty, smelly, offensive—an evil habit, and one the harmfulness of which gradually becometh apparent to all. Every qualified physician hath ruled—and this hath also been proven by tests—that one of the components of tobacco is a deadly poison, and that the smoker is vulnerable to many and various diseases. This is why smoking hath been plainly set forth as repugnant from the standpoint of hygiene.

129.8 The Báb, at the outset of His mission, explicitly prohibited tobacco, and the friends one and all abandoned its use. But since those were times when dissimulation was permitted, and every individual who abstained from smoking was exposed to harassment, abuse and even death—the friends, in order not to advertise their beliefs, would smoke. Later on, the Book of Aqdas was revealed, and since smoking tobacco was not specifically forbidden there, the believers did not give it up. The Blessed Beauty, however, always expressed repugnance for it, and although, in the early days, there were reasons why He would smoke a little tobacco, in time He completely renounced it, and those sanctified souls who followed Him in all things also abandoned its use.

My meaning is that in the sight of God, smoking tobacco is deprecated, abhorrent, filthy in the extreme; and, albeit by degrees, highly injurious to health. It is also a waste of money and time, and maketh the user a prey to a noxious addiction. To those who stand firm in the Covenant, this habit is therefore censured both by reason and experience, and renouncing it will bring relief and peace of mind to all men. Furthermore, this will make it possible to have a fresh mouth and unstained fingers, and hair that is free of a foul and repellent smell. On receipt of this missive, the friends will surely, by whatever means and even over a period of time, forsake this pernicious habit. Such is my hope. 129.9

As to opium, it is foul and accursed. God protect us from the punishment He inflicteth on the user. According to the explicit Text of the Most Holy Book, it is forbidden, and its use is utterly condemned. Reason showeth that smoking opium is a kind of insanity, and experience attesteth that the user is completely cut off from the human kingdom. May God protect all against the perpetration of an act so hideous as this, an act which layeth in ruins the very foundation of what it is 129.10

to be human, and which causeth the user to be dispossessed for ever and ever. For opium fasteneth on the soul, so that the user's conscience dieth, his mind is blotted away, his perceptions are eroded. It turneth the living into the dead. It quencheth the natural heat. No greater harm can be conceived than that which opium inflicteth. Fortunate are they who never even speak the name of it; then think how wretched is the user.

129.11   O ye lovers of God! In this, the cycle of Almighty God, violence and force, constraint and oppression, are one and all condemned. It is, however, mandatory that the use of opium be prevented by any means whatsoever, that perchance the human race may be delivered from this most powerful of plagues. And otherwise, woe and misery to whoso falleth short of his duty to his Lord.*

129.12   O Divine Providence! Bestow Thou in all things purity and cleanliness upon the people of Bahá. Grant that they be freed from all defilement, and released from all addictions. Save them from committing any repugnant act, unbind them from the chains of every evil habit, that they may live pure and free, wholesome and cleanly, worthy to serve at Thy Sacred Threshold and fit to be related to their Lord. Deliver them from intoxicating

---

* cf. Qur'án 39:57

drinks and tobacco, save them, rescue them, from this opium that bringeth on madness, suffer them to enjoy the sweet savors of holiness, that they may drink deep of the mystic cup of heavenly love and know the rapture of being drawn ever closer unto the Realm of the All-Glorious. For it is even as Thou hast said: "All that thou hast in thy cellar will not appease the thirst of my love—bring me, O cup-bearer, of the wine of the spirit a cup full as the sea!"

O ye, God's loved ones! Experience hath shown 129.13 how greatly the renouncing of smoking, of intoxicating drink, and of opium, conduceth to health and vigor, to the expansion and keenness of the mind and to bodily strength. There is today a people* who strictly avoid tobacco, intoxicating liquor and opium. This people is far and away superior to the others, for strength and physical courage, for health, beauty and comeliness. A single one of their men can stand up to ten men of another tribe. This hath proved true of the entire people: that is, member for member, each individual of this community is in every respect superior to the individuals of other communities.

Make ye then a mighty effort, that the purity 129.14 and sanctity which, above all else, are cherished by

---

* Possibly 'Abdu'l-Bahá was referring to the Sikhs; the description appears to apply to them.

'Abdu'l-Bahá, shall distinguish the people of Bahá; that in every kind of excellence the people of God shall surpass all other human beings; that both outwardly and inwardly they shall prove superior to the rest; that for purity, immaculacy, refinement, and the preservation of health, they shall be leaders in the vanguard of those who know. And that by their freedom from enslavement, their knowledge, their self-control, they shall be first among the pure, the free and the wise.

130.1   130. O thou distinguished physician! . . . Praise be to God that thou hast two powers: one to undertake physical healing and the other spiritual healing. Matters related to man's spirit have a great effect on his bodily condition. For instance, thou shouldst impart gladness to thy patient, give him comfort and joy, and bring him to ecstasy and exultation. How often hath it occurred that this hath caused early recovery. Therefore, treat thou the sick with both powers. Spiritual feelings have a surprising effect on healing nervous ailments.

131.1   131. When giving medical treatment turn to the Blessed Beauty, then follow the dictates of thy heart. Remedy the sick by means of heavenly joy and spiritual exultation, cure the sorely afflicted by imparting to them blissful glad tidings and heal the wounded through His resplendent bestowals. When at the bedside of a patient, cheer and gladden his heart and enrapture his spirit through celestial power. Indeed, such a heavenly breath quickeneth every moldering bone and reviveth the spirit of every sick and ailing one.

132. Although ill health is one of the unavoidable conditions of man, truly it is hard to bear. The bounty of good health is the greatest of all gifts. 132.1

133. There are two ways of healing sickness, material means and spiritual means. The first is by the treatment of physicians; the second consisteth in prayers offered by the spiritual ones to God and in turning to Him. Both means should be used and practiced. 133.1

Illnesses which occur by reason of physical causes should be treated by doctors with medical remedies; those which are due to spiritual causes disappear through spiritual means. Thus an illness caused by affliction, fear, nervous impressions, will be healed more effectively by spiritual rather than by physical treatment. Hence, both kinds of treatment should be followed; they are not contradictory. Therefore thou shouldst also accept physical 133.2

remedies inasmuch as these too have come from the mercy and favor of God, Who hath revealed and made manifest medical science so that His servants may profit from this kind of treatment also. Thou shouldst give equal attention to spiritual treatments, for they produce marvelous effects.

133.3 Now, if thou wishest to know the true remedy which will heal man from all sickness and will give him the health of the divine kingdom, know that it is the precepts and teachings of God. Focus thine attention upon them.

134.1 134. O thou who art attracted to the fragrant breathings of God! I have read thy letter addressed to Mrs. Lua Getsinger. Thou hast indeed examined with great care the reasons for the incursion of disease into the human body. It is certainly the case that sins are a potent cause of physical ailments. If humankind were free from the defilements of sin and waywardness, and lived according to a natural, inborn equilibrium, without following wherever their passions led, it is undeniable that diseases would no longer take the ascendant, nor diversify with such intensity.

134.2 But man hath perversely continued to serve his lustful appetites, and he would not content himself with simple foods. Rather, he prepared for himself food that was compounded of many ingredients, of substances differing one from the other. With this, and with the perpetrating of vile and ignoble acts, his attention was engrossed, and he abandoned the temperance and moderation of a natural way of life. The result was the engendering of diseases both violent and diverse.

For the animal, as to its body, is made up of the same constituent elements as man. Since, however, the animal contenteth itself with simple foods and striveth not to indulge its importunate urges to any great degree, and committeth no sins, its ailments relative to man's are few. We see clearly, therefore, how powerful are sin and contumacy as pathogenic factors. And once engendered these diseases become compounded, multiply, and are transmitted to others. Such are the spiritual, inner causes of sickness. 134.3

The outer, physical causal factor in disease, however, is a disturbance in the balance, the proportionate equilibrium of all those elements of which the human body is composed. To illustrate: the body of man is a compound of many constituent substances, each component being present in a prescribed amount, contributing to the essential equilibrium of the whole. So long as these constituents remain in their due proportion, according to the natural bal- 134.4

213

ance of the whole—that is, no component suffereth a change in its natural proportionate degree and balance, no component being either augmented or decreased—there will be no physical cause for the incursion of disease.

134.5   For example, the starch component must be present to a given amount, and the sugar to a given amount. So long as each remaineth in its natural proportion to the whole, there will be no cause for the onset of disease. When, however, these constituents vary as to their natural and due amounts—that is, when they are augmented or diminished—it is certain that this will provide for the inroads of disease.

134.6   This question requireth the most careful investigation. The Báb hath said that the people of Bahá must develop the science of medicine to such a high degree that they will heal illnesses by means of foods. The basic reason for this is that if, in some component substance of the human body, an imbalance should occur, altering its correct, relative proportion to the whole, this fact will inevitably result in the onset of disease. If, for example, the starch component should be unduly augmented, or the sugar component decreased, an illness will take control. It is the function of a skilled physician to determine which constituent of his patient's body hath suffered diminution, which hath been augmented. Once he hath discovered this, he must prescribe a food containing the diminished element in considerable amounts, to reestablish the body's essential equilibrium. The patient, once his constitution is again in balance, will be rid of his disease.

The proof of this is that while other animals have never studied medical science, nor carried on researches into diseases or medicines, treatments or cures—even so, when one of them falleth a prey to sickness, nature leadeth it, in fields or desert places, to the very plant which, once eaten, will rid the animal of its disease. The explanation is that if, as an example, the sugar component in the animal's body hath decreased, according to a natural law the animal hankereth after an herb that is rich in sugar. Then, by a natural urge, which is the appetite, among a thousand different varieties of plants across the field, the animal will discover and consume that herb which containeth a sugar component in large amounts. Thus the essential balance of the substances composing its body is reestablished, and the animal is rid of its disease. 134.7

This question requireth the most careful investigation. When highly skilled physicians shall fully examine this matter, thoroughly and perseveringly, 134.8

it will be clearly seen that the incursion of disease is due to a disturbance in the relative amounts of the body's component substances, and that treatment consisteth in adjusting these relative amounts, and that this can be apprehended and made possible by means of foods.

134.9 It is certain that in this wonderful new age the development of medical science will lead to the doctors' healing their patients with foods. For the sense of sight, the sense of hearing, of taste, of smell, of touch—all these are discriminative faculties, their purpose being to separate the beneficial from whatever causeth harm. Now, is it possible that man's sense of smell, the sense that differentiates odors, should find some odor repugnant, and that odor be beneficial to the human body? Absurd! Impossible! In the same way, could the human body, through the faculty of sight—the differentiator among things visible—benefit from gazing upon a revolting mass of excrement? Never! Again, if the sense of taste, likewise a faculty that selecteth and rejecteth, be offended by something, that thing is certainly not beneficial; and if, at the outset, it may yield some advantage, in the long run its harmfulness will be established.

134.10 And likewise, when the constitution is in a state of equilibrium, there is no doubt that whatever is relished will be beneficial to health. Observe how an animal will graze in a field where there are a hundred thousand kinds of herbs and grasses, and how, with its sense of smell, it snuffeth up the odors of the plants, and tasteth them with its sense of taste; then it consumeth whatever herb is pleasurable to these senses, and benefiteth therefrom. Were it not for this power of selectivity, the animals would all be dead in a single day; for there are a great many poisonous plants, and animals know nothing of the pharmacopoeia. And yet, observe what a reliable set of scales they have, by means of which to differentiate the good from the injurious. Whatever constituent of their body hath decreased, they can rehabilitate by seeking out and consuming some plant that hath an abundant store of that diminished element; and thus the equilibrium of their bodily components is reestablished, and they are rid of their disease.

At whatever time highly skilled physicians 134.11 shall have developed the healing of illnesses by means of foods, and shall make provision for simple foods, and shall prohibit humankind from living as slaves to their lustful appetites, it is certain that the incidence of chronic and diversified illnesses will abate, and the general health of all mankind will be much improved. This is destined to come about. In the same way, in the character, the conduct and the manners of men, universal modifications will be made.

135.1   135. According to the explicit decree of Bahá'u'lláh one must not turn aside from the advice of a competent doctor. It is imperative to consult one even if the patient himself be a well-known and eminent physician. In short, the point is that you should maintain your health by consulting a highly skilled physician.

136.1   136. It is incumbent upon everyone to seek medical treatment and to follow the doctor's instructions, for this is in compliance with the divine ordinance, but, in reality, He Who giveth healing is God.

137.1   137. O thou who art voicing the praises of thy Lord! I have read thy letter, wherein thou didst express astonishment at some of the laws of God, such as that concerning the hunting of innocent animals, creatures who are guilty of no wrong.

137.2   Be thou not surprised at this. Reflect upon the inner realities of the universe, the secret wisdoms involved, the enigmas, the interrelationships, the rules that govern all. For every part of the universe is connected with every other part by ties that are very powerful and admit of no imbalance, nor any slackening whatever. In the physical realm of creation, all things are eaters and eaten: the plant drinketh in the mineral, the animal doth crop and swallow down the plant, man doth feed upon the animal, and the mineral devoureth the body of man. Physical bodies are transferred past one barrier after another, from one life to another, and all things are subject to transformation and change, save only the essence of existence itself—since it is constant and immutable, and upon it is founded the life of every species and kind, of every contingent reality throughout the whole of creation.

Whensoever thou dost examine, through a microscope, the water man drinketh, the air he doth breathe, thou wilt see that with every breath of air, man taketh in an abundance of animal life, and with every draught of water, he also swalloweth down a great variety of animals. How could it ever be possible to put a stop to this process? For all creatures are eaters and eaten, and the very fabric of life is reared upon this fact. Were it not so, the ties that interlace all created things within the universe would be unraveled. 137.3

And further, whensoever a thing is destroyed, and decayeth, and is cut off from life, it is pro- 137.4

moted into a world that is greater than the world it knew before. It leaveth, for example, the life of the mineral and goeth forward into the life of the plant; then it departeth out of the vegetable life and ascendeth into that of the animal, following which it forsaketh the life of the animal and riseth into the realm of human life, and this is out of the grace of thy Lord, the Merciful, the Compassionate.

137.5   I beg of God that He will assist thee to comprehend the mysteries that lie at the heart of creation, and will draw away the veil from before thine eyes and thy sister's, that the well-guarded secret may be disclosed unto thee, and the hidden mystery be revealed as clear as the sun at noonday; that He will aid thy sister and thy husband to enter the Kingdom of God, and will heal thee of every ill, whether physical or spiritual, that assaileth one in this life.

138.1   138. O ye beloved of the Lord! The Kingdom of God is founded upon equity and justice, and also upon mercy, compassion, and kindness to every living soul. Strive ye then with all your heart to treat compassionately all humankind—except for those who have some selfish, private motive, or some disease of the soul. Kindness cannot be shown the tyrant, the deceiver, or the thief, because, far from awakening them to the error of their ways, it maketh them to continue in their perversity as before. No matter how much kindliness ye may expend upon the liar, he will but lie the more, for he believeth you to be deceived, while ye understand him but too well, and only remain silent out of your extreme compassion.

Briefly, it is not only their fellow human beings 138.2 that the beloved of God must treat with mercy and compassion, rather must they show forth the utmost loving-kindness to every living creature. For in all physical respects, and where the animal spirit is concerned, the selfsame feelings are shared by animal and man. Man hath not grasped this truth, however, and he believeth that physical sensations are confined to human beings, wherefore is he unjust to the animals, and cruel.

And yet in truth, what difference is there when 138.3 it cometh to physical sensations? The feelings are one and the same, whether ye inflict pain on man or on beast. There is no difference here whatever. And indeed ye do worse to harm an animal, for man hath a language, he can lodge a complaint, he can cry out and moan; if injured he can have recourse to the authorities and these will protect him from his aggressor. But the hapless beast is mute, able neither to express its hurt nor take its case to the authorities. If a man inflict a thousand ills upon a beast, it can neither ward him off with speech nor hale him into court. Therefore is it essential that ye show forth the utmost consideration to the animal, and that ye be even kinder to him than to your fellow man.

138.4 Train your children from their earliest days to be infinitely tender and loving to animals. If an animal be sick, let the children try to heal it, if it be hungry, let them feed it, if thirsty, let them quench its thirst, if weary, let them see that it rests.

138.5 Most human beings are sinners, but the beasts are innocent. Surely those without sin should receive the most kindness and love—all except animals which are harmful, such as bloodthirsty wolves, such as poisonous snakes, and similar pernicious creatures, the reason being that kindness to these is an injustice to human beings and to other animals as well. If, for example, ye be tenderhearted toward a wolf, this is but tyranny to a sheep, for a wolf will destroy a whole flock of sheep. A rabid dog, if given the chance, can kill a thousand animals and men. Therefore, compassion shown to wild and ravening beasts is cruelty to the peaceful ones—and so the harmful must be dealt with. But to blessed animals the utmost kindness must be shown, the more the better. Tenderness and loving-kindness are basic principles of God's heavenly Kingdom. Ye should most carefully bear this matter in mind.

139. O thou handmaid of God! The heavenly glad tidings must be delivered with the utmost dignity and magnanimity. And until a soul ariseth with qualities which are essential for the bearer of these tidings, his words will take no effect. 139.1

O bondswoman of God! The human spirit possesseth wondrous powers, but it should be reinforced by the Holy Spirit. What thou hearest other than this is pure imagination. If, however, it be assisted by the bounty of the Holy Spirit, then will its strength be a thing to marvel at. Then will that human spirit uncover realities, and unravel mysteries. Turn thy heart fully to the Holy Spirit, and invite others to do the same; then shall ye witness wonderful results. 139.2

O handmaid of God! The stars in the sky do not exert any spiritual influence on this world of dust; but all the members and parts of the universe are very strongly linked together in that limitless space, and this connection produceth a reciprocity of material effects. Outside the bounty of the Holy Spirit, whatsoever thou hearest as to the effect of trances, or the mediums' trumpets, conveying the 139.3

singing voices of the dead, is imagination pure and simple. As to the bounty of the Holy Spirit, however, relate whatsoever thou wilt—it cannot be overstated; believe, therefore, whatsoever thou hearest of this. But the persons referred to, the trumpet-people, are entirely shut out from this bounty and receive no portion thereof; their way is an illusion.

139.4 O handmaid of God! Prayers are granted through the universal Manifestations of God. Nevertheless, where the wish is to obtain material things, even where the heedless are concerned, if they supplicate, humbly imploring God's help— even their prayer hath an effect.

139.5 O handmaid of God! Although the reality of Divinity is sanctified and boundless, the aims and needs of the creatures are restricted. God's grace is like the rain that cometh down from heaven: the water is not bounded by the limitations of form, yet on whatever place it poureth down, it taketh on limitations—dimensions, appearance, shape—according to the characteristics of that place. In a square pool, the water, previously unconfined, becometh a square; in a six-sided pool it becometh a hexagon, in an eight-sided pool an octagon, and so forth. The rain itself hath no geometry, no limits, no form, but it taketh on one form or another, according to the restrictions of its vessel. In the same way, the Holy Essence of the Lord God is boundless, immeasurable, but His graces and splendors become finite in the creatures, because of their limitations, wherefore the prayers of given persons will receive favorable answers in certain cases.

O handmaid of God! It is with the Lord Christ even as with Adam. Did the first human being who came into existence on this earth have a father or mother? It is certain that he had neither. But Christ lacked only a father. 139.6

O handmaid of God! The prayers which were revealed to ask for healing apply both to physical and spiritual healing. Recite them, then, to heal both the soul and the body. If healing is right for the patient, it will certainly be granted; but for some ailing persons, healing would only be the cause of other ills, and therefore wisdom doth not permit an affirmative answer to the prayer. 139.7

O handmaid of God! The power of the Holy Spirit healeth both physical and spiritual ailments. 139.8

O handmaid of God! It is recorded in the Torah: And I will give you the valley of Achor for a door of hope. This valley of Achor is the city of 'Akká, and whoso hath interpreted this otherwise is of those who know not. 139.9

140.1   140. Thou didst ask as to the transfiguration of Jesus, with Moses and Elias and the Heavenly Father on Mount Tabor, as referred to in the Bible. This occurrence was perceived by the disciples with their inner eye, wherefore it was a secret hidden away, and was a spiritual discovery of theirs. Otherwise, if the intent be that they witnessed physical forms, that is, witnessed that transfiguration with their outward eyes, then there were many others at hand on that plain and mountain, and why did they fail to behold it? And why did the Lord charge them that they should tell no man? It is clear that this was a spiritual vision and a scene of the Kingdom. Wherefore did the Messiah bid them to keep this hidden, "till the Son of Man were risen from the dead,"*—that is, until the Cause of God should be exalted, and the Word of God prevail, and the reality of Christ rise up.

141.1   141. O thou yearning flame, thou who art afire with the love of God! I have read thy letter, and its contents, well-expressed and eloquent, delighted my heart, showing as they did thy deep sincerity in the Cause of God, thy persevering steps along the pathway of His Kingdom, and thy staunch-

---

* Matthew 17:1–19; Mark 9:2–9; Luke 9:28–36

ness in His Faith—for of all great things, this is the greatest in His sight.

How many a soul hath turned itself unto the 141.2 Lord and entered into the protective shadow of His Word, and become famed throughout the world—for example, Judas Iscariot. And then, when the tests grew harsh and the violence thereof intensified, their feet slipped on the pathway and they turned backward from the Faith after having acknowledged its truth, and they denied it, and fell away from harmony and love into mischief and hate. Thus became visible the power of tests, which maketh mighty pillars to tremble and shake.

Judas Iscariot was the greatest of the disciples, 141.3 and he summoned the people to Christ. Then it seemed to him that Jesus was showing increasing regard to the Apostle Peter, and when Jesus said, "Thou art Peter, and upon this rock I will build My church," these words addressed to Peter, and this singling out of Peter for special honor, had a marked effect on the Apostle, and kindled envy within the heart of Judas. For this reason he who had once drawn nigh did turn aside, and he who had believed in the Faith denied it, and his love changed to hate, until he became a cause of the crucifixion of that glorious Lord, that manifest Splendor. Such is the outcome of envy, the chief reason why men turn aside from the Straight Path. So hath it occurred, and will occur, in this great Cause. But it doth not matter, for it engendereth loyalty in the rest, and maketh souls to arise who waver not, who are fixed and unshakable as the mountains in their love for the Manifest Light.

141.4 Convey thou unto the handmaids of the Merciful the message that when a test turneth violent they must stand unmoved, and faithful to their love for Bahá. In winter come the storms, and the great winds blow, but then will follow spring in all its beauty, adorning hill and plain with perfumed plants and red anemones, fair to see. Then will the birds trill out upon the branches their songs of joy, and sermonize in lilting tones from the pulpits of the trees. Erelong shall ye bear witness that the lights are streaming forth, the banners of the realm above are waving, the sweet scents of the All-Merciful are wafted abroad, the hosts of the Kingdom are marching down, the angels of heaven are rushing forward, and the Holy Spirit is breathing upon all those regions. On that day thou shalt behold the waverers, men and women alike, frustrated of their hopes and in manifest loss. This is decreed by the Lord, the Revealer of Verses.

141.5 As to thee, blessed art thou, for thou art steadfast in the Cause of God, firm in His Covenant. I beg of Him to bestow upon thee a spiritual soul, and the life of the Kingdom, and to make thee a leaf verdant and flourishing on the Tree of Life, that thou mayest serve the handmaids of the Merciful with spirituality and good cheer.

Thy generous Lord will assist thee to labor in His vineyard and will cause thee to be the means of spreading the spirit of unity among His handmaids. He will make thine inner eye to see with the light of knowledge, He will forgive thy sins and transform them into goodly deeds. Verily He is the Forgiving, the Compassionate, the Lord of immeasurable grace. 141.6

142. O thou dear handmaid of God! Praise thou God, because thou art favored at His Holy Threshold, and cherished in the Kingdom of His might. Thou art the head of an assembly which is the very imprint of the Company on high, the mirror image of the all-glorious realm. Strive thou with heart and soul, in prayerful humility and self-effacement, to uphold the Law of God and spread His sweet savors abroad. Endeavor thou to become the true president of the assemblies of spiritual souls, and a companion to the angels in the realm of the All-Merciful. 142.1

Thou didst ask as to the tenth to the seventeenth verses of the twenty-first chapter of Saint John the Divine's Revelation. Know thou that ac- 142.2

cording to mathematical principles, the firmament of this earth's brilliant daystar hath been divided among twelve constellations, which they call the twelve zodiacal signs. In the same way, the Sun of Truth shineth out from and sheddeth its bounties through twelve stations of holiness, and by these heavenly signs are meant those stainless and unsullied personages who are the very wellsprings of sanctity, and the dawning-points proclaiming the oneness of God.

142.3   Consider how in the days of the Interlocutor (Moses), there were twelve holy beings who were leaders of the twelve tribes; and likewise in the dispensation of the Spirit (Christ), note that there were twelve Apostles gathered within the sheltering shade of that supernal Light, and from those splendid dawning-points the Sun of Truth shone forth even as the sun in the sky. Again, in the days of Muḥammad, observe that there were twelve dawning-points of holiness, the manifestors of God's confirming help. Such is the way of it.

142.4   Accordingly did Saint John the Divine tell of twelve gates in his vision, and twelve foundations. By "that great city, the holy Jerusalem, descending out of heaven from God" is meant the holy Law of God, and this is set forth in many Tablets and still to be read in the Scriptures of the Prophets of the past: for instance, that Jerusalem was seen going out into the wilderness.

The meaning of the passage is that this heavenly Jerusalem hath twelve gates, through which the blessed enter into the City of God. These gates are souls who are as guiding stars, as portals of knowledge and grace; and within these gates there stand twelve angels. By "angel" is meant the power of the confirmations of God—that the candle of God's confirming power shineth out from the lamp-niche of those souls—meaning that every one of those beings will be granted the most vehement confirming support. 142.5

These twelve gates surround the entire world, that is they are a shelter for all creatures. And further, these twelve gates are the foundation of the City of God, the heavenly Jerusalem, and on each one of these foundations is written the name of one of the Apostles of Christ. That is to say, each one maketh manifest the perfections, the joyous message, and the excellency of that holy Being. 142.6

In brief, the Scripture saith: "And he that talked with me had a rod made out of gold, that is, a measure, wherewith he measured the city and the gates thereof and the towers thereof." The meaning is that certain personages guided the people with a staff grown out of the earth, and shepherded them 142.7

with a rod, like unto the rod of Moses. Others trained and shepherded the people with a rod of iron, as in the Dispensation of Muḥammad. And in this present cycle, because it is the mightiest of Dispensations, that rod grown out of the vegetable kingdom and that rod of iron will be transformed into a rod of purest gold, taken from out the endless treasure houses in the Kingdom of the Lord. By this rod will the people be trained.

142.8   Note well the difference: at one time the Teachings of God were as a staff, and by this means the Holy Scriptures were spread abroad, the Law of God was promulgated and His Faith established. Then followed a time when the staff of the true Shepherd was as iron. And today, in this new and splendid age, the rod is even as pure gold. How wide is the difference here! Know, then, how much ground hath been gained by the Law of God and His Teachings in this dispensation, how they have reached such heights that they far transcend the dispensations gone before: truly this rod is purest gold, while those of other days were of iron and wood.

142.9   This is a brief answer that hath been written for thee, because there was no time for more. It is certain that thou wilt forgive me. The handmaids of God must rise to such a station that they will, by themselves and unaided, comprehend these inner meanings, and be able to expound at full length

every single word; a station where, out of the truth
of their inmost hearts, a spring of wisdom will well
up, and jet forth even as a fountain that leapeth
from its own original source.

143. O thou who hast drawn nigh unto the   143.1
spirit of Christ in the Kingdom of God! Verily the
body is composed of physical elements, and every
composite must needs be decomposed. The spirit,
however, is a single essence, fine and delicate, in-
corporeal, everlasting, and of God. For this reason
whoso looketh for Christ in His physical body
hath looked in vain, and will be shut away from
Him as by a veil. But whoso yearneth to find Him
in the spirit will grow from day to day in joy and
desire and burning love, in closeness to Him, and
in beholding Him clear and plain. In this new and
wondrous day, it behooveth thee to seek after the
spirit of Christ.

Verily the heaven into which the Messiah rose up   143.2
was not this unending sky, rather was His heaven
the Kingdom of His beneficent Lord. Even as He
Himself hath said, "I came down from heaven,"*
and again, "The Son of Man is in heaven."† Hence
it is clear that His heaven is beyond all directional

---

* John 6:38
† John 3:13

points; it encircleth all existence, and is raised up for those who worship God. Beg and implore thy Lord to lift thee up into that heaven, and give thee to eat of its food, in this age of majesty and might.

143.3 Know thou that the people, even unto this day, have failed to unravel the hidden secrets of the Book. They imagine that Christ was excluded from His heaven in the days when He walked the earth, that He fell from the heights of His sublimity, and afterwards mounted to those upper reaches of the sky, to the heaven which doth not exist at all, for it is but space. And they are waiting for Him to come down from there again, riding upon a cloud, and they imagine that there are clouds in that infinite space and that He will ride thereon and by that means He will descend. Whereas the truth is that a cloud is but vapor that riseth out of the earth, and it doth not come down from heaven. Rather, the cloud referred to in the Gospel is the human body, so called because the body is as a veil to man, which, even as a cloud, preventeth him from beholding the Sun of Truth that shineth from the horizon of Christ.

143.4 I beg of God to open before thine eyes the gates of discoveries and perceptions, that thou mayest become informed of His mysteries in this most manifest of days.

I am most eager to meet thee, but the times are   143.5
not propitious. God willing, we shall let thee know
of a better time, when thou canst come rejoicing.

144. O lover of humankind! Thy letter hath   144.1
been received, and it telleth, God be praised, of
thy health and well-being. It appeareth, from thine
answer to a previous letter, that feelings of affection
were being established between thyself and the
friends.

One must see in every human being only that   144.2
which is worthy of praise. When this is done,
one can be a friend to the whole human race. If,
however, we look at people from the standpoint
of their faults, then being a friend to them is a
formidable task.

It happened one day in the time of Christ—may   144.3
the life of the world be a sacrifice unto Him—that
He passed by the dead body of a dog, a carcass reek-
ing, hideous, the limbs rotting away. One of those
present said: "How foul its stench!" And another
said: "How sickening! How loathsome!" To be brief,
each one of them had something to add to the list.

But then Christ Himself spoke, and He told them: 144.4
"Look at that dog's teeth! How gleaming white!"

The Messiah's sin-covering gaze did not for a   144.5
moment dwell upon the repulsiveness of that car-

rion. The one element of that dead dog's carcass which was not abomination was the teeth: and Jesus looked upon their brightness.

144.6   Thus is it incumbent upon us, when we direct our gaze toward other people, to see where they excel, not where they fail.

144.7   Praise be to God, thy goal is to promote the well-being of humankind and to help the souls to overcome their faults. This good intention will produce laudable results.

145.1   145. Thou didst write as to the question of spiritual discoveries. The spirit of man is a circumambient power that encompasseth the realities of all things. Whatsoever thou dost see about thee—wondrous products of human workmanship, inventions, discoveries and like evidences—each one of these was once a secret hidden away in the realm of the unknown. The human spirit laid that secret bare, and drew it forth from the unseen into the visible world. There is, for example, the power of steam, and photography and the phonograph, and wireless telegraphy, and advances in mathematics: each and every one of these was once a mystery, a closely guarded secret, yet the human spirit unraveled these secrets and brought them out of the invisible into the light of day. Thus is it clear that the human spirit is an all-encompassing power that exerteth its dominion over the inner essences of all created things, uncovering the well kept mysteries of the phenomenal world.

The divine spirit, however, doth unveil divine 145.2 realities and universal mysteries that lie within the spiritual world. It is my hope that thou wilt attain unto this divine spirit, so that thou mayest uncover the secrets of the other world, as well as the mysteries of the world below.

Thou didst ask as to chapter 14, verse 30 of 145.3 the Gospel of John, where the Lord Christ saith, "Hereafter I will not talk much with you: for the Prince of this world cometh, and hath nothing in Me." The Prince of this world is the Blessed Beauty; and "hath nothing in Me" signifieth: after Me all will draw grace from Me, but He is independent of Me, and will draw no grace from Me. That is, He is rich beyond any grace of Mine.

As to thy question regarding discoveries made 145.4 by the soul after it hath put off its human form: certainly, that world is a world of perceptions and discoveries, for the interposed veil will be lifted away and the human spirit will gaze upon souls that are above, below, and on a par with itself. It is similar to the condition of a human being in the womb, where his eyes are veiled, and all things are hidden away from him. Once he is born out of the uterine world and entereth this life, he findeth it, with relation to that of the womb, to be a place of perceptions and discoveries, and he observeth all things through his outer eye. In the same way, once he hath departed this life, he will behold in that world whatsoever was hidden from him here: but there he will look upon and comprehend all things with his inner eye. There will he gaze on his fellows and his peers, and those in the ranks above him, and those below. As for what is meant by the equality of souls in the all-highest realm, it is this: the souls of the believers, at the time when they first become manifest in the world of the body, are equal, and each is sanctified and pure. In this world, however, they will begin to differ one from another, some achieving the highest station, some a middle one, others remaining at the lowest stage of being. Their equal status is at the beginning of their existence; the differentiation followeth their passing away.

145.5 Thou didst write as to Seir. Seir is a locality near Nazareth in Galilee.

145.6 As to the statement of Job, chapter 19, verses 25–27, "I know that my Redeemer liveth, and that He shall stand at the latter day upon the earth," the meaning here is: I shall not be abased, I have a Sustainer and a Guardian, and my Helper, my Defender will in the end be made manifest. And although now my flesh be weak and clothed with worms, yet shall I be healed, and with these mine own eyes, that is, mine inner sight, I shall behold Him. This did Job say after they had reproached him, and he himself had lamented the harms that his tribulations had wreaked upon him. And even when, from the terrible inroads of the sickness, his body was covered with worms, he sought to tell those about him that still he would be fully healed, and that in his very body, with his very eyes, he would gaze on his Redeemer.

As to the woman in the Revelation of Saint 145.7 John, chapter 12, who fled into the wilderness, and the great wonder appearing in the heavens—that woman clothed with the sun, with the moon under her feet: what is meant by the woman is the Law of God. For according to the terminology of the Holy Books, this reference is to the Law, the woman being its symbol here. And the two luminaries, the sun and the moon, are the two thrones, the Turkish and the Persian, these two being under the rule of the Law of God. The sun is the symbol of the Persian Empire, and the moon, that is, the crescent, of the Turkish. The twelve-fold crown is the twelve

Imáms, who, even as the Apostles, supported the Faith of God. The newborn Child is the Beauty of the Adored One,* come forth out of the Law of God. He then saith that the woman fled into the wilderness, that is, the Law of God was carried out of Palestine to the desert of Ḥijáz, where it remained 1260 years—that is, until the advent of the promised Child. And as is well known, in the Holy Books, every day is accounted as one year.

146.1　146. O thou handmaid afire with the love of God! I have considered thine excellent letter, and thanked God for thy safe arrival in that great city. I beg of Him, through His unfailing aid, to cause this return of thine to exert a powerful effect. Such a thing can only come about if thou dost divest thyself of all attachment to this world, and dost put on the vesture of holiness; if thou dost limit all thy thoughts and all thy words to the remembrance of God and His praise; to spreading His sweet savors abroad, and performing righteous acts; and if thou dost devote thyself to awakening the heedless and restoring sight to the blind, hearing to the deaf, speech to the mute, and through the power of the spirit, giving life to the dead.

---

* The Báb, cf. *Some Answered Questions,* chap. XIII.

For even as Christ said of them in the Gospel, 146.2
the people are blind, they are deaf, they are dumb;
and He said: "I will heal them."

Be thou kind and compassionate to thine en- 146.3
feebled mother, and speak to her of the Kingdom,
that her heart may rejoice.

Give thou my greetings to Miss Ford. Convey to 146.4
her the glad tidings that these are the days of the
Kingdom of God. Say unto her: Blessed art thou
for thy noble aims, blessed art thou for thy goodly
deeds, blessed art thou for thy spiritual nature. Verily do I love thee on account of these thine aims
and qualities and deeds. Tell her further: Remember
the Messiah, and His days on earth, and His abasement, and His tribulations, and how the people
paid Him no mind. Remember how the Jews would
hold Him up to ridicule, and mock at Him, and
address Him with: "Peace be upon thee, King of the
Jews! Peace be upon thee, King of Kings!" How they
would say that He was mad, and would ask how the
Cause of that crucified One could ever spread out to
the easts of the world and the wests thereof. None
followed Him then, save only a few souls who were
fishermen, carpenters, and other plain folk. Alas,
alas, for such delusions!

And see what happened then: how their mighty 146.5
banners were reversed, and in their place His most

exalted standard lifted up; how all the bright stars in that heaven of honor and pride did set; how they sank in the west of all that vanisheth—while His brilliant Orb still shineth down out of skies of undying glory, as the centuries and the ages roll by. Be ye then admonished, ye that have eyes to see! Erelong shall ye behold even greater things than this.

146.6   Know thou that all the powers combined have not the power to establish universal peace, nor to withstand the overmastering dominion, at every time and season, of these endless wars. Erelong, however, shall the power of heaven, the dominion of the Holy Spirit, hoist on the high summits the banners of love and peace, and there above the castles of majesty and might shall those banners wave in the rushing winds that blow out of the tender mercy of God.

146.7   Convey thou my greetings to Mrs. Florence, and tell her: The diverse congregations have given up the ground of their belief, and adopted doctrines that are of no account in the sight of God. They are even as the Pharisees who both prayed and fasted, and then did sentence Jesus Christ to death. By the life of God! This thing is passing strange!

146.8   As to thee, O handmaid of God, softly recite thou this commune to thy Lord, and say unto Him:

O God, my God! Fill up for me the cup of 146.9
detachment from all things, and in the assembly of Thy splendors and bestowals, rejoice me
with the wine of loving Thee. Free me from the
assaults of passion and desire, break off from
me the shackles of this nether world, draw me
with rapture unto Thy supernal realm, and
refresh me amongst the handmaids with the
breathings of Thy holiness.

O Lord, brighten Thou my face with the 146.10
lights of Thy bestowals, light Thou mine eyes
with beholding the signs of Thine all-subduing
might; delight my heart with the glory of Thy
knowledge that encompasseth all things, gladden Thou my soul with Thy soul-reviving tidings of great joy, O Thou King of this world
and the Kingdom above, O Thou Lord of
dominion and might, that I may spread abroad
Thy signs and tokens, and proclaim Thy
Cause, and promote Thy Teachings, and serve
Thy Law, and exalt Thy Word.

Thou art verily the Powerful, the Ever-Giv- 146.11
ing, the Able, the Omnipotent.

As to the fundamentals of teaching the Faith: 146.12
know thou that delivering the Message can be

accomplished only through goodly deeds and spiritual attributes, an utterance that is crystal clear and the happiness reflected from the face of that one who is expounding the Teachings. It is essential that the deeds of the teacher should attest the truth of his words. Such is the state of whoso doth spread abroad the sweet savors of God and the quality of him who is sincere in his faith.

146.13 Once the Lord hath enabled thee to attain this condition, be thou assured that He will inspire thee with words of truth, and will cause thee to speak through the breathings of the Holy Spirit.

147.1 147. Reflect upon the past events of the time of Christ, and the present events shall become clear and manifest.

148.1 148. O ye sons and daughters of the Kingdom! Thankful, the birds of the spirit seek only to fly in the high heavens and to sing out their songs with wondrous art. But the pitiable earthworms love only to tunnel into the ground, and what a mighty struggle they make to get themselves down into its depths! Even so are the sons of earth. Their highest aim is to augment their means of continuing on, in this vanishing world, this death in life; and this despite the fact that they are bound hand and foot by a thousand cares and sorrows, and never safe from danger, not even for the twinkling of an eye; never at any time secure, even from sudden death. Wherefore, after a brief span, are they utterly effaced, and no sign remaineth to tell of them, and no word of them is ever heard again.

Then let you engage in the praise of Bahá'u'lláh, 148.2 for it is through His grace and succor that ye have become sons and daughters of the Kingdom; it is thanks to Him that ye are now songsters in the meadows of truth, and have soared upward to the heights of the glory that abideth forever. Ye have found your place in the world that dieth not; the breaths of the Holy Spirit have blown upon you; ye have taken on another life, ye have gained access to the Threshold of God.

Wherefore, with great gladness, establish ye 148.3 spiritual assemblies, and engage ye in uttering the praise and glorification of the Lord, and calling Him Holy and Most Great. Lift up to the realm of the All-Glorious your suppliant cries for help, and voice ye at every moment a myriad thanks for having won this abounding favor and exceeding grace.

149. O thou who hast eyes to see! That which 149.1 thou didst witness is the very truth, and it pertaineth to the realm of vision.

149.2　　The perfume is intimately commingled and blended with the bud, and once the bud hath opened the sweet scent of it is spread abroad. The herb is not without its fruit, although it seemeth so, for in this garden of God every plant exerteth its own influence and hath its own properties, and every plant can even match the laughing, hundred-petalled rose in rejoicing the sense with its fragrance. Be thou assured of this. Although the pages of a book know nothing of the words and the meanings traced upon them, even so, because of their connection with these words, friends pass them reverently from hand to hand. This connection, furthermore, is purest bounty.

149.3　　When the human soul soareth out of this transient heap of dust and riseth into the world of God, then veils will fall away, and verities will come to light, and all things unknown before will be made clear, and hidden truths be understood.

149.4　　Consider how a being, in the world of the womb, was deaf of ear and blind of eye, and mute of tongue; how he was bereft of any perceptions at all. But once, out of that world of darkness, he passed into this world of light, then his eye saw, his ear heard, his tongue spoke. In the same way, once he hath hastened away from this mortal place into the Kingdom of God, then he will be born in the spirit; then the eye of his perception will open, the ear of his soul will hearken, and all the truths of which he was ignorant before will be made plain and clear.

An observant traveler passing along a way will 149.5 certainly recall his discoveries to mind, unless some accident befall him and efface the memory.

150. O thou handmaid aflame with the fire of 150.1 God's love! Grieve thou not over the troubles and hardships of this nether world, nor be thou glad in times of ease and comfort, for both shall pass away. This present life is even as a swelling wave, or a mirage, or drifting shadows. Could ever a distorted image on the desert serve as refreshing waters? No, by the Lord of Lords! Never can reality and the mere semblance of reality be one, and wide is the difference between fancy and fact, between truth and the phantom thereof.

Know thou that the Kingdom is the real world, 150.2 and this nether place is only its shadow stretching out. A shadow hath no life of its own; its existence is only a fantasy, and nothing more; it is but images reflected in water, and seeming as pictures to the eye.

Rely upon God. Trust in Him. Praise Him, and 150.3 call Him continually to mind. He verily turneth trouble into ease, and sorrow into solace, and toil into utter peace. He verily hath dominion over all things.

150.4 If thou wouldst hearken to my words, release thyself from the fetters of whatsoever cometh to pass. Nay rather, under all conditions thank thou thy loving Lord, and yield up thine affairs unto His Will that worketh as He pleaseth. This verily is better for thee than all else, in either world.

151.1 151. O thou believer in the oneness of God! Know thou that nothing profiteth a soul save the love of the All-Merciful, nothing lighteth up a heart save the splendor that shineth from the realm of the Lord.

151.2 Forsake thou every other concern, let oblivion overtake the memory of all else. Confine thy thoughts to whatever will lift up the human soul to the Paradise of heavenly grace, and make every bird of the Kingdom wing its way unto the Supreme Horizon, the central point of everlasting honor in this contingent world.

152.1 152. As to the question regarding the soul of a murderer, and what his punishment would be, the answer given was that the murderer must expiate his crime: that is, if they put the murderer to death, his death is his atonement for his crime, and following the death, God in His justice will impose no second penalty upon him, for divine justice would not allow this.

153. O thou handmaid of God! In this day, 153.1 to thank God for His bounties consisteth in possessing a radiant heart, and a soul open to the promptings of the spirit. This is the essence of thanksgiving.

As for offering thanks by speaking out or writ- 153.2 ing, although this is indeed acceptable, yet when compared with that other thanksgiving, it is only a semblance and unreal; for the essential thing is these intimations of the spirit, these emanations from the deep recess of the heart. It is my hope that thou wilt be favored therewith.

Regarding one's lack of capacity and one's un- 153.3 deserving on the Day of Resurrection, this does not cause one to be shut out from gifts and bounties; for this is not the Day of Justice but the Day of Grace, while justice is allotting to each whatever is his due. Then look thou not at the degree of thy capacity, look thou at the boundless favor of Bahá'-u'lláh; all-encompassing is His bounty, and consummate His grace.

I ask of God that with His assistance and strong 153.4 support thou mayest teach the inner meanings of the Torah with eloquence, understanding, vigor and skill. Turn thy face toward the Kingdom of God, ask for the bestowals of the Holy Spirit, speak, and the confirmations of the Spirit will come.

153.5 As for that mighty solar orb which thou didst behold in thy dream, that was the Promised One, and its spreading rays were His bounties, and the translucent surface of the mass of water signifieth hearts that are undefiled and pure, while the surging waves denote the great excitement of those hearts and the fact that they were shaken and deeply moved, that is, the waves are the stirrings of the spirit and holy intimations of the soul. Praise thou God that in the world of the dream thou hast witnessed such disclosures.

153.6 With reference to what is meant by an individual becoming entirely forgetful of self: the intent is that he should rise up and sacrifice himself in the true sense, that is, he should obliterate the promptings of the human condition, and rid himself of such characteristics as are worthy of blame and constitute the gloomy darkness of this life on earth—not that he should allow his physical health to deteriorate and his body to become infirm.

153.7 I do earnestly and humbly supplicate at the Holy Threshold that heavenly blessings and divine forgiveness will encompass thy dear mother, as well as thy loving sisters and relatives. Especially do I pray on behalf of thy betrothed, who hath suddenly hastened away from this world into the next.

154. O thou son of the Kingdom! Thy most agreeable letters, with their pleasing style, ever gladden our hearts. When the song is of the Kingdom, it rejoiceth the soul. 154.1

Praise thou God that thou hast travelled to that country* for the purpose of raising up His Word and spreading abroad the holy fragrance of His Kingdom, and that thou art serving as a gardener in the gardens of heaven. Erelong shall thine efforts be crowned with success. 154.2

O thou son of the Kingdom! All things are beneficial if joined with the love of God; and without His love all things are harmful, and act as a veil between man and the Lord of the Kingdom. When His love is there, every bitterness turneth sweet, and every bounty rendereth a wholesome pleasure. For example, a melody, sweet to the ear, bringeth the very spirit of life to a heart in love with God, yet staineth with lust a soul engrossed in sensual desires. And every branch of learning, conjoined with the love of God, is approved and 154.3

---

* Germany

worthy of praise; but bereft of His love, learning is barren—indeed, it bringeth on madness. Every kind of knowledge, every science, is as a tree: if the fruit of it be the love of God, then is it a blessed tree, but if not, that tree is but dried-up wood, and shall only feed the fire.

154.4   O thou loyal servant of God and thou spiritual healer of man! Whensoever thou dost attend a patient, turn thy face toward the Lord of the heavenly Kingdom, ask the Holy Spirit to come to thine aid, then heal thou the sickness.

155.1   155. O thou flame of God's love! What thou hast written hath brought great joy, for thy letter was as a garden from which roses of inner meanings spread abroad the sweet exhalations of the love of God. In the same way, my answers will serve as rainshowers and dew, to bestow on those spiritual plants that have blossomed in the garden of thy heart more freshness and delicate beauty than words can tell.

155.2   Thou didst write of afflictive tests that have assailed thee. To the loyal soul, a test is but God's grace and favor; for the valiant doth joyously press forward to furious battle on the field of anguish, when the coward, whimpering with fright, will tremble and shake. So too, the proficient student, who hath with great competence mastered his subjects and committed them to memory, will happily exhibit his skills before his examiners on the day of his tests. So too will solid gold wondrously gleam and shine out in the assayer's fire.

It is clear, then, that tests and trials are, for sanctified 155.3 souls, but God's bounty and grace, while to the weak, they are a calamity, unexpected and sudden.

These tests, even as thou didst write, do but 155.4 cleanse the spotting of self from off the mirror of the heart, till the Sun of Truth can cast its rays thereon; for there is no veil more obstructive than the self, and however tenuous that veil may be, at the last it will completely shut a person out, and deprive him of his portion of eternal grace.

O thou enraptured handmaid of the Lord! 155.5 When the believers, men and women, pass in thought before my eyes, I feel myself warmed at the fire of God's love, and I pray that the Almighty will succor those holy souls with His invisible hosts. Praised be the Lord that the prophecies of all His Manifestations have now been clearly fulfilled, in this greatest of all days, this holy and blessed age.

O thou enraptured handmaid of God! Near- 155.6 ness is verily of the soul, not of the body; and the help that is sought, and the help that cometh, is not material but of the spirit; nevertheless it is my hope that thou wilt attain to nearness in every sense. The bounties of God will verily encompass a sanctified soul even as the sun's light doth the moon and stars: be thou assured of this.

155.7   Waft thou to each one of the believers, men and women alike, fragrant breaths of holiness on behalf of 'Abdu'l-Bahá. Inspire them all and urge them on to shed abroad the sweet savors of the Lord.

156.1   156. O thou servant of the Holy Threshold! We have read what flowed out from thy pen in thy love for God, and found the contents of thy letter most pleasing. My hope is that through the bounty of God, the breaths of the All-Merciful will at all times refresh and renew thee.

156.2   Thou didst write of reincarnation. A belief in reincarnation goeth far back into the ancient history of almost all peoples, and was held even by the philosophers of Greece, the Roman sages, the ancient Egyptians, and the great Assyrians. Nevertheless such superstitions and sayings are but absurdities in the sight of God.

156.3   The major argument of the reincarnationists was this, that according to the justice of God, each must receive his due: whenever a man is afflicted with some calamity, for example, this is because of some wrong he hath committed. But take a child that is still in its mother's womb, the embryo but newly formed, and that child is blind, deaf, lame, defective—what sin hath such a child committed, to deserve its afflictions? They answer that, although to outward seeming the child, still in the womb, is guilty of no sin—nevertheless he perpetrated some wrong when in his previous form, and thus he came to deserve his punishment.

These individuals, however, have overlooked the following point. If creation went forward according to only one rule, how could the all-encompassing Power make Itself felt? How could the Almighty be the One Who "doeth as He pleaseth and ordaineth as He willeth"?* 156.4

Briefly, a return is indeed referred to in the Holy Scriptures, but by this is meant the return of the qualities, conditions, effects, perfections, and inner realities of the lights which recur in every dispensation. The reference is not to specific, individual souls and identities. 156.5

It may be said, for instance, that this lamplight is last night's come back again, or that last year's rose hath returned to the garden this year. Here the reference is not to the individual reality, the fixed identity, the specialized being of that other rose, rather doth 156.6

---

* cf. Qur'án 3:35; 2:254

it mean that the qualities, the distinctive characteristics of that other light, that other flower, are present now, in these. Those perfections, that is, those graces and gifts of a former springtime are back again this year. We say, for example, that this fruit is the same as last year's; but we are thinking only of the delicacy, bloom and freshness, and the sweet taste of it; for it is obvious that that impregnable center of reality, that specific identity, can never return.

156.7 What peace, what ease and comfort did the Holy Ones of God ever discover during Their sojourn in this nether world, that They should continually seek to come back and live this life again? Doth not a single turn at this anguish, these afflictions, these calamities, these body blows, these dire straits, suffice, that They should wish for repeated visits to the life of this world? This cup was not so sweet that one would care to drink of it a second time.

156.8 Therefore do the lovers of the Abhá Beauty wish for no other recompense but to reach that station where they may gaze upon Him in the Realm of Glory, and they walk no other path save over desert sands of longing for those exalted heights. They seek that ease and solace which will abide forever, and those bestowals that are sanctified beyond the understanding of the worldly mind.

When thou lookest about thee with a percep-   156.9
tive eye, thou wilt note that on this dusty earth all
humankind are suffering. Here no man is at rest
as a reward for what he hath performed in former
lives; nor is there anyone so blissful as seemingly
to pluck the fruit of bygone anguish. And if a human life, with its spiritual being, were limited to
this earthly span, then what would be the harvest
of creation? Indeed, what would be the effects and
the outcomes of Divinity Itself? Were such a no-
tion true, then all created things, all contingent realities, and this whole world of being—all would
be meaningless. God forbid that one should hold
to such a fiction and gross error.

For just as the effects and the fruitage of the   156.10
uterine life are not to be found in that dark and narrow place, and only when the child is transferred to
this wide earth do the benefits and uses of growth
and development in that previous world become
revealed—so likewise reward and punishment,
heaven and hell, requital and retribution for actions
done in this present life, will stand revealed in that
other world beyond. And just as, if human life in the
womb were limited to that uterine world, existence
there would be nonsensical, irrelevant—so too if
the life of this world, the deeds here done and their

fruitage, did not come forth in the world beyond, the whole process would be irrational and foolish.

156.11 Know then that the Lord God possesseth invisible realms which the human intellect can never hope to fathom nor the mind of man conceive. When once thou hast cleansed the channel of thy spiritual sense from the pollution of this worldly life, then wilt thou breathe in the sweet scents of holiness that blow from the blissful bowers of that heavenly land.

156.12 The Glory rest upon thee, and upon whosoever turneth toward and gazeth on the Kingdom of the All-Glorious, which the Lord hath sanctified beyond the understanding of those who are neglectful of Him, and hath hid from the eyes of those who show Him pride.

157.1 157. O ye who are strongly attracted! O ye who are mindful! O ye who are advancing unto the Kingdom of God! Verily with all my heart and soul and with all lowliness do I supplicate the Lord God to make of you ensigns of guidance, banners of righteousness, wellsprings of understanding and knowledge, that through you He may lead the seekers unto the straight path and guide them to the broad way of truth in this mightiest of ages.

157.2 O ye loved ones of God! Know ye that the world is even as a mirage rising over the sands, that the thirsty mistaketh for water. The wine of this world is but a vapor in the desert, its pity and compassion but toil and trouble, the repose it proffereth only weariness and sorrow. Abandon it to those who belong to it, and turn your faces unto the Kingdom of your Lord the All-Merciful, that His grace and bounty may cast their dawning splendors over you, and a heavenly table may be sent down for you, and your Lord may bless you, and shower His riches upon you to gladden your bosoms and fill your hearts with bliss, to attract your minds, and cleanse your souls, and console your eyes.

O ye loved ones of God! Is there any giver save 157.3
God? He singleth out for His mercy whomsoever He willeth. Erelong will He open before you the gates of His knowledge and fill up your hearts with His love. He will cheer your souls with the gentle winds of His holiness and make bright your faces with the splendors of His lights, and exalt the memory of you amongst all peoples. Your Lord is verily the Compassionate, the Merciful.

He will come to your aid with invisible hosts, 157.4
and support you with armies of inspiration from the Concourse above; He will send unto you sweet perfumes from the highest Paradise, and waft over you the pure breathings that blow from the rose gardens of the Company on high. He will breathe into your hearts the spirit of life, cause you to enter

the Ark of salvation, and reveal unto you His clear tokens and signs. Verily is this abounding grace. Verily is this the victory that none can deny.

158.1   158. Grieve thou not over the ascension of my beloved Breakwell, for he hath risen unto a rose garden of splendors within the Abhá Paradise, sheltered by the mercy of his mighty Lord, and he is crying at the top of his voice: "O that my people could know how graciously my Lord hath forgiven me, and made me to be of those who have attained His Presence!"*

158.2   *O Breakwell, O my dear one!*
Where now is thy fair face? Where is thy fluent tongue? Where thy clear brow? Where thy bright comeliness?

158.3   *O Breakwell, O my dear one!*
Where is thy fire, blazing with God's love? Where is thy rapture at His holy breaths? Where are thy praises, lifted unto Him? Where is thy rising up to serve His Cause?

158.4   *O Breakwell, O my dear one!*
Where are thy beauteous eyes? Thy smiling lips? The princely cheek? The graceful form?

---

* cf Qur'án 36:25

O Breakwell, O my dear one!   158.5

Thou hast quit this earthly world and risen upward to the Kingdom, thou hast reached unto the grace of the invisible realm, and offered thyself at the threshold of its Lord.

O Breakwell, O my dear one!   158.6

Thou hast left the lamp that was thy body here, the glass that was thy human form, thy earthy elements, thy way of life below.

O Breakwell, O my dear one!   158.7

Thou hast lit a flame within the lamp of the Company on high, thou hast set foot in the Abhá Paradise, thou hast found a shelter in the shadow of the Blessed Tree, thou hast attained His meeting in the haven of Heaven.

O Breakwell, O my dear one!   158.8

Thou art now a bird of Heaven, thou hast quit thine earthly nest, and soared away to a garden of holiness in the kingdom of thy Lord. Thou hast risen to a station filled with light.

O Breakwell, O my dear one!   158.9

Thy song is even as birdsong now, thou pourest forth verses as to the mercy of thy Lord; of Him Who forgiveth ever, thou wert a thankful servant, wherefore hast thou entered into exceeding bliss.

158.10   *O Breakwell, O my dear one!*
Thy Lord hath verily singled thee out for His love, and hath led thee into His precincts of holiness, and made thee to enter the garden of those who are His close companions, and hath blessed thee with beholding His beauty.

158.11   *O Breakwell, O my dear one!*
Thou hast won eternal life, and the bounty that faileth never, and a life to please thee well, and plenteous grace.

158.12   *O Breakwell, O my dear one!*
Thou art become a star in the supernal sky, and a lamp amid the angels of high Heaven; a living spirit in the most exalted Kingdom, throned in eternity.

158.13   *O Breakwell, O my dear one!*
I ask of God to draw thee ever closer, hold thee ever faster; to rejoice thy heart with nearness to His presence, to fill thee with light and still more light, to grant thee still more beauty, and to bestow upon thee power and great glory.

O Breakwell, O my dear one! 158.14

At all times do I call thee to mind. I shall never forget thee. I pray for thee by day, by night; I see thee plain before me, as if in open day.

O Breakwell, O my dear one! 158.15

159. As to thy question, doth every soul without exception achieve life everlasting? Know thou that immortality belongeth to those souls in whom hath been breathed the spirit of life from God. All save these are lifeless—they are the dead, even as Christ hath explained in the Gospel text. He whose eyes the Lord hath opened will see the souls of men in the stations they will occupy after their release from the body. He will find the living ones thriving within the precincts of their Lord, and the dead sunk down in the lowest abyss of perdition. 159.1

Know thou that every soul is fashioned after the nature of God, each being pure and holy at his birth. Afterwards, however, the individuals will vary according to what they acquire of virtues or vices in this world. Although all existent beings are in their very nature created in ranks or degrees, for capacities are various, nevertheless every individual is born holy and pure, and only thereafter may he become defiled. 159.2

159.3 And further, although the degrees of being are various, yet all are good. Observe the human body, its limbs, its members, the eye, the ear, the organs of smell, of taste, the hands, the fingernails. Notwithstanding the differences among all these parts, each one within the limitations of its own being participateth in a coherent whole. If one of them faileth it must be healed, and should no remedy avail, that part must be removed.

160.1 160. O thou sincere and loyal handmaid of the Lord! I have read thy letter. Thou art truly attached to the Kingdom and devoted to the All-Glorious Horizon. I beg of God in His bounty to make thee to burn ever more brightly in the fire of His love, as each day passeth by.

160.2 Thou wert, it appeareth, in doubt as to whether to write, or to teach the Faith. Teaching the Faith is essential, and for the present teaching is preferable for thee. Whensoever thou dost find an opportunity, loose thy tongue and guide the human race.

160.3 Thou didst ask as to acquiring knowledge: read thou the Books and Tablets of God, and the articles written to demonstrate the truth of this Faith. Included among them are the *Íqán*, which hath been translated into English, the works of Mírzá Abu'l-Faḍl, and those of some others among the believers. In the days to come a great number of holy Tablets and other sacred writings will be translated, and thou shouldst read these as well. Likewise, ask thou of God that the magnet of His love should draw unto thee the knowledge of Him. Once a soul becometh holy in all things, purified, sanctified, the gates of the knowledge of God will open wide before his eyes.

Thou hast written of the dear handmaid of God, Mrs. Goodall. That soul enraptured of God is truly serving the Faith at all times, and doing whatever she can to scatter abroad the heavenly splendors. If she continue in this same way, very great results will follow in a time to come. The main thing is to remain staunch and firmly rooted, and persevere to the end. It is my hope that through the high endeavors of the handmaids of the Lord, those foothills and that ocean* shore will grow so bright with the love of God as to cast their beams to the ends of the earth. 160.4

Thou didst ask whether, at the advent of the Kingdom of God, every soul was saved. The Sun of Truth hath shone forth in splendor over all the world, and its luminous rising is man's salvation and his eternal life—but only he is of the saved who hath opened wide the eye of his discernment and beheld that glory. 160.5

---

* The Pacific

160.6　　Likewise didst thou ask whether, in this Bahá'í Dispensation, the spiritual will ultimately prevail. It is certain that spirituality will defeat materialism, that the heavenly will subdue the human, and that through divine education the masses of mankind generally will take great steps forward in all degrees of life—except for those who are blind and deaf and mute and dead. How can such as they understand the light? Though the sun's rays illumine every darkest corner of the globe, still the blind can have no share in the glory, and though the rain of heavenly mercy come down in torrents over all the earth, no shrub or flower will bloom from a barren land.

161.1　　161. O thou who seekest the Kingdom of heaven! This world is even as the body of man, and the Kingdom of God is as the spirit of life. See how dark and narrow is the physical world of man's body, and what a prey it is to diseases and ills. On the other hand, how fresh and bright is the realm of the human spirit. Judge thou from this metaphor how the world of the Kingdom hath shone down, and how its laws have been made to work in this nether realm. Although the spirit is hidden from view, still its commandments shine out like rays of light upon the world of the human body. In the same way, although the Kingdom of heaven is hidden from the sight of this unwitting people, still, to him who seeth with the inner eye, it is plain as day.

Wherefore dwell thou ever in the Kingdom, 161.2 and be thou oblivious of this world below. Be thou so wholly absorbed in the emanations of the spirit that nothing in the world of man will distract thee.

162. O ye dear friends of 'Abdu'l-Bahá! At all 162.1 times do I await your good news, longing as I do to hear that ye are making progress from day to day, and are becoming ever more illumined by the light of guidance.

The blessings of Bahá'u'lláh are a shoreless sea, 162.2 and even life everlasting is only a dewdrop therefrom. The waves of that sea are continually lapping against the hearts of the friends, and from those waves there come intimations of the spirit and ardent pulsings of the soul, until the heart giveth way, and willing or not, turneth humbly in prayer unto the Kingdom of the Lord. Wherefore do all ye can to disengage your inner selves, that ye may at every moment reflect new splendors from the Sun of Truth.

Ye live, all of you, within the heart of 'Abdu'l- 162.3 Bahá, and with every breath do I turn my face toward the Threshold of Oneness and call down blessings upon you, each and all.

163.1   163. O ye two seekers after truth! Your letter was received and its contents noted. As for the letters ye had previously sent, not all were received, while some reached here at a time when the cruelty of the oppressors had so intensified that it was not possible to send a reply. Now this present letter is here, and we are able to answer it, and I have therefore set about writing, in spite of much pressing business, so that ye will know that ye are loved amongst us, and also accepted in the Kingdom of God.

163.2   Your questions, however, can be answered only briefly, since there is no time for a detailed reply. The answer to the first question: the souls of the children of the Kingdom, after their separation from the body, ascend unto the realm of everlasting life. But if ye ask as to the place, know ye that the world of existence is a single world, although its stations are various and distinct. For example, the mineral life occupieth its own plane, but a mineral entity is without any awareness at all of the vegetable kingdom, and indeed, with its inner tongue denieth that there is any such kingdom. In the same way, a vegetable entity knoweth noth-

ing of the animal world, remaining completely
heedless and ignorant thereof, for the stage of the
animal is higher than that of the vegetable, and
the vegetable is veiled from the animal world and
inwardly denieth the existence of that world—all
this while animal, vegetable and mineral dwell
together in the one world. In the same way the
animal remaineth totally unaware of that power
of the human mind which graspeth universal ideas
and layeth bare the secrets of creation—so that a
man who liveth in the east can make plans and
arrangements for the west; can unravel mysteries;
although located on the continent of Europe can
discover America; although sited on the earth can
lay hold of the inner realities of the stars of heaven.
Of this power of discovery which belongeth to the
human mind, this power which can grasp abstract
and universal ideas, the animal remaineth totally
ignorant, and indeed denieth its existence.

In the same way, the denizens of this earth are   163.3
completely unaware of the world of the Kingdom
and deny the existence thereof. They ask, for
example: "Where is the Kingdom? Where is the
Lord of the Kingdom?" These people are even as
the mineral and the vegetable, who know nothing whatever of the animal and the human realm;
they see it not; they find it not. Yet the mineral and

vegetable, the animal and man, are all living here together in this world of existence.

163.4   As to the second question: the tests and trials of God take place in this world, not in the world of the Kingdom.

163.5   The answer to the third question is this, that in the other world the human reality doth not assume a physical form, rather doth it take on a heavenly form, made up of elements of that heavenly realm.

163.6   And the answer to the fourth question: the center of the Sun of Truth is in the supernal world—the Kingdom of God. Those souls who are pure and unsullied, upon the dissolution of their elemental frames, hasten away to the world of God, and that world is within this world. The people of this world, however, are unaware of that world, and are even as the mineral and the vegetable that know nothing of the world of the animal and the world of man.

163.7   The answer to the fifth question is this: Bahá'u'lláh hath raised up the tabernacle of the oneness of mankind. Whoso seeketh shelter under this roof will certainly come forth from other dwellings.

163.8   And to the sixth question: if on some point or other a difference ariseth among two conflicting groups, let them refer to the Center of the Covenant for a solution to the problem.

And the seventh question: Bahá'u'lláh hath   163.9
been made manifest to all mankind and He hath
invited all to the table of God, the banquet of Divine bounty. Today, however, most of those who
sit at that table are the poor, and this is why Christ
hath said blessed are the poor, for riches do prevent
the rich from entering the Kingdom; and again,
He saith, "It is easier for a camel to go through the
eye of a needle, than for a rich man to enter into
the Kingdom of God."* If, however, the wealth
of this world, and worldly glory and repute, do
not block his entry therein, that rich man will be
favored at the Holy Threshold and accepted by the
Lord of the Kingdom.

In brief, Bahá'u'lláh hath become manifest to   163.10
educate all the peoples of the world. He is the Universal Educator, whether of the rich or the poor,
whether of black or white, or of peoples from east
or west, or north or south.

Among those who visit 'Akká, some have made   163.11
great forward strides. Lightless candles, they were
set alight; withered, they began to bloom; dead,
they were recalled to life and went home with tidings of great joy. But others, in truth, have simply
passed through; they have only taken a tour.

---

* Matthew 19:24; Mark 10:25

163.12 O ye twain who are strongly attracted to the Kingdom, thank ye God that ye have made your home a Bahá'í center and a gathering place for the friends.

164.1 164. O ye two faithful and assured souls! The letter was received. Praise be to God, it imparted good tidings. California is ready for the promulgation of the Teachings of God. My hope is that ye may strive with heart and soul that the sweet scent may perfume the nostrils. . . .

164.2 Convey on my behalf to Mrs. Chase respectful greetings and say: "Mr. Chase is a twinkling star above the horizon of Truth, but at present it is still behind the clouds; soon these shall be dispersed and the radiance of that star shall illumine the state of California. Appreciate thou this bounty that thou hast been his wife and companion in life."

164.3 Every year on the anniversary of the ascension* of that blessed soul the friends must visit his tomb on behalf of 'Abdu'l-Bahá and in the utmost lowliness and humility should with all respect lay on his grave wreaths of flowers and spend all the day in quiet prayer, while turning their faces toward the Kingdom of Signs and mentioning and praising the attributes of that illustrious person.

---

* 30 September 1912

165. O my God! O my God! Verily Thy servant, humble before the majesty of Thy divine supremacy, lowly at the door of Thy oneness, hath believed in Thee and in Thy verses, hath testified to Thy word, hath been enkindled with the fire of Thy love, hath been immersed in the depths of the ocean of Thy knowledge, hath been attracted by Thy breezes, hath relied upon Thee, hath turned his face to Thee, hath offered his supplications to Thee, and hath been assured of Thy pardon and forgiveness. He hath abandoned this mortal life and hath flown to the kingdom of immortality, yearning for the favor of meeting Thee.

165.1

O Lord, glorify his station, shelter him under the pavilion of Thy supreme mercy, cause him to enter Thy glorious paradise, and perpetuate his existence in Thine exalted rose garden, that he may plunge into the sea of light in the world of mysteries.

165.2

Verily, Thou art the Generous, the Powerful, the Forgiver and the Bestower.

165.3

O thou assured soul, thou maidservant of God . . . ! Be not grieved at the death of thy respected husband. He hath, verily, attained the meeting of his Lord at the seat of Truth in the presence of the potent King. Do not suppose that thou hast lost

165.4

him. The veil shall be lifted and thou shalt behold his face illumined in the Supreme Concourse. Just as God, the Exalted, hath said, "Him will We surely quicken to a happy life." Supreme importance should be attached, therefore, not to this first creation but rather to the future life.

166.1   166. O servant of Bahá! Be self-sacrificing in the path of God, and wing thy flight unto the heavens of the love of the Abhá Beauty, for any movement animated by love moveth from the periphery to the center, from space to the Daystar of the universe. Perchance thou deemest this to be difficult, but I tell thee that such cannot be the case, for when the motivating and guiding power is the divine force of magnetism it is possible, by its aid, to traverse time and space easily and swiftly. Glory be upon the people of Bahá.

167.1   167. Thou hadst asked about fate, predestination and will. Fate and predestination consist in the necessary and indispensable relationships which exist in the realities of things. These relationships have been placed in the realities of existent beings through the power of creation and every incident is a consequence of the necessary relationship. For example, God hath created a relation between the sun and the terrestrial globe that the rays of the sun should shine and the soil should yield. These relationships constitute predestination, and the manifestation thereof in the plane of existence is fate. Will is that active force which controlleth these relationships and these incidents. Such is the epitome of the explanation of fate and predestination. I have no time for a detailed explanation. Ponder over this; the reality of fate, predestination and will shall be made manifest.

168. O thou lady of the Kingdom! Praise thou God that in this age, the age of the dispensation of Bahá'u'lláh, thou hast been awakened, hast been made aware of the Manifestation of the Lord of Hosts. All the people of the world are buried in the graves of nature, or are slumbering, heedless and unaware. Just as Christ saith: "I may come when you are not aware. The coming of the Son of Man is like the coming of a thief into a house, the owner of which is utterly unaware." 168.1

In brief, my hope is that from the bounties of Bahá'u'lláh, thou mayest daily advance in the Kingdom, that thou mayest become a heavenly angel, confirmed by the breaths of the Holy Spirit, and mayest erect a structure that shall eternally remain firm and unshakable. . . . 168.2

168.3   These days are very precious; grasp the present opportunity and ignite a candle that shall never be extinguished, and which shall pour out its light eternally illuminating the world of mankind!

169.1   169. O ye two patient souls! Your letter was received. The death of that beloved youth and his separation from you have caused the utmost sorrow and grief; for he winged his flight in the flower of his age and the bloom of his youth to the heavenly nest. But he hath been freed from this sorrow-stricken shelter and hath turned his face toward the everlasting nest of the Kingdom, and, being delivered from a dark and narrow world, hath hastened to the sanctified realm of light; therein lieth the consolation of our hearts.

169.2   The inscrutable divine wisdom underlieth such heartrending occurrences. It is as if a kind gardener transferreth a fresh and tender shrub from a confined place to a wide open area. This transfer is not the cause of the withering, the lessening or the destruction of that shrub; nay, on the contrary, it maketh it to grow and thrive, acquire freshness and delicacy, become green and bear fruit. This hidden secret is well known to the gardener, but those souls who are unaware of this bounty suppose that the gardener, in his anger and wrath, hath uprooted the shrub. Yet to those who are aware, this concealed fact is manifest, and this predestined decree is considered a bounty. Do not feel grieved or disconsolate, therefore, at the ascension of that bird of faithfulness; nay, under all circumstances pray for that youth, supplicating for him forgiveness and the elevation of his station.

I hope that ye will attain the utmost patience, composure and resignation, and I entreat and implore at the Threshold of Oneness, begging for forgiveness and pardon. My hope from the infinite bounties of God is that He may shelter this dove of the garden of faith, and cause him to abide on the branch of the Supreme Concourse, that he may sing in the best of melodies the praise and glorification of the Lord of Names and Attributes.   169.3

170. O thou seeker of the Kingdom! Thy letter was received. Thou hast written of the severe calamity that hath befallen thee—the death of thy respected husband. That honorable man hath been so subjected to the stress and strain of this world that his greatest wish was for deliverance from it. Such is this mortal abode: a storehouse of afflictions and suffering. It is ignorance that binds man to it, for no comfort can be secured by any soul in this world, from monarch down to the most hum-   170.1

ble commoner. If once this life should offer a man a sweet cup, a hundred bitter ones will follow; such is the condition of this world. The wise man, therefore, doth not attach himself to this mortal life and doth not depend upon it; at some moments, even, he eagerly wisheth for death that he may thereby be freed from these sorrows and afflictions. Thus it is seen that some, under extreme pressure of anguish, have committed suicide.

170.2   As to thy husband, rest assured. He will be immersed in the ocean of pardon and forgiveness and will become the recipient of bounty and favor. Strive thine utmost to give his child a Bahá'í training so that when he attaineth maturity he may be merciful, illumined and heavenly.

171.1   171. O thou beloved maidservant of God, although the loss of a son is indeed heartbreaking and beyond the limits of human endurance, yet one who knoweth and understandeth is assured that the son hath not been lost but, rather, hath stepped from this world into another, and she will find him in the divine realm. That reunion shall be for eternity, while in this world separation is inevitable and bringeth with it a burning grief.

171.2   Praise be unto God that thou hast faith, art turning thy face toward the everlasting Kingdom and believest in the existence of a heavenly world. Therefore be thou not disconsolate, do not languish, do not sigh, neither wail nor weep; for agitation and mourning deeply affect his soul in the divine realm.

That beloved child addresseth thee from the 171.3 hidden world: "O thou kind Mother, thank divine Providence that I have been freed from a small and gloomy cage and, like the birds of the meadows, have soared to the divine world—a world which is spacious, illumined, and ever gay and jubilant. Therefore, lament not, O Mother, and be not grieved; I am not of the lost, nor have I been obliterated and destroyed. I have shaken off the mortal form and have raised my banner in this spiritual world. Following this separation is everlasting companionship. Thou shalt find me in the heaven of the Lord, immersed in an ocean of light."

172. Praise be to God, thy heart is engaged in 172.1 the commemoration of God, thy soul is gladdened by the glad tidings of God and thou art absorbed in prayer. The state of prayer is the best of conditions, for man is then associating with God. Prayer verily bestoweth life, particularly when offered in private and at times, such as midnight, when freed from daily cares.

173.1   173. Those souls that, in this day, enter the divine kingdom and attain everlasting life, although materially dwelling on earth, yet in reality soar in the realm of heaven. Their bodies may linger on earth but their spirits travel in the immensity of space. For as thoughts widen and become illumined, they acquire the power of flight and transport man to the kingdom of God.

174.1   174. O ye spiritual friends of 'Abdu'l-Bahá! The letter ye had written hath been noted; its contents were most pleasing and bespoke your firmness and steadfastness in the Cause of God.

174.2   That Assembly resteth in the sheltering shade of the Lord of all bounties, and it is my hope that, as beseemeth that body, it will be favored and invigorated by the breathings of the Holy Spirit, and that day by day ye will love God in ever greater measure, and become more tightly bound to the Beauty that abideth forever, to Him Who is the Light of the world. For love of God and spiritual attraction do cleanse and purify the human heart and dress and adorn it with the spotless garment of holiness; and once the heart is entirely attached to the Lord, and bound over to the Blessed Perfection, then will the grace of God be revealed.

174.3   This love is not of the body but completely of the soul. And those souls whose inner being is lit by the love of God are even as spreading rays of light, and they shine out like stars of holiness in a pure and crystalline sky. For true love, real love, is the love for God, and this is sanctified beyond the notions and imaginings of men.

Let God's beloved, each and every one, be the 174.4 essence of purity, the very life of holiness, so that in every country they may become famed for their sanctity, independence of spirit, and meekness. Let them be cheered by draughts from the eternal cup of love for God, and make merry as they drink from the wine-vaults of Heaven. Let them behold the Blessed Beauty, and feel the flame and rapture of that meeting, and be struck dumb with awe and wonder. This is the station of the sincere; this is the way of the loyal; this is the brightness that shineth on the faces of those nigh unto God.

Wherefore must the friends of God, with utter 174.5 sanctity, with one accord, rise up in the spirit, in unity with one another, to such a degree that they will become even as one being and one soul. On such a plane as this, physical bodies play no part, rather doth the spirit take over and rule; and when its power encompasseth all then is spiritual union achieved. Strive ye by day and night to cultivate your unity to the fullest degree. Let your thoughts dwell on your own spiritual development, and close your eyes to the deficiencies of other souls.

Act ye in such wise, showing forth pure and goodly deeds, and modesty and humility, that ye will cause others to be awakened.

174.6 Never is it the wish of 'Abdu'l-Bahá to see any being hurt, nor will He make anyone to grieve; for man can receive no greater gift than this, that he rejoice another's heart. I beg of God that ye will be bringers of joy, even as are the angels in Heaven.

175.1 175. Mortal charm shall fade away, roses shall give way to thorns, and beauty and youth shall live their day and be no more. But that which eternally endureth is the Beauty of the True One, for its splendor perisheth not and its glory lasteth forever; its charm is all-powerful and its attraction infinite. Well is it then with that countenance that reflecteth the splendor of the Light of the Beloved One! The Lord be praised, thou hast been illumined with this Light, hast acquired the pearl of true knowledge, and hast spoken the Word of Truth.

176.1 176. O thou who art attracted to the Kingdom of God! Every soul seeketh an object and cherisheth a desire, and day and night striveth to attain his aim. One craveth riches, another thirsteth for glory and still another yearneth for fame, for art, for prosperity and the like. Yet finally all are doomed to loss and disappointment. One and all they leave behind them all that is theirs and empty-handed hasten to the realm beyond, and all their labors shall be in vain. To dust they shall all return, denuded, depressed, disheartened and in utter despair.

But, praised be the Lord, thou art engaged 176.2 in that which secureth for thee a gain that shall eternally endure; and that is naught but thine attraction to the Kingdom of God, thy faith, and thy knowledge, the enlightenment of thine heart, and thine earnest endeavor to promote the Divine Teachings.

Verily this gift is imperishable and this wealth is 176.3 a treasure from on high!

177. O living flame of heavenly love! Thine heart 177.1 hath been so fired with the love of God that from ten thousand leagues afar its warmth and radiance may be felt and seen. The fire lit by mortal hand imparteth light and warmth to but a little space, whereas that sacred flame which the Hand of God hath kindled, though burning in the east, will set aflame the west and give warmth to both the north and the south; nay, it shall rise from this world to glow with the hottest flame in the realms on high, flooding with light the Kingdom of eternal glory.

177.2 Happy art thou to have obtained so heavenly a gift. Blessed art thou to be favored with His divine bestowals.

177.3 The glory of God rest upon thee and upon them that hold fast unto the sure handle of His Will and holy Covenant.

178.1 178. O maidservant of God! Thy letter dated 9 December 1918 was received. Its contents were noted. Never lose thy trust in God. Be thou ever hopeful, for the bounties of God never cease to flow upon man. If viewed from one perspective they seem to decrease, but from another they are full and complete. Man is under all conditions immersed in a sea of God's blessings. Therefore, be thou not hopeless under any circumstances, but rather be firm in thy hope.

178.2 Attendance at the gatherings of the friends is specifically to keep them alert, vigilant, loving and attracted to the divine Kingdom.

178.3 If thou hast a full and eager desire to travel to Phillsburg, Montana, thou art permitted, perchance thou mayest be able to ignite a candle amid that group of miners and may make them awake and vigilant so that they may turn to God and may acquire a share from the Bounty of the divine Kingdom.

179. Strive as much as ye can to turn wholly 179.1
toward the Kingdom, that ye may acquire innate
courage and ideal power.

180. I hope that in this nether world thou shalt 180.1
attain unto heavenly light, thou wilt free the souls
from the gloom of nature, which is the animal kingdom, and cause them to reach lofty stations in the
human kingdom. Today all people are immersed
in the world of nature. That is why thou dost see
jealousy, greed, the struggle for survival, deception,
hypocrisy, tyranny, oppression, disputes, strife, bloodshed, looting and pillaging, which all emanate from
the world of nature. Few are those who have been
freed from this darkness, who have ascended from
the world of nature to the world of man, who have
followed the divine Teachings, have served the world
of humanity, are resplendent, merciful, illumined
and like unto a rose garden. Strive thine utmost to
become godlike, characterized with His attributes,
illumined and merciful, that thou mayest be freed
from every bond and become attached at heart to
the Kingdom of the incomparable Lord. This is
Bahá'í bounty, and this is heavenly light.

181. Regarding the statement in The Hidden 181.1
Words, that man must renounce his own self, the

meaning is that he must renounce his inordinate desires, his selfish purposes and the promptings of his human self, and seek out the holy breathings of the spirit, and follow the yearnings of his higher self, and immerse himself in the sea of sacrifice, with his heart fixed upon the beauty of the All-Glorious.

181.2   As for the reference in The Hidden Words regarding the Covenant entered into on Mount Párán, this signifieth that in the sight of God the past, the present and the future are all one and the same—whereas, relative to man, the past is gone and forgotten, the present is fleeting, and the future is within the realm of hope. And it is a basic principle of the Law of God that in every Prophetic Mission, He entereth into a Covenant with all believers—a Covenant that endureth until the end of that Mission, until the promised day when the Personage stipulated at the outset of the Mission is made manifest. Consider Moses, He Who conversed with God. Verily, upon Mount Sinai, Moses entered into a Covenant regarding the Messiah, with all those souls who would live in the day of the Messiah. And those souls, although they appeared many centuries after Moses, were nevertheless—so far as the Covenant, which is outside time, was concerned—present there with Moses. The Jews, however, were heedless of this and remembered it not, and thus they suffered a great and clear loss.

As to the reference in the Arabic Hidden Words 181.3 that the human being must become detached from self, here too the meaning is that he should not seek out anything whatever for his own self in this swiftly passing life, but that he should cut the self away, that is, he should yield up the self and all its concerns on the field of martyrdom, at the time of the coming of the Lord.

182. O ye who are holding fast unto the Cov- 182.1 enant and Testament! This day, from the realms of the All-Glorious, from the Kingdom of Holiness where hosannas of glorification and praise rise up, the Company on high direct their gaze upon you. Whensoever their gaze lighteth upon gatherings of those who are steadfast in the Covenant and Testament, then do they utter their cry, "Glad tidings! Glad tidings!" Then, exulting, do they lift up their voices, and shout, "O ye spiritual communion! O ye gathering of God! Blessed are ye! Glad tidings be unto you! Bright be your faces, and be ye of good cheer, for ye cling to the Covenant of the Beloved of all the worlds, ye are on fire with the wine of His Testament. Ye have plighted your troth to

the Ancient of Days, ye have drunk deep from the chalice of loyalty. Ye have guarded and defended the Cause of God; ye have not been a cause of dividing up His Word; ye have not brought His Faith low, but have striven to glorify His Holy Name; ye have not allowed the Blessed Cause to be exposed to the derision of the people. Ye have not permitted the Designated Station to be humbled, nor been willing to see the Center of Authority discredited or exposed to mockery and persecution. Ye have striven to keep the Word whole and one. Ye have passed through the portals of mercy. Ye have not let the Blessed Beauty slip from your minds, to fade unremembered."

182.2 The Glory rest upon you.

183.1 183. O thou daughter of the Kingdom! Thy letter was received. It was like the melody of the divine nightingale, whose song delighteth the hearts. This is because its contents indicated faith, assurance and firmness in the Covenant and the Testament. Today the dynamic power of the world of existence is the power of the Covenant which like unto an artery pulsateth in the body of the contingent world and protecteth Bahá'í unity.

183.2 The Bahá'ís are commanded to establish the oneness of mankind; if they cannot unite around one point how will they be able to bring about the unity of mankind?

The purpose of the Blessed Beauty in entering 183.3 into this Covenant and Testament was to gather all existent beings around one point so that the thoughtless souls, who in every cycle and generation have been the cause of dissension, may not undermine the Cause. He hath, therefore, commanded that whatever emanateth from the Center of the Covenant is right and is under His protection and favor, while all else is error.

Praise be to God, thou art firm in the Covenant 183.4 and the Testament.

184. O ye blessed souls! Although ye are un- 184.1 dergoing crucial tests in view of the repeated and assiduous attempts of some people to shake the faith of the friends in Los Angeles, yet ye are under the guarding eye of the bounty of Bahá'u'lláh and are assisted by legions of angels.

Walk, therefore, with a sure step and engage with 184.2 the utmost assurance and confidence in the promulgation of the divine fragrances, the glorification of the Word of God and firmness in the Covenant. Rest ye assured that if a soul ariseth in the utmost perseverance and raiseth the Call of the Kingdom and resolutely promulgateth the Covenant, be he an insignificant ant he shall be enabled to drive away the formidable elephant from the arena, and if he be a feeble moth he shall cut to pieces the plumage of the rapacious vulture.

184.3 Endeavor, therefore, that ye may scatter and disperse the army of doubt and of error with the power of the holy utterances. This is my exhortation and this is my counsel. Do not quarrel with anybody, and shun every form of dispute. Utter the Word of God. If he accepteth it, the desired purpose is attained, and if he turneth away leave him to himself and trust to God.

184.4 Such is the attribute of those who are firm in the Covenant.

185.1 185. O ye friends and maidservants of the Merciful! From the Spiritual Assembly of Los Angeles a letter hath been received. It was indicative of the fact that the blessed souls in California, like unto an immovable mountain, are withstanding the gale of violation, have, like unto blessed trees, been planted in the soil of the Covenant and are most firm and steadfast. The hope is entertained, therefore, that through the blessings of the Sun of Truth they may daily increase in their firmness and steadfastness. The tests of every dispensation are in direct proportion to the greatness of the Cause, and as heretofore such a manifest Covenant, written by the Supreme Pen, hath not been entered upon, the tests are proportionately more severe. These trials cause the feeble souls to waver while those who are firm are not affected. These agitations of the violators are no more than the foam of the ocean, which is one of its inseparable features; but the ocean of the Covenant shall surge and shall cast ashore the bodies of the dead, for it cannot retain them. Thus it is seen that the ocean of the Covenant hath surged and surged until it hath thrown out the dead bodies—souls that are deprived of the Spirit of God and are lost in passion and self and are seeking leadership. This foam of the ocean shall not endure and shall soon disperse and vanish, while the ocean of the Covenant shall eternally surge and roar. . . .

From the early days of creation down to the present time, throughout all the divine dispensations, such a firm and explicit Covenant hath not been entered upon. In view of this fact is it possible for this foam to remain on the surface of the ocean of the Covenant? No, by God! The violators are trampling upon their own dignity, are uprooting their own foundations and are proud at being upheld by flatterers who exert a great effort to shake the faith of feeble souls. But this action of theirs is 185.2

of no consequence; it is a mirage and not water, foam and not the sea, mist and not a cloud, illusion and not reality. All this ye shall soon see.

185.3   Praise be to God, ye are firm and steadfast; be ye thankful that like unto blessed trees ye are firmly planted in the soil of the Covenant. It is sure that every firm one will grow, will yield new fruits and will increase daily in freshness and grace. Reflect upon all the writings of Bahá'u'lláh, whether epistles or prayers, and ye shall surely come across a thousand passages wherein Bahá'u'lláh prays: "O God! Bring to naught the violators of the Covenant and defeat the oppressors of the Testament." "He who denieth the Covenant and the Testament is rejected by God, and he who remaineth firm and steadfast therein is favored at the Threshold of Oneness." Such sayings and prayers abound, refer to them and ye shall know.

185.4   Never be depressed. The more ye are stirred by violation, the more deepen ye in firmness and steadfastness, and be assured that the divine hosts shall conquer, for they are assured of the victory of the Abhá Kingdom. Throughout all regions the standard of firmness and steadfastness is upraised and the flag of violation is debased, for only a few weak souls have been led away by the flattery and the specious arguments of the violators who are outwardly with the greatest care exhibiting firmness but inwardly are engaged in agitating souls. Only a few who are the leaders of those who stir and agitate are outwardly known as violators while the rest, through subtle means, deceive the souls, for outwardly they assert their firmness and steadfastness in the Covenant but when they come across responsive ears they secretly sow the seeds of suspicion. The case of all of them resembleth the violation of the Covenant by Judas Iscariot and his followers. Consider: hath any result or trace remained after them? Not even a name hath been left by his followers and although a number of Jews sided with him it was as if he had no followers at all. This Judas Iscariot who was the leader of the apostles betrayed Christ for thirty pieces of silver. Take heed, O ye people of perception!

At this time these insignificant violators will surely betray the Center of the Covenant for the large sum which by every subtle means they have begged. It is now thirty years since Bahá'u'lláh ascended, and in that time these violators have striven with might and main. What have they achieved? Under all conditions those who have remained firm in the Covenant have conquered, while the violators have met defeat, disappointment and dejection. After the ascension of 'Abdu'l-Bahá, no trace of them shall 185.5

remain. These souls are ignorant of what will happen and are proud of their own fancies.

185.6   In short, O ye friends of God and maidservants of the Merciful! The hand of divine bounty hath placed upon your heads a jewelled crown, the precious gems of which shall shine eternally over all regions. Appreciate this bounty, loose your tongues in praise and thanksgiving, and engage in the promulgation of the divine teachings, for this is the spirit of life and the means of salvation.

186.1   186. O thou who art firm in the Covenant! Three consecutive letters have been received from thee. From their contents it became known that in Cleveland the hearts are afflicted by the murky breaths of the Covenant-breakers and harmony hath decreased among the friends. Gracious God! A hundred times it hath been foretold that the violators are lying in ambush and by every means desire to cause dissension among the friends so that this dissension may end in violation of the Covenant. How is it that, notwithstanding this warning, the friends have neglected this explicit statement?

186.2   The point at issue is clear, direct and of utmost brevity. Either Bahá'u'lláh was wise, omniscient and aware of what would ensue, or was ignorant and in error. He entered, by His supreme pen, into such a firm Covenant and Testament with all the Bahá'ís, first with the Aghṣán, the Afnán and His kindred, and commanded them to obey and turn toward Him. By His supreme pen He hath explicitly declared that the object of the following verse of the *Kitáb-i-Aqdas* is the Most Great Branch:

"When the ocean of My presence hath ebbed   186.3
and the Book of My Revelation is ended, turn your faces toward Him Whom God hath purposed, Who hath branched from this Ancient Root." Its meaning briefly is this: that after My ascension it is incumbent upon the Aghṣán, the Afnán and the kindred, and all the friends of God, to turn their faces to Him Who hath branched from the Ancient Root.

He also plainly saith in the *Kitáb-i-Aqdas*: "O ye   186.4
people of the world! When the Mystic Dove will have winged its flight from its Sanctuary of Praise and sought its far-off goal, its hidden habitation, refer ye whatsoever ye understand not in the Book to Him Who hath branched from this mighty Stock." Addressing all the people of the world He saith: When the Mystic Dove flieth away from the orchard of praise to the Most Supreme and Invisible Station—that is, when the Blessed Beauty turneth away from the contingent world towards the invisible realm—refer whatever ye do not un-

derstand in the Book to Him Who hath branched from the Ancient Root. That is, whatever He saith is the very truth.

186.5 And in the Book of the Covenant He explicitly saith that the object of this verse "Who hath branched from this Ancient Root" is the Most Mighty Branch. And He commandeth all the Aghṣán, the Afnán, the kindred and the Bahá'ís to turn toward Him. Now, either one must say that the Blessed Beauty hath made a mistake, or He must be obeyed. 'Abdu'l-Bahá hath no command for the people to obey save the diffusion of the fragrances of God, the exaltation of His Word, the promulgation of the oneness of the world of humanity, the establishment of universal peace, and other of the commands of God. These are divine commands and have nothing to do with 'Abdu'l-Bahá. Whoever wisheth may accept them, and anyone who rejecteth them may do as he pleaseth.

186.6 Now some of the mischief-makers, with many stratagems, are seeking leadership, and in order to reach this position they instil doubts among the friends that they may cause differences, and that these differences may result in their drawing a party to themselves. But the friends of God must be awake and must know that the scattering of these doubts hath as its motive personal desires and the achievement of leadership.

Do not disrupt Bahá'í unity, and know that this 186.7
unity cannot be maintained save through faith in
the Covenant of God.

Thou hast the desire to travel that thou mayest 186.8
spread the fragrances of God. This is highly suitable. Assuredly divine confirmations will assist thee
and the power of the Covenant and Testament
will secure for thee triumph and victory.

187. O thou who art firm in the Covenant! Thy 187.1
letter was received. Thou hast expressed satisfac-
tion with the Convention, that this gathering hath
been the means of the elevation of the Cause of
God and the demonstration of the power of His
Word. The greatness of the Cause will clear away
these differences and may be compared to health in
the body of man which, when established, cureth
all disease and weakness. Our hope is that no trace
of opposition may remain; but some of the friends
in America are restless in their fresh ambitions and
strive and seek under the ground and in the air to
discover anything that breedeth dissension.

Praise be to God, all such doors are closed in 187.2
the Cause of Bahá'u'lláh for a special authoritative
Center hath been appointed—a Center that sol-
veth all difficulties and wardeth off all differences.
The Universal House of Justice, likewise, wardeth
off all differences and whatever it prescribeth must

be accepted and he who transgresseth is rejected. But this Universal House of Justice which is the Legislature hath not yet been instituted.

187.3 Thus it is seen that no means for dissension hath been left, but carnal desires are the cause of difference as it is the case with the violators. These do not doubt the validity of the Covenant but selfish motives have dragged them to this condition. It is not that they do not know what they do—they are perfectly aware and still they exhibit opposition.

187.4 In short, the ocean of the Covenant is tumultuous and wide. It casteth ashore the foam of violation and thus rest ye assured. Be engaged in the furtherance of the Mashriqu'l-Adhkár and prepare the means for the diffusion of the divine fragrances. Be not engaged in anything but this, for otherwise thou shalt dissipate thine attention and the work will not advance.

188.1 188. O ye the cherished loved ones of 'Abdu'l-Bahá! It is a long time now since my inward ear hath heard any sweet melodies out of certain regions, or my heart been gladdened; and this despite the fact that ye are ever present in my thoughts and standing clearly visible before my sight. Filled to overflowing is the goblet of my heart with the wine of the love I bear you, and my yearning to set eyes

upon you streameth like the spirit through my arteries and veins. From this it is clear how great is my
affliction. At this time and throughout this tempest
of calamities now tossing its waves to high heaven,
cruel and incessant darts are being hurled against
me from every point of the compass, and at every
moment, here in the Holy Land, terrifying news is
received, and every day bringeth its quota of hor-
ror. The Center of Sedition had imagined that it
needed but his arrogant rebellion to bring down
the Covenant and Testament in ruins; it needed
but this, so he thought, to turn the righteous away
from the Holy Will. Wherefore he sent out far and
wide his leaflets of doubt, devising many a secret
scheme. Now he would cry out that God's edifice
had been subverted and His divine commands
annulled, and that accordingly, the Covenant and
Testament was abolished. Again he would set himself to sighing and groaning that he was being held
a prisoner and was kept hungry and thirsty day
and night. Another day he would raise an uproar,
saying that the oneness of God had been denied,
since another Manifestation had been proclaimed,
prior to the expiration of a thousand years.

When he saw that his calumnies had no effect, 188.2
he gradually formed a plan to incite a disturbance.
He began stirring up mischief, and went knocking
at every door. He started making false accusations to

the officials of the Government. He approached some of the foreigners, made himself their intimate, and together with them prepared a document and presented it to the Seat of the Sultanate, bringing consternation to the authorities. Among the many slanderous charges was this, that this hapless one had raised up a standard of revolt, a flag bearing the words *Yá Bahá'u'l-Abhá*; that I had paraded this throughout the countryside, to every city, town and village, and even among the desert tribes, and had summoned all the inhabitants to unite under this flag.

188.3   O my Lord, verily I seek refuge with Thee from the very thought of such an act, which is contrary to all the commandments of Bahá'u'lláh, and which would indeed be a mighty wrong that none but a grievous sinner would ever perpetrate. For Thou hast made it incumbent upon us to obey the rulers and kings.

188.4   Another of his slanders was that the Shrine on Mount Carmel was a fortress that I had built strong and impregnable—this when the building under construction compriseth six rooms—and that I had named it Medina the Resplendent, while I had named the Holy Tomb* Mecca the Glorified. Yet another of his calumnies was that I had established

---

* at Bahjí

an independent sovereignty, and that—God forbid! God forbid! God forbid! —I had summoned all the believers to join me in this massive wrongdoing. How dire, O my Lord, is his slander!

Yet again, he claimeth that since the Holy Shrine 188.5 hath become a point visited by pilgrims from all over the world, great damage will accrue to this Government and people. He, the Center of Sedition, averreth that he himself hath had no hand in all these matters, that he is a Sunní of the Sunnites and a devoted follower of Abú-Bakr and 'Umar, and regardeth Bahá'u'lláh as only a pious man and a mystic; all these things, he saith, were set afoot by this wronged one.

To be brief, a Commission of Investigation was 188.6 appointed by the Sultán, may the glory of his reign endure. The Commission journeyed hither and immediately upon arrival betook themselves to the house of one of the accusers. They then summoned the group who, working with my brother, had prepared the accusatory document and asked them whether it was true. The group explained the contents of the document, stated that everything they had reported therein was nothing but the truth, and added further accusations. Thus they functioned at one and the same time as plaintiffs, witnesses, and judge.

The Commission hath now returned to the seat 188.7 of the Caliphate, and reports of a most frightful nature are coming in daily from that city. However, praised be God, 'Abdu'l-Bahá remaineth composed and unperturbed. To none do I bear ill will because of this defamation. I have made all my affairs conditioned upon His irresistible Will and I am waiting, indeed in perfect happiness, to offer my life and prepared for whatever dire affliction may be in store. Praise be to God, the loving believers also accept and remain submissive to God's Will, content with it, radiantly acquiescent, offering thanks.

188.8   The Center of Sedition hath imagined that once the blood of this wronged one is spilled out, once I have been cast away on the wide desert sands or drowned in the Mediterranean Sea—nameless, gone without trace, with none to tell of me—then would he at last have a field where he could urge his steed ahead, and with his mallet of lies and doubts, hit hard at the polo ball of his ambitions, and carry off the prize.

188.9   Far from it! For even if the sweet musk-scent of faithfulness should pass, and leave no trace behind, who would be drawn by the stench of perfidy? And even if some gazelle of heaven were to be ripped apart by dogs and wolves, who would go running to seek out a ravening wolf? Even should the day of the Mystic Nightingale draw to its close, who would ever lend his ear to the raven's croak, or the cawing of the crow? What an empty supposition is his! What a foolish presumption! "Their works are like the vapor in a desert which the thirsty dreameth to be water, until when he cometh unto it, he findeth nothing."*

O ye loved ones of God! Be ye firm of foot, and fixed of heart, and through the power of the Blessed Beauty's help, stand ye committed to your purpose. Serve ye the Cause of God. Face ye all nations of the world with the constancy and the endurance of the people of Bahá, that all men may be astounded and ask how this could be, that your hearts are as wellsprings of confidence and faith, and as mines so rich in the love of God. Be ye so, that ye shall neither fail nor falter on account of these tragedies in the Holy Land; let not these dread events make you despondent. And if all the believers be put to the sword, and only one be left, let that one cry out in the name of the Lord and tell the joyous tidings; let that one rise up and confront all the peoples of the earth. 188.10

Gaze ye not upon the dire happenings at this Illumined Spot. The Holy Land is in danger at all times, and here, the tide of calamities is ever 188.11

* Qur'án 24:39

at the flood; for this upraised call hath now been heard around the world, and the fame of it hath gone forth to the ends of the earth. It is because of this that foes, both from within and from without, have turned themselves with subtlety and craft to spreading slander. It is clear that such a place as this would be exposed to danger, for there is no defender here, none to arise and take our side in the face of calumny: here are only a few souls that are homeless, hapless, held captive in this stronghold. No champion have they; there is none to succor them, none to ward off the arrows of lies, the darts of defamation that are hurled against them: none except God.

188.12 It behooveth you to ponder on all those well-beloved ones who hastened to the holy field of sacrifice, those precious souls who offered up their lives. Bear ye in mind what streams of sacred blood were poured away, how many a righteous heart was commingled with its gore, how many a breast was the target of tyranny's spear, how many a chaste body was ripped to shreds. How then could it be right for us even to think of saving ourselves! To curry favor with stranger or kin, and make a show of compromise! Should we not, rather, take the pathway of the righteous, and follow in the footsteps of those great ones gone before?

These few brief days shall pass away, this present life shall vanish from our sight; the roses of this world shall be fresh and fair no more, the garden of this earth's triumphs and delights shall droop and fade. The spring season of life shall turn into the autumn of death, the bright joy of palace halls give way to moonless dark within the tomb. And therefore is none of this worth loving at all, and to this the wise will not anchor his heart.   188.13

He who hath knowledge and power will rather seek out the glory of heaven, and spiritual distinction, and the life that dieth not. And such a one longeth to approach the sacred Threshold of God; for in the tavern of this swiftly passing world the man of God will not lie drunken, nor will he even for a moment take his ease, nor stain himself with any fondness for this earthly life.   188.14

Nay rather, the friends are stars in the high heavens of guidance, celestial bodies in the skies of divine grace, who with all their powers put the dark to flight. They break down the foundations of malevolence and hate. They cherish but one desire for the world and all its peoples: well-being and peace. By them, the ramparts of warfare and aggression are battered down. They have truthfulness and honest dealing and friendship for their goal, and kindness even toward a vicious foe; until   188.15

at last they change this prison of treachery, the world, into a mansion of utmost trust, and turn this jail-house of hatred and malevolence and spite, into God's Paradise.

188.16   O ye loving friends! Strive ye with heart and soul to make this world the mirror image of the Kingdom, that this nether world may teem with the blessings of the world of God, that the voices of the Company on high may be raised in acclamation, and signs and tokens of the bounties and bestowals of Bahá'u'lláh may encompass all the earth.

188.17   Jináb-i-Amín hath expressed the greatest admiration for you honored men and enlightened women, naming and commending you each by each, telling at length of the firmness and constancy ye all have shown, saying that, God be praised, in all Persia the men and women are standing together, straight, strong, unmovable—a mighty edifice solidly raised up; and that ye are engaged with love and joy in spreading abroad the sweet savors of the Lord.

188.18   These were tidings of great joy, especially as they have reached me in these days of extreme peril. For the dearest wish of this wronged one is that the friends be spiritual of heart and illumined of mind, and once this grace is granted me, calamity, however afflictive, is but bounty pouring down upon me, like copious rain.

O God, my God! Thou seest me plunged in   188.19 an ocean of anguish, held fast to the fires of tyranny, and weeping in the darkness of the night. Sleepless I toss and turn upon my bed, mine eyes straining to behold the morning light of faithfulness and trust. I agonize even as a fish, its inward parts afire as it leapeth about in terror upon the sand, yet I ever look for Thy bestowals to appear from every side.

O God, my God! Make thou the believers   188.20 in other lands to partake of Thine abounding grace, deliver Thou, by Thine unfailing help and bounty, whoso among Thy loved ones in the farthermost climes sigheth over the bitter cruelty of his foe. O Lord, they are the captives of Thy love, the prisoners taken by Thy troops. They are the birds that fly in the heavens of Thy guidance, the whales that swim in the ocean of Thy bestowals, the stars that sparkle on the horizon of Thy gifts. They are the defenders of the fortress of Thy law. They are the banners of Thy remembrance amongst men. They are the deep wells of Thy divine compassion, the fountains of Thy favors, the wellsprings of Thy grace.

188.21 Keep them ever in safety beneath Thine all-protecting eye. Assist them to exalt Thy Word; make Thou their hearts to be constant in Thy love; strengthen Thou their backs that they may serve Thee well; in servitude, strengthen Thou their powers.

188.22 Spread Thou through them Thy sweet savors far and wide; expound through them Thy Holy Writ; make known through them Thine Utterance; fulfill through them Thy Words; through them pour out Thy mercy.

188.23 Thou art verily the Mighty, the Powerful. Thou art verily the Clement, the Compassionate.

189.1 189. Today, every wise, vigilant and foresighted person is awakened, and to him are unveiled the mysteries of the future which show that nothing save the power of the Covenant is able to stir and move the heart of humanity, just as the New and Old Testaments propounded throughout all regions the Cause of Christ and were the pulsating power in the body of the human world. A tree that hath a root shall bear fruit, while the tree that hath none, no matter how high and hardy it may be, will eventually wither, perish and become but a log fit for the fire.

189.2 The Covenant of God is like unto a vast and fathomless ocean. A billow shall rise and surge therefrom and shall cast ashore all accumulated foam.

Praise be to God that the highest wish enter- 189.3
tained by heedful souls is the exaltation of the Word
of God and the propagation of divine fragrances.
This is, verily, the secure and firm foundation.

Now, like unto the morn, the light of the Sun 189.4
of Truth hath been shed abroad. Effort must be
made that slumbering souls may be awakened,
the heedless become vigilant, and that the divine
teachings, which constitute the spirit of this age,
may reach the ears of the people of the world, may
be propagated in the press and set forth with brilliance and eloquence in the assemblages of men.

One's conduct must be like the conduct of 189.5
Paul, and one's faith similar to that of Peter. This
musk-scented breeze shall perfume the nostrils of
the people of the world, and this spirit shall resuscitate the dead.

The offensive odor of violation hath temporar- 189.6
ily arrested the onward movement of the Cause,
for otherwise the divine teachings, like unto the
rays of the sun, would immediately spread and
permeate all regions.

Thou intendest to print and publish the ad- 189.7
dresses of 'Abdu'l-Bahá which thou hast compiled.
This is indeed very advisable. This service shall
cause thee to acquire an effulgent face in the Abhá
Kingdom, and shall make thee the object of the
praise and gratitude of the friends in the East as

well as in the West. But it is to be undertaken with the utmost care, so that the exact text may be reproduced and will exclude all deviations and corruptions committed by former translators.

190.1   190. Thou seest me, O my God, bowed down in lowliness, humbling myself before Thy commandments, submitting to Thy sovereignty, trembling at the might of Thy dominion, fleeing from Thy wrath, entreating Thy grace, relying upon Thy forgiveness, shaking with awe at Thy fury. I implore Thee with a throbbing heart, with streaming tears and a yearning soul, and in complete detachment from all things, to make Thy lovers as rays of light across Thy realms, and to aid Thy chosen servants to exalt Thy Word, that their faces may turn beauteous and bright with splendor, that their hearts may be filled with mysteries, and that every soul may lay down its burden of sin. Guard them then from the aggressor, from him who hath become a shameless and blasphemous doer of wrong.

190.2   Verily Thy lovers thirst, O my Lord; lead them to the wellspring of bounty and grace. Verily, they hunger; send down unto them Thy heavenly table. Verily, they are naked; robe them in the garments of learning and knowledge.

190.3   Heroes are they, O my Lord, lead them to the field of battle. Guides are they, make them to speak

out with arguments and proofs. Ministering servants are they, cause them to pass round the cup
that brimmeth with the wine of certitude. O my
God, make them to be songsters that carol in fair
gardens, make them lions that couch in the thick-
ets, whales that plunge in the vasty deep.

Verily Thou art He of abounding grace. There   190.4
is none other God save Thee, the Mighty, the
Powerful, the Ever-Bestowing.

O ye my spiritual friends! For some time now   190.5
the pressures have been severe, the restrictions as
shackles of iron. This hapless wronged one was
left single and alone, for all the ways were barred.
Friends were forbidden access to me, the trusted
were shut away, the foe compassed me about, the
evil watchers were fierce and bold. At every instant,
fresh affliction. At every breath, new anguish. Both
kin and stranger on the attack; indeed, onetime
lovers, faithless and unpitying, were worse than
foes as they rose up to harass me. None was there
to defend 'Abdu'l-Bahá, no helper, no protector,
no ally, no champion. I was drowning in a shoreless sea, and ever beating upon my ears were the
raven-croaking voices of the disloyal.

At every daybreak, triple darkness. At eventide,   190.6
stone-hearted tyranny. And never a moment's peace,
and never any balm for the spear's red wounds. From
moment to moment, word would come of my exile

to the Fezzan sands; from hour to hour, I was to be cast into the endless sea. Now they would say that these homeless wanderers were ruined at last; again that the cross would soon be put to use. This wasted frame of mine was to be made the target for bullet or arrow; or again, this failing body was to be cut to ribbons by the sword.

190.7 Our alien acquaintances could not contain themselves for joy, and our treacherous friends exulted. "Praise be to God," one would exclaim, "Here is our dream come true." And another, "God be thanked, our spearhead found the heart."

190.8 Affliction beat upon this captive like the heavy rains of spring, and the victories of the malevolent swept down in a relentless flood, and still 'Abdu'l-Bahá remained happy and serene, and relied on the grace of the All-Merciful. That pain, that anguish, was a paradise of all delights; those chains were the necklace of a king on a throne in heaven. Content with God's will, utterly resigned, my heart surrendered to whatever fate had in store, I was happy. For a boon companion, I had great joy.

190.9 Finally a time came when the friends turned inconsolable, and abandoned all hope. It was then the morning dawned, and flooded all with unending light. The towering clouds were scattered, the dismal shadows fled. In that instant the fetters fell away, the chains were lifted off the neck of this homeless one and hung round the neck of the foe. Those dire straits were changed to ease, and on the horizon of God's bounties the sun of hope rose up. All this was out of God's grace and His bestowals.

And yet, from one point of view, this wanderer 190.10 was saddened and despondent. For what pain, in the time to come, could I seek comfort? At the news of what granted wish could I rejoice? There was no more tyranny, no more affliction, no tragical events, no tribulations. My only joy in this swiftly passing world was to tread the stony path of God and to endure hard tests and all material griefs. For otherwise, this earthly life would prove barren and vain, and better would be death. The tree of being would produce no fruit; the sown field of this existence would yield no harvest. Thus it is my hope that once again some circumstance will make my cup of anguish to brim over, and that beauteous Love, that Slayer of souls, will dazzle the beholders again. Then will this heart be blissful, this soul be blessed.

O Divine Providence! Lift to Thy lovers' 190.11 lips a cup brimful of anguish. To the yearners on Thy pathway, make sweetness but a sting, and poison honey-sweet. Set Thou our heads for ornaments on the points of spears. Make Thou our hearts the targets for pitiless arrows and darts. Raise Thou this withered soul to life on the martyr's field, make Thou his faded heart to drink the draught of tyranny, and thus grow fresh and fair once more. Make him to be drunk with the wine of Thine Eternal Covenant, make him a reveler holding high his cup. Help him to fling away his life; grant that for Thy sake, he be offered up.

190.12   Thou art the Mighty, the Powerful. Thou art the Knower, the Seer, the Hearer.

191.1   191. O thou who hast been sore afflicted on the pathway of the Covenant! Anguish and torment, when suffered on the pathway of the Lord, Him of manifest signs, is only favor and grace; affliction is but mercy, and grief a gift from God. Poison is sugar on the tongue, and wrath is kindness, nourishing the soul.

191.2   Then praise thou Him, the loving Provider, for having ordained this dire affliction, which is but bounty unalloyed.

191.3   If I, like Abraham, through flames must go,
Or yet like John* a bloodstained road must run;

---

* John the Baptist

If, Joseph-like, Thou'd cast me in a well,
Or shut me up within a prison cell—
Or make me e'en as poor as Mary's Son—
I will not go from Thee,
But ever stand
My soul and body bowed to Thy command.

192. Today, the Lord of Hosts is the defender of   192.1
the Covenant, the forces of the Kingdom protect
it, heavenly souls tender their services, and heavenly angels promulgate and spread it broadcast. If
it is considered with insight, it will be seen that all
the forces of the universe, in the last analysis serve
the Covenant. In the future it shall be made evident and manifest. In view of this fact, what can
these weak and feeble souls achieve? Hardy plants
that are destitute of roots and are deprived of the
outpourings of the cloud of mercy will not last.
What then may be expected from feeble weeds? . . .

193. It is daybreak, and from the rising-point   193.1
of the invisible realms of God, the light of unity
is dawning; and streaming and beating down from
the hidden world of the Kingdom of oneness there
cometh a flood of abounding grace. Glad tidings
of the Kingdom are sounding from every side,
and wafting in from every direction are the first
morning signs of the exalting of God's Word and

the upraising of His Cause. The word of unity is spreading, the verses of oneness are being sung, the sea of God's bestowals is tossing high its waves, and in plunging cataracts His blessings are pouring down.

193.2   The confirmations of Him Who is the Ever-Forgiving have wrapped every clime in light, the armies of the Company on high are rushing forward to do battle at the side of the friends of the Lord and carry the day, the fame of the Ancient Beauty—may my life be offered up for His loved ones—resoundeth from pole to pole and word of the Holy Cause hath spread to east and west.

193.3   All these things bring joy to the heart, and yet 'Abdu'l-Bahá is sunk deep in an ocean of grief, and pain and anguish have so affected my limbs and members that utter weakness hath overtaken my whole body. Note ye that when, singly and alone, with none to second me, I upraised the call of God around the world, the peoples thereof rose up to oppose, to dispute, to deny. On one side, it is clear how the religionists of the past have mounted their attack at all points; again, there cometh word of the lying mockers and the extreme limits to which they are going to pull out the Divine Tree by the roots. What malicious and slanderous charges they bring against the Ancient Beauty, what pamphlets filled with wicked and depraved allegations they are busily writing and spreading against the Most Great Name! And now, in deepest secrecy, they are straining every nerve to deal this Faith a fearsome blow.

Again have the prideful devised all manner of plots and schemes to completely disable the Cause of God and to erase the name of 'Abdu'l-Bahá from the Book of Life.

And now, added to all these tribulations, these miseries, these enemy attacks, there hath arisen a dust cloud of ill will amongst the believers themselves. This in spite of the fact that the Cause of the Ancient Beauty is the very essence of love, the very channel of oneness, existing only that all may become the waves of one sea, and bright stars of the same endless sky, and pearls within the shell of singleness, and gleaming jewels quarried from the mines of unity; that they may become servants one to another, adore one another, bless one another, praise one another; that each one may loose his tongue and extol the rest without exception, each one voice his gratitude to all the rest; that all should lift up their eyes to the horizon of glory, and remember that they are linked to the Holy Threshold; that they should see nothing but good in one another, hear nothing but praise of one another, and speak no word of one another save only to praise.

193.4

193.5

193.6   There are indeed certain ones who tread this way of righteousness, and God be thanked, these are strengthened and supported by heavenly power in every land. But others have not arisen as they ought to this gloried and exalted station, and this doth lay upon the heart of 'Abdu'l-Bahá a heavy burden of grief, of inconceivable grief. For no tempest more perilous than this could ever assail the Cause of God, nor could anything else so diminish the influence of His Word.

193.7   It behooveth all the beloved of God to become as one, to gather together under the protection of a single flag, to stand for a uniform body of opinion, to follow one and the same pathway, to hold fast to a single resolve. Let them forget their divergent theories and put aside their conflicting views since, God be praised, our purpose is one, our goal is one. We are the servants of one Threshold, we all draw our nourishment from the same one Source, we all are gathered in the shade of the same high Tabernacle, we all are sheltered under the one celestial Tree.

193.8   O beloved of the Lord! If any soul speak ill of an absent one, the only result will clearly be this: he will dampen the zeal of the friends and tend to make them indifferent. For backbiting is divisive, it is the leading cause among the friends of a disposition to withdraw. If any individual should speak ill of one who is absent, it is incumbent on his hearers, in a spiritual and friendly manner, to stop him, and say in effect: would this detraction serve any useful purpose? Would it please the Blessed Beauty, contribute to the lasting honor of the friends, promote the holy Faith, support the Covenant, or be of any possible benefit to any soul? No, never! On the contrary, it would make the dust to settle so thickly on the heart that the ears would hear no more, and the eyes would no longer behold the light of truth.

If, however, a person setteth about speaking 193.9 well of another, opening his lips to praise another, he will touch an answering chord in his hearers and they will be stirred up by the breathings of God. Their hearts and souls will rejoice to know that, God be thanked, here is a soul in the Faith who is a focus of human perfections, a very embodiment of the bounties of the Lord, one whose tongue is eloquent, and whose face shineth, in whatever gathering he may be, one who hath victory upon his brow, and who is a being sustained by the sweet savors of God.

Now which is the better way? I swear this by the 193.10 beauty of the Lord: whensoever I hear good of the friends, my heart filleth up with joy; but whensoever I find even a hint that they are on bad terms one with another, I am overwhelmed by grief. Such is the condition of 'Abdu'l-Bahá. Then judge from this where your duty lieth.

193.11 God be praised, wherever we turn, the Ancient Beauty hath opened wide the gates of grace, and hath in unmistakable words announced glad tidings of victory through the Lord's sustaining help. Through love hath He carried off the hearts of the believers, and He hath entrusted their triumph to the armies of the Concourse on high.

193.12 Now amidst all the peoples of the world must the beloved arise, with a heart even as the daystar, a strong inward urge, a shining brow, a musk-scented breath, a tongue speaking ever of God, an exposition crystal-clear, a high resolve, a power born of heaven, a spiritual character, a confirmation nothing short of the divine. Let them one and all become as a splendor on the horizon of heaven, and in the skies of the world a dazzling star. Let them be fruitful trees in the celestial bowers, sweet-scented blooms in the divine gardens; let them be verses of perfection on the page of the universe, words of oneness in the Book of Life. This is the first age, and the early beginnings of the dispensation of the Most Great Light, wherefore, within this century, virtues must be acquired, goodly qualities must be perfected within this span of time. In these very days the Abhá Paradise must pitch its pavilions on the plains of the world. The lights of reality must now be revealed, and the secrets of God's bestowals must now be made known, and now must the olden grace shine forth and this world change into the pleasure-ground of heaven, the garden of God. And out of pure hearts, and through heavenly bounties, all the perfections, qualities and attributes of the divine must now be made manifest.

At all times doth 'Abdu'l-Bahá supplicate and with tears entreat the Almighty at the sacred Threshold, and crieth out: 193.13

O Thou kind Lord! We are servants of Thy Threshold, taking shelter at Thy holy Door. We seek no refuge save only this strong pillar, turn nowhere for a haven but unto Thy safekeeping. Protect us, bless us, support us, make us such that we shall love but Thy good pleasure, utter only Thy praise, follow only the pathway of truth, that we may become rich enough to dispense with all save Thee, and receive our gifts from the sea of Thy beneficence, that we may ever strive to exalt Thy Cause and to spread Thy sweet savors far 193.14

and wide, that we may become oblivious of self and occupied only with Thee, and disown all else and be caught up in Thee.

193.15   O Thou Provider, O Thou Forgiver! Grant us Thy grace and loving-kindness, Thy gifts and Thy bestowals, and sustain us, that we may attain our goal. Thou art the Powerful, the Able, the Knower, the Seer; and verily Thou art the Generous, and verily Thou art the All-Merciful, and verily Thou art the Ever-Forgiving, He to Whom repentance is due, He Who forgiveth even the most grievous of sins.

194.1   194. O ye the sincere loved ones of the Abhá Beauty! In these days the Cause of God, the world over, is fast growing in power and, day by day, is spreading further and further to the utmost bounds of the earth. Its enemies, therefore, from all the kindreds and peoples of the world, are growing aggressive, malevolent, envious and bitterly hostile. It is incumbent upon the loved ones of God to exercise the greatest care and prudence in all things, whether great or small, to take counsel together and unitedly resist the onslaught of the stirrers up of strife and the movers of mischief. They must endeavor to consort in a friendly spirit with everyone, must follow moderation in their conduct, must have respect and consideration one for another and show loving-kindness and tender regard to all the peoples of the world. They must be patient and long-suffering, that they may grow to become the divine magnets of the Abhá Kingdom and acquire the dynamic power of the hosts of the realm on high.

The fleeting hours of man's life on earth pass swiftly by and the little that still remaineth shall come to an end, but that which endureth and lasteth for evermore is the fruit that man reapeth from his servitude at the Divine Threshold. Behold the truth of this saying, how abundant and glorious are the proofs thereof in the world of being! 194.2

The glory of glories rest upon the people of Bahá! 194.3

195. O thou exalted bough of the divine Lote-Tree! . . . When thou art disdained and rejected by the wicked doers be not cast down; and at the power and stiffneckedness of the presumptuous be neither vexed nor sick at heart; for such is the way of heedless souls, from time out of mind. "O the misery of men! No Messenger cometh unto them but they laugh Him to scorn!"* 195.1

---

* Qur'án 36:29

195.2   Indeed, the attacks and the obstructiveness of the ignorant but cause the Word of God to be exalted, and spread His signs and tokens far and wide. Were it not for this opposition by the disdainful, this obduracy of the slanderers, this shouting from the pulpits, this crying and wailing of great and small alike, these accusations of unbelief leveled by the ignorant, this uproar from the foolish—how could news of the advent of the Primal Point and the bright dawning of the Daystar of Bahá ever have reached to east and west? How else could the planet have been rocked from pole to pole? How else could Persia have become the focal point of scattering splendors, and Asia Minor the radiating heart of the beauty of the Lord? However else could the flame of the Manifestation have spread into the south? By what means could the cries of God have been heard in the far north? How else could His summons have been heard in the continents of America and of Africa the dark? How else could the cockcrow of Heaven have penetrated those ears? How else could the sweet parrots of India have come upon this sugar, or nightingales have lifted up their warblings out of the land of 'Iráq? What else could set the east and west to dancing, how else could this Consecrated Spot become the throne of the Beauty of God? How else could Sinai behold this burning brightness, how could the Advent's flame adorn that mount? How else could the Holy Land be made the footstool of God's beauty, and the holy vale of Towa* become the site of excellence and grace, the sacred spot where Moses put off His shoes? How could the breaths of heaven be carried across the Vale of Holiness, how could the sweet-scented, airy streams that blow out of the Abhá gardens ever be perceived by those that dwell on the Verdant Isle? How else could the pledges of the Prophets, the joyous tidings of the holy Seers of old, the stirring promises given unto this Sacred Place by the Manifestations of God, ever have been fulfilled?

How else could the Tree of Anísá have been 195.3 planted here, the flag of the Testament be flown, the intoxicating cup of the Covenant be lifted to these lips? All these blessings and bestowals, the very means of proclaiming the Faith, have come about through the scorn of the ignorant, the opposition of the foolish, the stubbornness of the dull-witted, the violence of the aggressor. Had it not been for these things, the news of the Báb's advent would not, to this day, have reached even into lands hard by. Wherefore we should never

---

* Qur'án 20:12. Also referred to as the "Sacred Vale."

grieve over the blindness of the unwitting, the attacks of the foolish, the hostility of the low and base, the heedlessness of the divines, the charges of infidelity brought against us by the empty of mind. Such too was their way in ages past, nor would it be thus if they were of those who know; but they are benighted, and they come not close to understanding what is told them.*

195.4 Wherefore doth it befit thyself, an offshoot of the Holy Tree of God, branched out from that mighty Trunk—and it behooveth ourselves as well—so to burn, through the sustaining grace of the Ancient Beauty—may my life be offered up for His Most Holy Shrine—with this kindled flame out of heaven, that we will light the fire of God's love from pole to pole. Let us take for our example the great and sacred Tree of the exalted Báb—may my life be offered up for Him. Like Him let us bare our breasts to the shafts of agony, like Him make our hearts to be targets for the spears decreed by God. Let us, like candles, burn away; as moths, let us scorch our wings; as the field larks, vent our plaintive cries; as the nightingales, burst forth in lamentations.

195.5 Even as the clouds let us shed down tears, and as the lightning flashes let us laugh at our cours-

---

* cf. Qur'án 4:80

ings through east and west. By day, by night, let us think but of spreading the sweet savors of God. Let us not keep on forever with our fancies and illusions, with our analyzing and interpreting and circulating of complex dubieties. Let us put aside all thoughts of self; let us close our eyes to all on earth, let us neither make known our sufferings nor complain of our wrongs. Rather let us become oblivious of our own selves, and drinking down the wine of heavenly grace, let us cry out our joy, and lose ourselves in the beauty of the All-Glorious.

O thou Afnán of the divine Lote-Tree! We must 195.6 strive, each one of us, to become as fecund boughs and to yield an ever sweeter and more wholesome fruit, that the branch may prove itself to be a continuation of the root, and the part be in harmony with the whole. It is my hope that out of the bounty of the Greatest Name and the loving-kindness of the Primal Point—may my soul be offered up for Them both—we shall become the means of exalting the Word of God around the world; that we may ever render services unto the Source of our Cause and spread over all the canopy of the true and holy zeal of the Lord. That from over the fields of grace, we may make zephyrs to blow, bringing to man the sweet scents that come from the gardens of God. That we may make of this world the

Abhá Paradise, and change this nether place into the Kingdom of Heaven.

195.7 It is true that every one of God's servants, and in particular those who are on fire with the Faith, have been allotted this task of servitude to Almighty God; still, the duty imposed upon us is greater than that which hath been laid upon the rest. To Him do we look for grace and favor and strength.

195.8 All praise and thanksgiving be unto the Blessed Beauty, for calling into action the armies of His Abhá Kingdom, and sending forth to us His never-interrupted aid, dependable as the rising stars. In every region of the earth hath He supported this single, lonely servant, at every moment hath He made known to me the signs and tokens of His love. He hath cast into a stupor all those who are clinging to their vain illusions, and made them infamous in the sight of high and low. He hath caused those who run after their fads and fancies to become objects of general reproach, and hath exposed the arrogant to public view; He hath made those of the friends who proved infirm of faith to serve as a warning to every beholder, and hath caused the leaders of those who waver to love but themselves and sink down in self-conceit. Meanwhile, by the power of His might, He hath made this broken-winged bird to rise up before all who dwell on earth. He hath shattered the serried ranks of the rebellious, and hath given the victory to the hosts of salvation, and breathed into the hearts of those who stand firm in the Covenant and Testament the breath of everlasting life.

Convey thou the greetings of Abhá to each one of the Afnán, branched from the Holy Tree. The glory rest upon thee and upon all the Afnán who remain faithful and true to the Covenant. 195.9

196. O thou who art steadfast in the Covenant! Thy letter of 9 September 1909 hath been received. Be thou neither grieved nor despondent over what hath come to pass. This trouble overtook thee as thou didst walk the path of God, wherefore it should bring thee joy. We addressed the friends in writing ere this, and made a verbal statement as well, to the effect that the friends in the West will unquestionably have their share of the calamities befalling the friends in the East. It is inevitable that, walking the pathway of Bahá'u'lláh, they too will become targets for persecution by the oppressors. 196.1

Consider how at the beginning of the Christian era the Apostles were afflicted, and what torments they endured in the pathway of Christ. Every day of their lives they were targets for the Pharisees' darts 196.2

of mockery, vilification and abuse. They bore great hardship; they saw prison; and most of them carried to their lips the sweet cup of martyrdom.

196.3　　Now ye, as well, must certainly become my partners to some slight degree, and accept your share of tests and sorrows. But these episodes shall pass away, while that abiding glory and eternal life shall remain unchanged forever. Moreover, these afflictions shall be the cause of great advancement.

196.4　　I ask of God that thou, His husbandman, shalt plough the hard and stony ground, and water it, and scatter seeds therein—for this will show how skilful is the farmer, while any man can sow and till where the ground is soft, and clear of brambles and thorns.

197.1　　197. O thou servant of God! Do not grieve at the afflictions and calamities that have befallen thee. All calamities and afflictions have been created for man so that he may spurn this mortal world—a world to which he is much attached. When he experienceth severe trials and hardships, then his nature will recoil and he will desire the eternal realm—a realm which is sanctified from all afflictions and calamities. Such is the case with the man who is wise. He shall never drink from a cup which is at the end distasteful, but, on the contrary, he will seek the cup of pure and limpid water. He will not taste of the honey that is mixed with poison.

Praise thou God, that thou hast been tried and hast experienced such a test. Be patient and grateful. Turn thy face to the divine Kingdom and strive that thou mayest acquire merciful characteristics, mayest become illumined and acquire the attributes of the Kingdom and of the Lord. Endeavor to become indifferent to the pleasures of this world and to its comfort, to remain firm and steadfast in the Covenant and to promulgate the Cause of God. 197.2

This is the cause of the exaltation of man, the cause of his glory and of his salvation. 197.3

198. O thou who art enamored of the breaths of God! I have read thy letter, which cried out with thy love for God and thine irresistible attraction to His Beauty, and its wondrous theme did cheer my heart. 198.1

The intent of what I wrote to thee in my previous letter was this, that when exalting the Word of God, there are trials to be met with, and calamities; and that in loving Him, at every moment there are hardships, torments, afflictions. 198.2

It behooveth the individual first to value these ordeals, willingly accept them, and eagerly welcome 198.3

them; only then should he proceed with teaching the Faith and exalting the Word of God.

198.4 In such a state, no matter what may befall him in his love for God—harassment, reproach, vilification, curses, beatings, imprisonment, death—he will never be cast down, and his passion for the Divine Beauty will but gain in strength. This was what I meant.

198.5 Otherwise, woe and misery to the soul that seeketh after comforts, riches, and earthly delights while neglecting to call God to mind! Because calamities encountered in God's pathway are, to 'Abdu'l-Bahá, but favor and grace, and in one of His Tablets the all-glorious Beauty hath declared: "I never passed a tree but Mine heart addressed it saying: 'O would that thou wert cut down in My name, and My body crucified upon thee!'" These were the words of the Most Great Name. This is His path. This is the way to His Realm of Might.

199.1 199. O ye sincere ones, ye longing ones, ye who are drawn as if magnetized, ye who have risen up to serve the Cause of God, to exalt His Word and scatter His sweet savors far and wide! I have read your excellent letter, beautiful as to style, eloquent as to words, profound as to meaning, and I praised God and thanked Him for having come to your aid and enabled you to serve Him in His wide-spreading vineyard.

Erelong shall your faces be bright with the radiance of your supplications and your worship of God, your prayers unto Him, and your humility and selflessness in the presence of the friends. He will make of your assemblage a magnet that will draw unto you the bright rays of divine confirmations that shine out from His kingdom of glory. 199.2

It is incumbent upon you to ponder in your hearts and meditate upon His words, and humbly to call upon Him, and to put away self in His heavenly Cause. These are the things that will make of you signs of guidance unto all mankind, and brilliant stars shining down from the all-highest horizon, and towering trees in the Abhá Paradise. 199.3

Know ye that 'Abdu'l-Bahá dwelleth in continual delight. To have been lodged in this faraway prison is for me exceeding joy. By the life of Bahá! This prison is my supernal paradise; it is my cherished goal, the comfort of my bosom, the bliss of my heart; it is my refuge, my shelter, my asylum, my safe haven, and within it do I exult amid the hosts of heaven and the Company on high. 199.4

Rejoice in my bondage, O ye friends of God, for it soweth the seeds of freedom; rejoice at my 199.5

imprisonment, for it is the wellspring of salvation; be ye glad on account of my travail, for it leadeth to eternal ease. By the Lord God! I would not exchange this prison for the throne of the whole world, nor give up this confinement for pleasures and pastimes in all the fair gardens on earth. My hope is that out of the Lord's abundant grace, His munificence and loving-kindness, I may, in His pathway, be hanged against the sky, that my heart may become the target for a thousand bullets, or that I may be cast into the depths of the sea, or be left to perish on desert sands. This is what I long for most; this is my supreme desire; it refresheth my soul, it is balm for my breast, it is the very solace of mine eyes.

199.6   As for you, O ye lovers of God, make firm your steps in His Cause, with such resolve that ye shall not be shaken though the direst of calamities assail the world. By nothing, under no conditions, be ye perturbed. Be ye anchored fast as the high mountains, be stars that dawn over the horizon of life, be bright lamps in the gatherings of unity, be souls humble and lowly in the presence of the friends, be innocent in heart. Be ye symbols of guidance and lights of godliness, severed from the world, clinging to the handhold that is sure and strong, spreading abroad the spirit of life, riding the Ark of salvation. Be ye daysprings of generosity, dawning-points of the mysteries of existence, sites where inspiration alighteth, rising-places of splendors, souls that are sustained by the Holy Spirit, enamored of the Lord, detached from all save Him, holy above the characteristics of humankind, clothed in the attributes of the angels of heaven, that ye may win for yourselves the highest bestowal of all, in this new time, this wondrous age.

By the life of Bahá! Only he who is severed 199.7 from the world shall achieve this ultimate grace, he who is a captive of divine love, empty of passion and self, from every aspect true unto his God, humble, lowly, supplicating, in tears, submissive in the presence of the Lord.

200. O my spiritual loved ones! At a time when 200.1 an ocean of trials and tribulations was surging up and flinging its waves to the heavens, when multitudes were assailing us and the tyrannical were inflicting upon us crushing wrongs—at such a time a band of individuals, intent on defaming us, allied themselves with our unkind brother, brought out a treatise that was filled with slanderous charges, and leveled accusations and calumnies against us.

In this way they alarmed and confused the 200.2 government authorities, and it is obvious what the condition of this captive then became, in this dilapidated fortress, and what terrible harm and mischief was done, far worse than words can tell. In spite of everything, this homeless prisoner remained inwardly tranquil and secure, trusting in the peerless Lord, yearning for whatever afflictions might have to be encountered in the pathway of God's love. For bolts of hate are, in our sight, but a gift of pearls from Him, and mortal poison but a healing draught.

200.3   Such was our state when a letter came to us from the American friends.* They had covenanted together, so they wrote, to remain at one in all things, and the signatories one and all had pledged themselves to make sacrifices in the pathway of the love of God, thus to achieve eternal life. At the very moment when this letter was read, together with the signatures at its close, 'Abdu'l-Bahá experienced a joy so vehement that no pen can describe it, and thanked God that friends have been raised up in that country who will live together in perfect harmony, in the best of fellowship, in full agreement, closely knit, united in their efforts.

200.4   The more this compact is reinforced, the happier and the better shall all things be, for it will draw unto itself the confirmations of God. If the

---

* This letter was signed by four hundred and twenty-two believers in America, and sent on 4 July 1905.

lovers of the Lord are hoping for grace to win as their friends the Company on high, they must do all they can to strengthen this compact, for such an alliance for brotherhood and unity is even as watering the Tree of Life: it is life everlasting.

O ye lovers of God! Make firm your steps; fulfill 200.5 your pledge to one another; go forth in harmony to scatter abroad the sweet savors of God's love, and to establish His Teachings, until ye breathe a soul into the dead body of this world, and bring true healing in the physical and spiritual realms to everyone who aileth.

O ye lovers of God! The world is even as a hu- 200.6 man being who is diseased and impotent, whose eyes can see no longer, whose ears have gone deaf, all of whose powers are corroded and used up. Wherefore must the friends of God be competent physicians who, following the holy Teachings, will nurse this patient back to health. Perhaps, God willing, the world will mend, and become permanently whole, and its exhausted faculties will be restored, and its person will take on such vigor, freshness and verdancy that it will shine out with comeliness and grace.

The first remedy of all is to guide the people 200.7 aright, so that they will turn themselves unto God, and listen to His counselings, and go forth with hearing ears and seeing eyes. Once this speedily effective draught is given them, then, in accordance with the Teachings, they must be led to acquire the characteristics and the behavior of the Concourse on high, and encouraged to seek out all the bounties of the Abhá Realm. They must cleanse their hearts from even the slightest trace of hatred and spite, and they must set about being truthful and honest, conciliatory and loving to all humankind—so that East and West will, even as two lovers, hold each other close; that hatred and hostility will perish from the earth, and universal peace be firmly rooted in their place.

200.8   O ye lovers of God! Be kind to all peoples; care for every person; do all ye can to purify the hearts and minds of men; strive ye to gladden every soul. To every meadow be a shower of grace, to every tree the water of life; be as sweet musk to the sense of humankind, and to the ailing be a fresh, restoring breeze. Be pleasing waters to all those who thirst, a careful guide to all who have lost their way; be father and mother to the orphan, be loving sons and daughters to the old, be an abundant treasure to the poor. Think ye of love and good fellowship as the delights of heaven, think ye of hostility and hatred as the torments of hell.

200.9   Indulge not your bodies with rest, but work with all your souls, and with all your hearts cry out and beg of God to grant you His succor and grace. Thus may ye make this world the Abhá Paradise, and this globe of earth the parade ground of the realm on high. If only ye exert the effort, it is certain that these splendors will shine out, these clouds of mercy will shed down their rain, these life-giving winds will rise and blow, this sweet-smelling musk will be scattered far and wide.

O ye lovers of God! Do not dwell on what is 200.10 coming to pass in this holy place, and be ye in no wise alarmed. Whatsoever may happen is for the best, because affliction is but the essence of bounty, and sorrow and toil are mercy unalloyed, and anguish is peace of mind, and to make a sacrifice is to receive a gift, and whatsoever may come to pass hath issued from God's grace.

See ye, therefore, to your own tasks: guide ye the 200.11 people and educate them in the ways of 'Abdu'l-Bahá. Deliver to mankind this joyous message from the Abhá Realm. Rest not, by day or night; seek ye no moment's peace. Strive ye with all your might to bring to men's ears these happy tidings. In your love for God and your attachment to 'Abdu'l-Bahá, accept ye every tribulation, every sorrow. Endure the aggressor's taunts, put up with the enemy's reproaches. Follow in the footsteps of 'Abdu'l-Bahá, and in the pathway of the Abhá Beauty, long at every moment to give up your lives. Shine out like the daystar, be unresting as the sea; even as the clouds of heaven, shed ye life upon field and hill, and like unto April winds, blow freshness through those human trees, and bring them to their blossoming.

201.1 201. O thou who art carried away by the love of God! The Sun of Truth hath risen above the horizon of this world and cast down its beams of guidance. Eternal grace is never interrupted, and a fruit of that everlasting grace is universal peace. Rest thou assured that in this era of the spirit, the Kingdom of Peace will raise up its tabernacle on the summits of the world, and the commandments of the Prince of Peace will so dominate the arteries and nerves of every people as to draw into His sheltering shade all the nations on earth. From springs of love and truth and unity will the true Shepherd give His sheep to drink.

201.2 O handmaid of God, peace must first be established among individuals, until it leadeth in the end to peace among nations. Wherefore, O ye Bahá'ís, strive ye with all your might to create, through the power of the Word of God, genuine love, spiritual communion and durable bonds among individuals. This is your task.

202. O ye lovers of truth, ye servants of hu- 202.1
mankind! Out of the flowering of your thoughts
and hopes, fragrant emanations have come my
way, wherefore an inner sense of obligation com-
pelleth me to pen these words.

Ye observe how the world is divided against 202.2
itself, how many a land is red with blood and its
very dust is caked with human gore. The fires of
conflict have blazed so high that never in early
times, not in the Middle Ages, not in recent centuries hath there ever been such a hideous war, a
war that is even as millstones, taking for grain the
skulls of men. Nay, even worse, for flourishing
countries have been reduced to rubble, cities have
been leveled with the ground, and many a once
prosperous village hath been turned into ruin. Fathers have lost their sons, and sons their fathers.
Mothers have wept away their hearts over dead
children. Children have been orphaned, women
left to wander, vagrants without a home. From every aspect, humankind hath sunken low. Loud are
the piercing cries of fatherless children; loud the
mothers' anguished voices, reaching to the skies.

And the breeding ground of all these tragedies 202.3
is prejudice: prejudice of race and nation, of religion, of political opinion; and the root cause of

prejudice is blind imitation of the past—imitation in religion, in racial attitudes, in national bias, in politics. So long as this aping of the past persisteth, just so long will the foundations of the social order be blown to the four winds, just so long will humanity be continually exposed to direst peril.

202.4   Now, in such an illumined age as ours, when realities previously unknown to man have been laid bare, and the secrets of created things have been disclosed, and the Morn of Truth hath broken and lit up the world—is it admissible that men should be waging a frightful war that is bringing humanity down to ruin? No, by the Lord God!

202.5   Christ Jesus summoned all mankind to amity and peace. Unto Peter He said: "Put up thy sword into the sheath."* Such was the bidding and counsel of the Lord Christ; and yet today the Christians one and all have drawn their swords from out the scabbard. How wide is the discrepancy between such acts and the clear Gospel text!

202.6   Sixty years ago Bahá'u'lláh rose up, even as the Daystar, over Persia. He declared that the skies of the world were dark, that this darkness boded evil, and that terrible wars would come. From the prison at 'Akká, He addressed the German Emperor in the clearest of terms, telling him that a

_____

* John 18:11

great war was on the way and that his city of Berlin would break forth in lamentation and wailing. Likewise did He write to the Turkish sovereign, although He was that Sultán's victim and a captive in his prison—that is, He was being held prisoner in the Fortress at 'Akká—and clearly stated that Constantinople would be overtaken by a sudden and radical change, so great that the women and children of that city would mourn and cry aloud. In brief, He addressed such words to all the monarchs and the presidents, and everything came to pass, exactly as He had foretold.

There have issued, from His mighty Pen, various teachings for the prevention of war, and these have been scattered far and wide. 202.7

The first is the independent investigation of truth; for blind imitation of the past will stunt the mind. But once every soul inquireth into truth, society will be freed from the darkness of continually repeating the past. 202.8

His second principle is the oneness of mankind: that all men are the sheep of God, and God is their loving Shepherd, caring most tenderly for all without favoring one or another. "No difference canst thou see in the creation of the God of mercy;"* all are His servants, all implore His grace. 202.9

---

* Qur'án 67:3

202.10   His third teaching is that religion is a mighty stronghold, but that it must engender love, not malevolence and hate. Should it lead to malice, spite, and hate, it is of no value at all. For religion is a remedy, and if the remedy bring on disease, then put it aside. Again, as to religious, racial, national and political bias: all these prejudices strike at the very root of human life; one and all they beget bloodshed, and the ruination of the world. So long as these prejudices survive, there will be continuous and fearsome wars.

202.11   To remedy this condition there must be universal peace. To bring this about, a Supreme Tribunal must be established, representative of all governments and peoples; questions both national and international must be referred thereto, and all must carry out the decrees of this Tribunal. Should any government or people disobey, let the whole world arise against that government or people.

202.12   Yet another of the teachings of Bahá'u'lláh is the equality of men and women and their equal sharing in all rights. And there are many similar principles. It hath now become evident that these teachings are the very life and soul of the world.

202.13   Ye who are servants of the human race, strive ye with all your heart to deliver mankind out of this darkness and these prejudices that belong to the human condition and the world of nature, so that humanity may find its way into the light of the world of God.

Praise be to Him, ye are acquainted with the various laws, institutions and principles of the world; today nothing short of these divine teachings can assure peace and tranquillity to mankind. But for these teachings, this darkness shall never vanish, these chronic diseases shall never be healed; nay, they shall grow fiercer from day to day. The Balkans will remain discontented. Its restlessness will increase. The vanquished Powers will continue to agitate. They will resort to every measure that may rekindle the flame of war. Movements, newly born and worldwide in their range, will exert their utmost effort for the advancement of their designs. The Movement of the Left will acquire great importance. Its influence will spread. 202.14

Strive ye, therefore, with the help of God, with illumined minds and hearts and a strength born of heaven, to become a bestowal from God to man, and to call into being for all humankind, comfort and peace. 202.15

203. O thou who art enamored of the Covenant! The Blessed Beauty hath promised this servant that souls would be raised up who would be the very 203.1

embodiments of guidance, and banners of the Concourse on high, torches of God's oneness, and stars of His pure truth, shining in the heavens where God reigneth alone. They would give sight to the blind, and would make the deaf to hear; they would raise the dead to life. They would confront all the peoples of the earth, pleading their Cause with proofs of the Lord of the seven spheres.

203.2 It is my hope that in His bounty He will soon raise up these souls, that His Cause may be exalted. The lodestone which will attract this grace is staunchness in the Covenant. Render thou thanks unto God that thou art firmest of the firm.

203.3 O my God, aid Thou Thy servant to raise up the Word, and to refute what is vain and false, to establish the truth, to spread the sacred verses abroad, reveal the splendors, and make the morning's light to dawn in the hearts of the righteous.

203.4 Thou art verily the Generous, the Forgiving.

204.1 204. O phoenix of that immortal flame kindled in the sacred Tree! Bahá'u'lláh—may my life, my soul, my spirit be offered up as a sacrifice unto His lowly servants—hath, during His last days on earth, given the most emphatic promise that, through the outpourings of the grace of God and the aid and assistance vouchsafed from His

Kingdom on high, souls will arise and holy beings appear who, as stars, would adorn the firmament of divine guidance; illumine the dayspring of loving-kindness and bounty; manifest the signs of the unity of God; shine with the light of sanctity and purity; receive their full measure of divine inspiration; raise high the sacred torch of faith; stand firm as the rock and immoveable as the mountain; and grow to become luminaries in the heavens of His Revelation, mighty channels of His grace, means for the bestowal of God's bountiful care, heralds calling forth the name of the One true God, and establishers of the world's supreme foundation.

These shall labor ceaselessly, by day and by night, shall heed neither trials nor woe, shall suffer no respite in their efforts, shall seek no repose, shall disregard all ease and comfort, and, detached and unsullied, shall consecrate every fleeting moment of their lives to the diffusion of the divine fragrance and the exaltation of God's holy Word. Their faces will radiate heavenly gladness, and their hearts be filled with joy. Their souls will be inspired, and their foundation stand secure. They shall scatter in the world, and travel throughout all regions. They shall raise their voices in every assembly, and adorn and revive every gathering. They shall speak in every tongue, and interpret every hidden

204.2

347

meaning. They shall reveal the mysteries of the Kingdom, and manifest unto everyone the signs of God. They shall burn brightly even as a candle in the heart of every assembly, and beam forth as a star upon every horizon. The gentle breezes wafted from the garden of their hearts shall perfume and revive the souls of men, and the revelations of their minds, even as showers, will reinvigorate the peoples and nations of the world.

204.3   I am waiting, eagerly waiting for these holy ones to appear; and yet, how long will they delay their coming? My prayer and ardent supplication, at eventide and at dawn, is that these shining stars may soon shed their radiance upon the world, that their sacred countenances may be unveiled to mortal eyes, that the hosts of divine assistance may achieve their victory, and the billows of grace, rising from His oceans above, may flow upon all mankind. Pray ye also and supplicate unto Him that through the bountiful aid of the Ancient Beauty these souls may be unveiled to the eyes of the world.

204.4   The glory of God rest upon thee, and upon him whose face is illumined with that everlasting light that shineth from His Kingdom of Glory.

205.1   205. O ye respected souls! From the continual imitation of ancient and worn-out ways, the world had grown dark as darksome night. The fundamentals of the divine Teachings had passed from memory; their pith and heart had been totally forgotten, and the people were holding on to husks. The nations had, like tattered garments long outworn, fallen into a pitiful condition.

Out of this pitch blackness there dawned the morning splendor of the Teachings of Bahá'u'lláh. He hath dressed the world with a garment new and fair, and that new garment is the principles which have come down from God. 205.2

Now the new age is here and creation is reborn. Humanity hath taken on new life. The autumn hath gone by, and the reviving spring is here. All things are now made new. Arts and industries have been reborn, there are new discoveries in science, and there are new inventions; even the details of human affairs, such as dress and personal effects—even weapons—all these have likewise been renewed. The laws and procedures of every government have been revised. Renewal is the order of the day. 205.3

And all this newness hath its source in the fresh outpourings of wondrous grace and favor from the Lord of the Kingdom, which have renewed the world. The people, therefore, must be set completely free from their old patterns of thought, that 205.4

all their attention may be focused upon these new principles, for these are the light of this time and the very spirit of this age.

205.5 Unless these Teachings are effectively spread among the people, until the old ways, the old concepts, are gone and forgotten, this world of being will find no peace, nor will it reflect the perfections of the Heavenly Kingdom. Strive ye with all your hearts to make the heedless conscious, to waken those who sleep, to bring knowledge to the ignorant, to make the blind to see, the deaf to hear, and restore the dead to life.

205.6 It behooveth you to show forth such power, such endurance, as to astonish all beholders. The confirmations of the Kingdom are with you. Upon you be the glory of the All-Glorious.

206.1 206. Praise be to Him Who hath rent the dark asunder, hath blotted out the night, hath drawn aside the coverings and torn away the veils; Whose light thereupon shone out, Whose signs and tokens were spread abroad, and His mysteries laid bare. Then did His clouds part and loaded down the earth with His bounties and bestowals, and made all things sweet with rain, and caused the fresh greenery of knowledge and the hyacinths of certitude to spring forth and to shake and tremble for joy, till the whole world was scented with the fragrance of His holiness.

Salutations and praise, blessings and glory be 206.2 upon those divine realities, those sacred wind-flowers that have come forth out of this supreme bestowal, this flooding grace that hath roared like a clashing sea of gifts and bounties, tossing its waves to the high heavens.

O God, my God! Praise be unto Thee for 206.3 kindling the fire of divine love in the Holy Tree on the summit of the loftiest mount: that Tree which is "neither of the East nor of the West,"* that fire which blazed out till the flame of it soared upward to the Concourse on high, and from it those realities caught the light of guidance, and cried out: "Verily have we perceived a fire on the slope of Mount Sinai."†

O God, my God! Increase Thou this fire, as 206.4 day followeth day, till the blast of it setteth in motion all the earth. O Thou, my Lord! Kindle the light of Thy love in every heart, breathe into men's souls the spirit of Thy knowledge, gladden their breasts with the verses of Thy oneness. Call

---

* Qur'án 24:35
† cf. Qur'án 28:29

Thou to life those who dwell in their tombs, warn Thou the prideful, make happiness worldwide, send down Thy crystal waters, and in the assemblage of manifest splendors, pass round that cup which is "tempered at the camphor fountain."*

206.5   Verily, art Thou the Giving, the Forgiving, the Ever-Bestowing. Verily, art Thou the Merciful, the Compassionate.

206.6   O ye loved ones of God! The wine-cup of Heaven overfloweth, the banquet of God's Covenant is bright with festive lights, the dawn of all bestowals is breaking, the gentle winds of grace are blowing, and out of the invisible world come good tidings of bounties and gifts. In flower-spangled meadows hath the divine springtime pitched its tents, and the spiritual are inhaling sweet scents from the Sheba of the spirit, carried their way by the east wind. Now doth the mystic nightingale carol its odes, and buds of inner meaning are bursting into blossoms delicate and fair. The field larks are become the festival's musicians, and lifting wondrous voices they cry and sing to the melodies of the Company on high, "Blessed are ye! Glad Tidings! Glad Tidings!" And they urge on the revelers

---

* Qur'án 76:5

of the Abhá Paradise to drink their fill, and they eloquently hold forth upon the celestial tree, and utter their sacred cries. All this, that withered souls who tread the desert of the heedless, and faded ones lost in the sands of unconcern, may come to throbbing life again, and present themselves at the feasts and revels of the Lord God.

Praise be to Him! The renown of His Cause hath reached to east and west, and word of the power of the Abhá Beauty hath quickened north and south. That cry from the American continent is a choir of holiness, that shout from far and near that riseth even to the Company on high is "Yá Bahá'u'l-Abhá!" Now is the east lit up with a glory, and the west rose-sweet, and all the earth is fragrant with ambergris, and the winds that blow over the Holy Shrine are laden with musk. Erelong shall ye see that even the darkest lands are bright, and the continents of Europe and Africa have turned into gardens of flowers, and forests of blossoming trees. 206.7

But since the dawning of this Daystar was in Persia, and since from that orient the sun shone upon the west, it is our fondest hope that the flames of love's fire should blaze ever more vehemently in that land, and that there the splendor of this Holy Faith should grow ever more intense. May the tumult of God's Cause so shake that land 206.8

to its foundations, may the spiritual force of His Word so manifest itself, as to make Írán the core and focus of well-being and peace. May rectitude and conciliation, and love and trust, issuing forth from Írán, bring immortality to all on earth. May she raise on the highest summits the banner of public order, of purest spirituality, of universal peace.

206.9   O ye loved ones of God! In this, the Bahá'í dispensation, God's Cause is spirit unalloyed. His Cause belongeth not to the material world. It cometh neither for strife nor war, nor for acts of mischief or of shame; it is neither for quarrelling with other Faiths, nor for conflicts with the nations. Its only army is the love of God, its only joy the clear wine of His knowledge, its only battle the expounding of the Truth; its one crusade is against the insistent self, the evil promptings of the human heart. Its victory is to submit and yield, and to be selfless is its everlasting glory. In brief, it is spirit upon spirit:

> Unless ye must,
> Bruise not the serpent in the dust,
> How much less wound a man.
> And if ye can,
> No ant should ye alarm,
> Much less a brother harm.

Let all your striving be for this, to become the   206.10
source of life and immortality, and peace and
comfort and joy, to every human soul, whether
one known to you or a stranger, one opposed to
you or on your side. Look ye not upon the purity or impurity of his nature: look ye upon the
all-embracing mercy of the Lord, the light of
Whose grace hath embosomed the whole earth
and all who dwell thereon, and in the plenitude
of Whose bounty are immersed both the wise and
the ignorant. Stranger and friend alike are seated
at the table of His favor. Even as the believer, the
denier who turneth away from God doth at the
same time cup his hands and drink from the sea of
His bestowals.

It behooveth the loved ones of the Lord to be   206.11
the signs and tokens of His universal mercy and
the embodiments of His own excelling grace. Like
the sun, let them cast their rays upon garden and
rubbish heap alike, and even as clouds in spring,
let them shed down their rain upon flower and
thorn. Let them seek but love and faithfulness, let
them not follow the ways of unkindness, let their
talk be confined to the secrets of friendship and
of peace. Such are the attributes of the righteous,
such is the distinguishing mark of those who serve
His Threshold.

206.12   The Abhá Beauty endured the most afflictive of calamities. He bore countless agonies and ills. He enjoyed not a moment's peace, drew not an easeful breath. He wandered, homeless, over desert sands and mountain slopes; He was shut in a fortress, and a prison cell. But to Him, His pauper's mat of straw was an eternal throne of glory, and His heavy chains a sovereign's carcanet. By day, by night, He lived under a whirring sword, and He was ready from moment to moment for death on the cross. He bore all this that He might purify the world, and deck it out with the tender mercies of the Lord God; that He might set it at rest; that conflict and aggression might be put to flight, the lance and the keen blade be exchanged for loving fellowship, malevolence and war turn into safety and gentleness and love, that battlefields of hate and wrath should become gardens of delight, and places where once the blood-drenched armies clashed, be fragrant pleasure grounds; that warfare should be seen as shame, and the resort to arms, even as a loathsome sickness, be shunned by every people; that universal peace raise its pavilions on the loftiest mounts, and war be made to perish forever from the earth.

206.13   Wherefore must the loved ones of God, laboriously, with the waters of their striving, tend and nourish and foster this tree of hope. In whatsoever land they dwell, let them with a whole heart befriend and be companions to those who are either close to them, or far removed. Let them, with qualities like unto those of heaven, promote the institutions and the religion of God. Let them never lose heart, never be despondent, never feel afflicted. The more antagonism they meet, the more let them show their own good faith; the more torments and calamities they have to face, the more generously let them pass round the bounteous cup. Such is the spirit which will become the life of the world, such is the spreading light at its heart: and he who may be and do other than this is not worthy to serve at the Holy Threshold of the Lord.

O ye loved ones of God! The Sun of Truth is 206.14 shining down from invisible skies; know ye the value of these days. Lift up your heads, and grow ye cypress-tall in these swift-running streams. Take ye joy in the beauty of the narcissus of Najd, for night will fall and it will be no more. . . .

O ye loved ones of God! Praise be to Him, the 206.15 bright banner of the Covenant is flying higher every day, while the flag of perfidy hath been reversed, and hangeth at half-mast. The benighted attackers have been shaken to their core; they are now as ruined sepulchers, and even as blind creatures that dwell beneath the earth they creep and crawl about a corner of the tomb, and out of that hole, from time to time, like unto savage beasts, do they jibber and howl. Glory be to God! How can the darkness hope to overcome the light, how can a magician's cords hold fast "a serpent plain for all to see"? "Then lo! It swallowed up their lying wonders."* Alas for them! They have deluded themselves with a fable, and to indulge their appetites they have done away with their own selves. They gave up everlasting glory in exchange for human pride, and they sacrificed greatness in both worlds to the demands of the insistent self. This is that of which We have forewarned you. Erelong shall ye behold the foolish in manifest loss.

206.16   O my Lord and my Hope! Help Thou Thy loved ones to be steadfast in Thy mighty Covenant, to remain faithful to Thy manifest Cause, and to carry out the commandments Thou didst set down for them in Thy Book of Splendors; that they may become banners of guidance and lamps of the Company above, wellsprings of Thine infinite wisdom, and stars

---

* Qur'án 26:31; 26:44; the reference is to Moses' rod, and the enchanters.

that lead aright, as they shine down from the supernal sky.

Verily art Thou the Invincible, the Almighty, the All-Powerful. 206.17

207. O ye who have turned your faces toward 207.1
the Exalted Beauty! By night, by day, at morningtide and sunset, when darkness draweth on, and at early light I remember, and ever have remembered, in the realms of my mind and heart, the loved ones of the Lord. I beg of Him to bestow His confirmations upon those loved ones, dwellers in that pure and holy land, and to grant them successful outcomes in all things: that in their character, their behavior, their words, their way of life, in all they are and do, He will make them to achieve distinction among men; that He will gather them into the world community, their hearts filled with ecstasy and fervor and yearning love, with knowledge and certitude, with steadfastness and unity, their faces beauteous and bright.

O ye beloved of the Lord! This day is the day of 207.2
union, the day of the ingathering of all mankind. "Verily God loveth those who, as though they were a solid wall, do battle for His Cause in serried lines!"* Note that He saith "in serried lines"—mean-

___
* Qur'án 61:4

ing crowded and pressed together, one locked to the next, each supporting his fellows. To do battle, as stated in the sacred verse, doth not, in this greatest of all dispensations, mean to go forth with sword and spear, with lance and piercing arrow—but rather weaponed with pure intent, with righteous motives, with counsels helpful and effective, with godly attributes, with deeds pleasing to the Almighty, with the qualities of heaven. It signifieth education for all mankind, guidance for all men, the spreading far and wide of the sweet savors of the spirit, the promulgation of God's proofs, the setting forth of arguments conclusive and divine, the doing of charitable deeds.

207.3 Whensoever holy souls, drawing on the powers of heaven, shall arise with such qualities of the spirit, and march in unison, rank on rank, every one of those souls will be even as one thousand, and the surging waves of that mighty ocean will be even as the battalions of the Concourse on high. What a blessing that will be—when all shall come together, even as once separate torrents, rivers and streams, running brooks and single drops, when collected together in one place will form a mighty sea. And to such a degree will the inherent unity of all prevail, that the traditions, rules, customs and distinctions in the fanciful life of these populations will be effaced and vanish away like isolated drops, once the great sea of oneness doth leap and surge and roll.

I swear by the Ancient Beauty, that at such a   207.4
time overwhelming grace will so encircle all, and the sea of grandeur will so overflow its shores, that the narrowest strip of water will grow wide as an endless sea, and every merest drop will be even as the shoreless deep.

O ye loved ones of God! Struggle and strive to   207.5
reach that high station, and to make a splendor so to shine across these realms of earth that the rays of it will be reflected back from a dawning-point on the horizon of eternity. This is the very foundation of the Cause of God. This is the very pith of the Law of God. This is the mighty structure raised up by the Manifestations of God. This is why the orb of God's world dawneth. This is why the Lord establisheth Himself on the throne of His human body.

O ye loved ones of God! See how the Exalted   207.6
One*—may the souls of all on earth be a ransom for Him—for this high purpose made His blessed heart the target for affliction's spears; and because the real intent of the Ancient Beauty—for Him may the souls of the Concourse on high be offered

---

* The Báb

up—was to win this same supernal goal, the Exalted One bared His holy breast for a target to a myriad bullets fired by the people of malice and hate, and with utter meekness died the martyr's death. On the dust of this pathway the holy blood of thousands upon thousands of sacred souls gushed out, and many a time the blessed body of a loyal lover of God was hanged to the gallows tree.

207.7 The Abhá Beauty Himself—may the spirit of all existence be offered up for His loved ones—bore all manner of ordeals, and willingly accepted for Himself intense afflictions. No torment was there left that His sacred form was not subjected to, no suffering that did not descend upon Him. How many a night, when He was chained, did He go sleepless because of the weight of His iron collar; how many a day the burning pain of the stocks and fetters gave Him no moment's peace. From Níyávarán to Ṭihrán they made Him run—He, that embodied spirit, He Who had been accustomed to repose against cushions of ornamented silk—chained, shoeless, His head bared; and down under the earth, in the thick darkness of that narrow dungeon, they shut Him up with murderers, rebels and thieves. Ever and again they assailed Him with a new torment, and all were certain that from one moment to the next He would suffer a martyr's death. After some time they banished Him from His native land, and sent Him to countries alien and far away. During many a year in 'Iráq, no moment passed but the arrow of a new anguish struck His holy heart; with every breath a sword came down upon that sacred body, and He could hope for no moment of security and rest. From every side His enemies mounted their attack with unrelenting hate; and singly and alone He withstood them all. After all these tribulations, these body blows, they flung Him out of 'Iráq in the continent of Asia, to the continent of Europe, and in that place of bitter exile, of wretched hardships, to the wrongs that were heaped upon Him by the people of the Qur'án were now added the virulent persecutions, the powerful attacks, the plottings, the slanders, the continual hostilities, the hate and malice, of the people of the Bayán. My pen is powerless to tell it all; but ye have surely been informed of it. Then, after twenty-four years in this, the Most Great Prison, in agony and sore affliction, His days drew to a close.

To sum it up, the Ancient Beauty was ever, dur- 207.8 ing His sojourn in this transitory world, either a captive bound with chains, or living under a sword, or subjected to extreme suffering and torment, or held in the Most Great Prison. Because of His physical weakness, brought on by His afflictions, His blessed body was worn away to a breath; it was light as a cobweb from long grieving. And His reason for shouldering this heavy load and enduring all this anguish, which was even as an ocean that hurleth its waves to high heaven—His reason for putting on the heavy iron chains and for becoming the very embodiment of utter resignation and meekness, was to lead every soul on earth to concord, to fellow feeling, to oneness; to make known amongst all peoples the sign of the singleness of God, so that at last the primal oneness deposited at the heart of all created things would bear its destined fruit, and the splendor of "No difference canst thou see in the creation of the God of Mercy,"* would cast abroad its rays.

207.9   Now is the time, O ye beloved of the Lord, for ardent endeavor. Struggle ye, and strive. And since the Ancient Beauty was exposed by day and night on the field of martyrdom, let us in our turn labor hard, and hear and ponder the counsels of God; let us fling away our lives, and renounce our brief and numbered days. Let us turn our eyes away from empty fantasies of this world's divergent forms, and serve instead this preeminent purpose, this grand design. Let us not, because of our own

---

* Qur'án 67:3

imaginings, cut down this tree that the hand of heavenly grace hath planted; let us not, with the dark clouds of our illusions, our selfish interests, blot out the glory that streameth from the Abhá Realm. Let us not be as barriers that wall out the rolling ocean of Almighty God. Let us not prevent the pure, sweet scents from the garden of the All-Glorious Beauty from blowing far and wide. Let us not, on this day of reunion, shut out the vernal downpour of blessings from on high. Let us not consent that the splendors of the Sun of Truth should ever fade and disappear. These are the admonitions of God, as set forth in His Holy Books, His Scriptures, His Tablets that tell out His counselings to the sincere.

The glory rest upon you, and God's mercy, and God's blessings. 207.10

208. O ye servants of the Sacred Threshold! 208.1
The triumphant hosts of the Celestial Concourse, arrayed and marshaled in the Realms above, stand ready and expectant to assist and assure victory to that valiant horseman who with confidence spurs on his charger into the arena of service. Well is it with that fearless warrior, who armed with the power of true Knowledge, hastens unto the field, disperses the armies of ignorance, and scatters the

hosts of error, who holds aloft the Standard of Divine Guidance, and sounds the Clarion of Victory. By the righteousness of the Lord! He hath achieved a glorious triumph and obtained the true victory.

209.1   209. O ye servants of the Blessed Beauty! . . . It is clear that in this day, confirmations from the unseen world are encompassing all those who deliver the divine Message. Should the work of teaching lapse, these confirmations would be entirely cut off, since it is impossible for the loved ones of God to receive assistance unless they teach.

209.2   Under all conditions, the teaching must be carried forward, but with wisdom. If the work cannot proceed openly, then let them teach in private, and thus engender spirituality and fellowship among the children of men. If, for example, each and every one of the believers would become a true friend to one of the unheeding, and, conducting himself with absolute rectitude, associate with this soul, treat him with the utmost kindness, himself exemplify the divine instructions he hath received, the good qualities and behavior patterns, and at all times act in accord with the admonitions of God—it is certain that little by little he will succeed in awakening that previously heedless individual, and in changing his ignorance to knowledge of the truth.

Souls are inclined toward estrangement. Steps 209.3
should first be taken to do away with this estrangement, for only then will the Word take effect. If a
believer showeth kindness to one of the neglectful,
and, with great love, gradually leadeth him to an
understanding of the validity of the Holy Cause,
so that he may come to know the fundamentals of
God's Faith and the implications thereof—such a
one will certainly be transformed, excepting only
those seldom-encountered individuals who are
even as ashes, whose hearts are "hard as rocks, or
harder still."*

If every one of the friends should strive in 209.4
this way to guide one soul aright, the number of
believers will double every year; and this can be
accomplished with prudence and wisdom, and no
harm whatever would result therefrom.

Furthermore, the teachers must travel about, 209.5
and if spreading the Message openly should cause
a disturbance, then instead, let them stimulate and
train the believers, inspire them, delight them, rejoice their hearts, revive and refresh them with the
sweet savors of holiness.

210. O ye roses in the garden of God's love! O 210.1
ye bright lamps in the assemblage of His knowl-

---

* Qur'án 2:69

edge! May the soft breathings of God pass over you, may the Glory of God illumine the horizon of your hearts. Ye are the waves of the deep sea of knowledge, ye are the massed armies on the plains of certitude, ye are the stars in the skies of God's compassion, ye are the stones that put the people of perdition to flight, ye are clouds of divine pity over the gardens of life, ye are the abundant grace of God's oneness that is shed upon the essences of all created things.

210.2   On the outspread tablet of this world, ye are the verses of His singleness; and atop lofty palace towers, ye are the banners of the Lord. In His bowers are ye the blossoms and sweet-smelling herbs, in the rose garden of the spirit the nightingales that utter plaintive cries. Ye are the birds that soar upward into the firmament of knowledge, the royal falcons on the wrist of God.

210.3   Why then are ye quenched, why silent, why leaden and dull? Ye must shine forth like the lightning, and raise up a clamoring like unto the great sea. Like a candle must ye shed your light, and even as the soft breezes of God must ye blow across the world. Even as sweet breaths from heavenly bowers, as musk-laden winds from the gardens of the Lord, must ye perfume the air for the people of knowledge, and even as the splendors shed by the true Sun, must ye illumine the hearts of humankind. For ye are the life-laden winds, ye are the jessamine-scents from the gardens of the saved. Bring then life to the dead, and awaken those who slumber. In the darkness of the world be ye radiant flames; in the sands of perdition, be ye wellsprings of the water of life, be ye guidance from the Lord God. Now is the time to serve, now is the time to be on fire. Know ye the value of this chance, this favorable juncture that is limitless grace, ere it slip from your hands.

Soon will our handful of days, our vanishing life, be gone, and we shall pass, empty-handed, into the hollow that is dug for those who speak no more; wherefore must we bind our hearts to the manifest Beauty, and cling to the lifeline that faileth never. We must gird ourselves for service, kindle love's flame, and burn away in its heat. We must loose our tongues till we set the wide world's heart afire, and with bright rays of guidance blot out the armies of the night, and then, for His sake, on the field of sacrifice, fling down our lives. 210.4

Thus let us scatter over every people the treasured gems of the recognition of God, and with the decisive blade of the tongue, and the sure arrows of knowledge, let us defeat the hosts of self and passion, and hasten onward to the site of martyr- 210.5

dom, to the place where we die for the Lord. And then, with flying flags, and to the beat of drums, let us pass into the realm of the All-Glorious, and join the Company on high.

210.6 Well is it with the doers of great deeds.

211.1 211. When the friends do not endeavor to spread the message, they fail to remember God befittingly, and will not witness the tokens of assistance and confirmation from the Abhá Kingdom nor comprehend the divine mysteries. However, when the tongue of the teacher is engaged in teaching, he will naturally himself be stimulated, will become a magnet attracting the divine aid and bounty of the Kingdom, and will be like unto the bird at the hour of dawn, which itself becometh exhilarated by its own singing, its warbling and its melody.

212.1 212. It is at such times that the friends of God avail themselves of the occasion, seize the opportunity, rush forth and win the prize. If their task is to be confined to good conduct and advice, nothing will be accomplished. They must speak out, expound the proofs, set forth clear arguments, draw irrefutable conclusions establishing the truth of the manifestation of the Sun of Reality.

213. The teaching work should under all condi- 213.1
tions be actively pursued by the believers because
divine confirmations are dependent upon it. Should
a Bahá'í refrain from being fully, vigorously and
wholeheartedly involved in the teaching work he
will undoubtedly be deprived of the blessings of
the Abhá Kingdom. Even so, this activity should be
tempered with wisdom—not that wisdom which
requireth one to be silent and forgetful of such an
obligation, but rather that which requireth one to
display divine tolerance, love, kindness, patience,
a goodly character, and holy deeds. In brief, encourage the friends individually to teach the Cause
of God and draw their attention to this meaning
of wisdom mentioned in the Writings, which is
itself the essence of teaching the Faith—but all
this to be done with the greatest tolerance, so that
heavenly assistance and divine confirmation may
aid the friends.

214. Follow thou the way of thy Lord, and say 214.1
not that which the ears cannot bear to hear, for such
speech is like luscious food given to small children.
However palatable, rare and rich the food may be,
it cannot be assimilated by the digestive organs of a
suckling child. Therefore unto every one who hath
a right, let his settled measure be given.

214.2   "Not everything that a man knoweth can be disclosed, nor can everything that he can disclose be regarded as timely, nor can every timely utterance be considered as suited to the capacity of those who hear it." Such is the consummate wisdom to be observed in thy pursuits. Be not oblivious thereof, if thou wishest to be a man of action under all conditions. First diagnose the disease and identify the malady, then prescribe the remedy, for such is the perfect method of the skilful physician.

215.1   215. My hope from the grace of the One true Lord is that thou wilt be enabled to spread the fragrances of God among the tribes. This is extremely important. . . .

215.2   If thou succeedest in rendering this service thou shalt excel and be the leader in the field.

216.1   216. Rest assured that the breathings of the Holy Spirit will loosen thy tongue. Speak, therefore; speak out with great courage at every meeting. When thou art about to begin thine address, turn first to Bahá'u'lláh, and ask for the confirmations of the Holy Spirit, then open thy lips and say whatever is suggested to thy heart; this, however, with the utmost courage, dignity and conviction. It is my hope that from day to day your gatherings will grow and flourish, and that those who are seeking after truth will hearken therein to reasoned arguments and conclusive proofs. I am with you heart and soul at every meeting; be sure of this.

217. The teacher, when teaching, must be him- 217.1 self fully enkindled, so that his utterance, like unto a flame of fire, may exert influence and consume the veil of self and passion. He must also be utterly humble and lowly so that others may be edified, and be totally self-effaced and evanescent so that he may teach with the melody of the Concourse on high—otherwise his teaching will have no effect.

218. O ye close and dear friends of 'Abdu'l-Bahá! 218.1
In the Orient scatter perfumes,
And shed splendors on the West.
Carry light unto the Bulgar,
And the Slav with life invest.

One year after the ascension of Bahá'u'lláh, there 218.2 came this verse from the lips of the Center of the Covenant. The Covenant-breakers found it strange indeed, and they treated it with scorn. Yet, praised be God, its effects are now manifest, its power revealed, its import clear; for by God's grace, today both East and West are trembling for joy, and now, from sweet waftings of holiness, the whole earth is scented with musk.

218.3 The Blessed Beauty, in unmistakable language, hath made this promise in His Book: "We behold you from Our realm of glory, and shall aid whosoever will arise for the triumph of Our Cause with the hosts of the Concourse on high and a company of Our favored angels."*

218.4 God be thanked, that promised aid hath been vouchsafed, as is plain for all to see, and it shineth forth as clear as the sun in the heavens.

218.5 Wherefore, O ye friends of God, redouble your efforts, strain every nerve, till ye triumph in your servitude to the Ancient Beauty, the Manifest Light, and become the cause of spreading far and wide the rays of the Daystar of Truth. Breathe ye into the world's worn and wasted body the fresh breath of life, and in the furrows of every region sow ye holy seed. Rise up to champion this Cause; open your lips and teach. In the meeting place of life be ye a guiding candle; in the skies of this world be dazzling stars; in the gardens of unity be birds of the spirit, singing of inner truths and mysteries.

218.6 Expend your every breath of life in this great Cause and dedicate all your days to the service of

---

* *Gleanings from the Writings of Bahá'u'lláh*, no. 72.

Bahá, so that in the end, safe from loss and deprivation, ye will inherit the heaped-up treasures of
the realms above. For the days of a man are full of
peril and he cannot rely on so much as a moment
more of life; and still the people, who are even
as a wavering mirage of illusions, tell themselves
that in the end they shall reach the heights. Alas
for them! The men of bygone times hugged these
same fancies to their breasts, until a wave flicked
over them and they returned to dust, and they
found themselves excluded and bereft—all save
those souls who had freed themselves from self
and had flung away their lives in the pathway of
God. Their bright star shone out in the skies of
ancient glory, and the handed-down memories of
all the ages are the proof of what I say.

Wherefore, rest ye neither day nor night and 218.7
seek no ease. Tell ye the secrets of servitude, follow
the pathway of service, till ye attain the promised
succor that cometh from the realms of God.

O friends! Black clouds have shrouded all this 218.8
earth, and the darkness of hatred and malice, of
cruelty and aggression and defilement is spreading far and wide. The people, one and all, live out
their lives in a heedless stupor and the chief virtues
of man are held to be his rapacity and his thirst
for blood. Out of all the mass of humankind God

hath chosen the friends, and He hath favored them with His guidance and boundless grace. His purpose is this, that we, all of us, should strive with our whole hearts to offer ourselves up, guide others to His path, and train the souls of men—until these frenzied beasts change to gazelles in the meadows of oneness, and these wolves to lambs of God, and these brutish creatures to angelic hosts; till the fires of hatred are quenched, and the flame coming out of the sheltered vale of the Holy Shrine doth shed its splendors; till the foul odor of the tyrant's dunghill is blown away, and yieldeth to the pure, sweet scents that stream from the rosebeds of faith and trust. On that day will the weak of intellect draw on the bounty of the divine, Universal Mind, and they whose life is but abomination will seek out these cleansing, holy breaths.

218.9 But there needs must be souls who will manifest such bestowals, there needs must be husbandmen to till these fields, gardeners for these gardens, there needs must be fish to swim in this sea, stars to gleam in these heavens. These ailing ones must be tended by spiritual physicians, these who are the lost need gentle guides—so that from such souls the bereft may receive their portion, and the deprived obtain their share, and the poor discover in such as they unmeasured wealth, and the seekers hear from them unanswerable proofs.

O my Lord, my Defender, my Help in peril! 218.10
Lowly do I entreat Thee, ailing do I come unto Thee to be healed, humbly do I cry out to Thee with my tongue, my soul, my spirit:

O God, my God! The gloom of night hath shrouded every region, and all the earth is shut away behind thick clouds. The peoples of the world are sunk in the black depths of vain illusions, while their tyrants wallow in cruelty and hate. I see nothing but the glare of searing fires that blaze upward from the nethermost abyss, I hear nothing save the thunderous roar that belloweth out from thousands upon thousands of fiery weapons of assault, while every land is crying aloud in its secret tongue: "My riches avail me nothing, and my sovereignty hath perished!"

O my Lord, the lamps of guidance have gone 218.12
out. The flames of passion are mounting high, and malevolence is ever gaining on the world. Malice and hate have overspread the face of the whole earth, and I find no souls except Thine own oppressed small band who are raising up this cry:

Make haste to love! Make haste to trust! Make 218.13
haste to give! To guidance come!

218.14   Come ye for harmony! To behold the Star of Day! Come here for kindliness, for ease! Come here for amity and peace!

218.15   Come and cast down your weapons of wrath, till unity is won! Come and in the Lord's true path each one help each one.

218.16   Verily with exceeding joy, with heart and soul, do these oppressed of Thine offer themselves up for all mankind in every land. Thou seest them, O my Lord, weeping over the tears Thy people shed, mourning the grief of Thy children, condoling with humankind, suffering because of the calamities that beset all the denizens of the earth.

218.17   O my Lord, wing them with victory that they may soar upward to salvation, strengthen their loins in service to Thy people, and their backs in servitude to Thy Threshold of Holiness.

218.18   Verily Thou art the Generous, verily Thou art the Merciful! There is none other God save Thee, the Clement, the Pitiful, the Ancient of Days!

219.1   219. O ye sons and daughters of the Kingdom! Your letter, which was surely inspired of heaven, hath been received. Its contents were most pleasing, its sentiments arising out of luminous hearts.

219.2   The believers in London are indeed steadfast and true, they are resolute, they are constant in service; when put to the test, they do not falter, nor doth their fire abate with the passage of time; rather, they are Bahá'ís. They are of heaven, they are filled with light, they are of God. Without any doubt they will become the cause of raising high the Word of God, and advancing the oneness of the world of man; of promoting the teachings of God, and spreading far and near the equality of every member of the human race.

It is easy to approach the Kingdom of Heaven, but hard to stand firm and staunch within it, for the tests are rigorous, and heavy to bear. But the English remain steadfast under all conditions, neither at the first sign of trouble do their footsteps slip. They are not changeable, playing fast and loose with some project and soon giving it up. They do not, for some trivial reason, fail in enthusiasm and zeal, their interest gone. No, in all they do, they are stable, rock-solid and staunch. 219.3

Although ye dwell in western lands, still, praise be to God, ye did hear His call from out the east and, even as Moses, did warm your hands at the fire kindled in the Asian Tree. Ye did find the true path, were lit like unto lamps, and have come into the Kingdom of God. And now have ye arisen, out of gratitude for these blessings, and ye are asking God's help for all the peoples of the earth, 219.4

that their eyes as well may behold the splendors of the Abhá Realm, and their hearts, even as mirrors, reflect the bright rays of the Sun of Truth.

219.5 It is my hope that the breaths of the Holy Spirit will so be breathed into your hearts that your tongues will disclose the mysteries, and set forth and expound the inner meanings of the Holy Books; that the friends will become physicians, and will, through the potent medicine of the heavenly Teachings, heal the long-standing diseases that afflict the body of this world; that they will make the blind to see, the deaf to hear, the dead to come alive; that they will awaken those who are sound asleep.

219.6 Rest ye assured that the confirmations of the Holy Spirit will descend upon you, and that the armies of the Abhá Kingdom will grant you the victory.

220.1 220. The Lord of all mankind hath fashioned this human realm to be a Garden of Eden, an earthly paradise. If, as it must, it findeth the way to harmony and peace, to love and mutual trust, it will become a true abode of bliss, a place of manifold blessings and unending delights. Therein shall be revealed the excellence of humankind, therein shall the rays of the Sun of Truth shine forth on every hand.

Remember how Adam and the others once 220.2
dwelt together in Eden. No sooner, however,
did a quarrel break out between Adam and Satan
than they were, one and all, banished from the
Garden, and this was meant as a warning to the
human race, a means of telling humankind that
dissension—even with the Devil—is the way to
bitter loss. This is why, in our illumined age, God
teacheth that conflicts and disputes are not allow-
able, not even with Satan himself.

Gracious God! Even with such a lesson before 220.3
him, how heedless is man! Still do we see his world
at war from pole to pole. There is war among the
religions; war among the nations; war among the
peoples; war among the rulers. What a welcome
change would it be, if only these black clouds
would lift from off the skies of the world, so that
the light of reality could be shed abroad! If only
the darksome dust of this continual fighting and
killing could settle forever, and the sweet winds
of God's loving-kindness could blow from out
the wellspring of peace. Then would this world
become another world, and the earth would shine
with the light of her Lord.

If there is any hope, it is solely in the bounties 220.4
of God: that His strengthening grace will come,
and the struggling and contending will cease, and

the acid bite of blood-dripping steel will be turned into the honey-dew of friendship and probity and trust. How sweet would that day be in the mouth, how fragrant as musk the scent thereof.

220.5 God grant that the new year will bring a promise of the new peace. May He enable this distinguished assemblage to conclude a fair treaty and establish a just covenant, that you may be blessed forever, across the unborn reaches of time.

[Addressed to the readers of *The Christian Commonwealth*, 1 January 1913]

221.1 221. O ye who are steadfast in the Covenant! The pilgrim hath made mention of each one of you, and hath asked for a separate letter addressed to each, but this wanderer in the wilderness of God's love is withheld from correspondence by a thousand preoccupations and concerns; and since out of the easts and the wests of the earth there poureth a mounting flood of letters upon him, it would be impossible to send a separate letter to each one, wherefore this one letter is addressed to each of you, that it may, as sealed wine, rejoice your souls and warm your hearts.

221.2 O ye steadfast loved ones! The grace of God is beating down upon mankind, even as the rains in spring, and the rays of the manifest Light have made this earth to be the envy of heaven. But alas, the blind are deprived of this bounty, the heedless are closed off from it, the withered despair of it, the faded are dying away—so that even as flooding waters, this endless stream of grace passeth back into its primal source in a hidden sea. Only a few receive this grace and take their share of it. Wherefore, let us put our hopes in whatever the strong arm of the Beloved can bring about.

We trust that in a time to come the slumberers will waken, and the heedless will be made aware, and the excluded will become initiates in the mysteries. Now must the friends work on with heart and soul and put forth a mighty effort, until the ramparts of dissension are toppled down and the glories of the oneness of humanity lead all to unity. 221.3

Today the one overriding need is unity and harmony among the beloved of the Lord, for they should have among them but one heart and soul and should, so far as in them lieth, unitedly withstand the hostility of all the peoples of the world; they must bring to an end the benighted prejudices of all nations and religions and must make known to every member of the human race that all are the leaves of one branch, the fruits of one bough. 221.4

Until such time, however, as the friends establish perfect unity among themselves, how can they summon others to harmony and peace? 221.5

> That soul which hath itself not come alive,
> Can it then hope another to revive?

221.6   Reflect ye as to other than human forms of life and be ye admonished thereby: those clouds that drift apart cannot produce the bounty of the rain, and are soon lost; a flock of sheep, once scattered, falleth prey to the wolf, and birds that fly alone will be caught fast in the claws of the hawk. What greater demonstration could there be that unity leadeth to flourishing life, while dissension and withdrawing from the others, will lead only to misery; for these are the sure ways to bitter disappointment and ruin.

221.7   The holy Manifestations of God were sent down to make visible the oneness of humanity. For this did They endure unnumbered ills and tribulations, that a community from amongst mankind's divergent peoples could gather within the shadow of the Word of God and live as one, and could, with delight and grace, demonstrate on earth the unity of humankind. Therefore must the desire of the friends be this, to bring together and unify all peoples, that all may receive a generous drink of this pure wine from this cup that is "tempered at the camphor fountain."* Let them

---

* Qur'án 76:5

make the differing populations to be as one and induce the hostile and murderous kindreds of the earth to love one another instead. Let them loose from their shackles the captives of sensual desires and cause the excluded to become intimates of the mysteries. Let them give to the bereft a share of the blessings of these days; let them guide the portionless to inexhaustible treasure. This grace can come about through words and ways and deeds that are of the Unseen Kingdom but, lacking such, it can never be.

The confirmations of God are the surety for   221.8
these blessings; the sacred bounty of God bestoweth these great gifts. The friends of God are supported by the Kingdom on high and they win their victories through the massed armies of the most great guidance. Thus for them every difficulty will be made smooth, every problem will most easily be solved.

Note ye how easily, where unity existeth in a   221.9
given family, the affairs of that family are conducted; what progress the members of that family make, how they prosper in the world. Their concerns are in order, they enjoy comfort and tranquillity, they are secure, their position is assured, they come to be envied by all. Such a family but addeth to its stature and its lasting honor, as day succeedeth day. And if we widen out the sphere of unity a little to include the inhabitants of a village

who seek to be loving and united, who associate with and are kind to one another, what great advances they will be seen to make, how secure and protected they will be. Then let us widen out the sphere a little more, let us take the inhabitants of a city, all of them together: if they establish the strongest bonds of unity among themselves, how far they will progress, even in a brief period, and what power they will exert. And if the sphere of unity be still further widened out, that is, if the inhabitants of a whole country develop peaceable hearts, and if with all their hearts and souls they yearn to cooperate with one another and to live in unity, and if they become kind and loving to one another, that country will achieve undying joy and lasting glory. Peace will it have, and plenty, and vast wealth.

221.10   Note then: if every clan, tribe, community, every nation, country, territory on earth should come together under the single-hued pavilion of the oneness of mankind, and by the dazzling rays of the Sun of Truth should proclaim the universality of man; if they should cause all nations and all creeds to open wide their arms to one another, establish a World Council, and proceed to bind the members of society one to another by strong mutual ties, what would happen then? There is no doubt whatsoever that the divine Beloved, in all His endearing beauty, and with Him a massive host of heavenly confirmations and human blessings and bestowals, would appear in His full glory before the assemblage of the world.

Wherefore, O ye beloved of the Lord, bestir yourselves, do all in your power to be as one, to live in peace, each with the others: for ye are all the drops from but one ocean, the foliage of one tree, the pearls from a single shell, the flowers and sweet herbs from the same one garden. And achieving that, strive ye to unite the hearts of those who follow other faiths. 221.11

For one another must ye give up even life itself. To every human being must ye be infinitely kind. Call none a stranger; think none to be your foe. Be ye as if all men were your close kin and honored friends. Walk ye in such wise that this fleeting world will change into a splendor and this dismal heap of dust become a palace of delights. Such is the counsel of 'Abdu'l-Bahá, this hapless servant. 221.12

222. O ye homeless and wanderers in the Path of God! Prosperity, contentment, and freedom, however much desired and conducive to the gladness of the human heart, can in no wise compare with the trials of homelessness and adversity in 222.1

the pathway of God; for such exile and banishment are blessed by the divine favor, and are surely followed by the mercy of Providence. The joy of tranquillity in one's home, and the sweetness of freedom from all cares shall pass away, whilst the blessing of homelessness shall endure forever, and its far-reaching results shall be made manifest.

222.2 Abraham's migration from His native land caused the bountiful gifts of the All-Glorious to be made manifest, and the setting of Canaan's brightest star unfolded to the eyes the radiance of Joseph. The flight of Moses, the Prophet of Sinai, revealed the Flame of the Lord's burning Fire, and the rise of Jesus breathed the breaths of the Holy Spirit into the world. The departure of Muḥammad, the Beloved of God, from the city of His birth was the cause of the exaltation of God's Holy Word, and the banishment of the Sacred Beauty led to the diffusion of the light of His divine Revelation throughout all regions.

222.3 Take ye good heed, O people of insight!

223.1 223. O ye sons and daughters of the Kingdom! Your letter was received. From its contents it was known that, praise be to God, your hearts are in the utmost purity and your souls rejoice in the glad tidings of God. The mass of the people are occupied with self and worldly desire, are immersed in the ocean of the nether world and are captives of the world of nature, save those souls who have been freed from the chains and fetters of the material world and, like unto swift-flying birds, are soaring in this unbounded realm. They are awake and vigilant, they shun the obscurity of the world of nature, their highest wish centereth on the eradication from among men of the struggle for existence, the shining forth of the spirituality and the love of the realm on high, the exercise of utmost kindness among peoples, the realization of an intimate and close connection between religions and the practice of the ideal of self-sacrifice. Then will the world of humanity be transformed into the Kingdom of God.

O ye friends, exert ye an effort! Every expenditure is in need of an income. This day, in the world of humanity, men are all the time expending, for war is nothing but the consumption of men and of wealth. At least engage ye in a deed of profit to the world of humanity that ye may partially compensate for that loss. Perchance, through the divine confirmations, ye may be assisted in promulgating amity and concord among men, in substituting love for enmity, in causing universal peace to result from universal war and in converting loss and rancor into profit and love. This wish will be realized through the power of the Kingdom.

224.1   224. O thou servant of God! Thy letter was received. Its contents were lofty and sublime, and its aim high and far-reaching. The world of humanity is in need of great improvement, for it is a material jungle wherein trees without fruit flourish and useless weeds abound. If at all there is a tree that beareth fruit it is overshadowed by the fruitless ones, and if a flower groweth in this jungle it is hidden and concealed. The world of mankind is in need of expert gardeners who may convert these forests into delectable rose gardens, may substitute for these barren trees ones that yield fruit, and may replace these useless weeds with roses and fragrant herbs. Thus active souls and vigilant people rest neither by day nor by night; they strive to be closely linked to the divine Kingdom and thereby become the manifestations of infinite bounty and ideal gardeners for these forests. Thus the world of humanity will be wholly transformed and the merciful bounties become manifest.

225.1   225. O ye concourse of the Kingdom of Abhá! Two calls to success and prosperity are being raised from the heights of the happiness of mankind, awakening the slumbering, granting sight to the blind, causing the heedless to become mindful, bestowing hearing upon the deaf, unloosing the tongue of the mute and resuscitating the dead.

The one is the call of civilization, of the progress 225.2 of the material world. This pertaineth to the world of phenomena, promoteth the principles of material achievement, and is the trainer for the physical accomplishments of mankind. It compriseth the laws, regulations, arts and sciences through which the world of humanity hath developed; laws and regulations which are the outcome of lofty ideals and the result of sound minds, and which have stepped forth into the arena of existence through the efforts of the wise and cultured in past and subsequent ages. The propagator and executive power of this call is just government.

The other is the soul-stirring call of God, Whose 225.3 spiritual teachings are safeguards of the everlasting glory, the eternal happiness and illumination of the world of humanity, and cause attributes of mercy to be revealed in the human world and the life beyond.

This second call is founded upon the instruc- 225.4 tions and exhortations of the Lord and the admonitions and altruistic emotions belonging to the realm of morality which, like unto a brilliant light, brighten and illumine the lamp of the realities of mankind. Its penetrative power is the Word of God.

225.5 However, until material achievements, physical accomplishments and human virtues are reinforced by spiritual perfections, luminous qualities and characteristics of mercy, no fruit or result shall issue therefrom, nor will the happiness of the world of humanity, which is the ultimate aim, be attained. For although, on the one hand, material achievements and the development of the physical world produce prosperity, which exquisitely manifests its intended aims, on the other hand dangers, severe calamities and violent afflictions are imminent.

225.6 Consequently, when thou lookest at the orderly pattern of kingdoms, cities and villages, with the attractiveness of their adornments, the freshness of their natural resources, the refinement of their appliances, the ease of their means of travel, the extent of knowledge available about the world of nature, the great inventions, the colossal enterprises, the noble discoveries and scientific researches, thou wouldst conclude that civilization conduceth to the happiness and the progress of the human world. Yet shouldst thou turn thine eye to the discovery of destructive and infernal machines, to the development of forces of demolition and the invention of fiery implements, which uproot the tree of life, it would become evident and manifest unto thee that civilization is conjoined with barbarism. Progress and barbarism go hand in hand, unless material civilization be confirmed by Divine Guidance, by the revelations of the All-Merciful and by godly virtues, and be reinforced by spiritual conduct, by the ideals of the Kingdom and by the outpourings of the Realm of Might.

225.7 Consider now, that the most advanced and civilized countries of the world have been turned into arsenals of explosives, that the continents of the globe have been transformed into huge camps and battlefields, that the peoples of the world have formed themselves into armed nations, and that the governments of the world are vying with each other as to who will first step into the field of carnage and bloodshed, thus subjecting mankind to the utmost degree of affliction.

225.8 Therefore, this civilization and material progress should be combined with the Most Great Guidance so that this nether world may become the scene of the appearance of the bestowals of the Kingdom, and physical achievements may be conjoined with the effulgences of the Merciful. This in order that the beauty and perfection of the world of man may be unveiled and be manifested before all in the utmost grace and splendor. Thus everlasting glory and happiness shall be revealed.

225.9   Praise be to God, throughout succeeding centuries and ages the call of civilization hath been
raised, the world of humanity hath been advancing and progressing day by day, various countries
have been developing by leaps and bounds, and
material improvements have increased, until the
world of existence obtained universal capacity to
receive the spiritual teachings and to hearken to the
Divine Call. The suckling babe passeth through
various physical stages, growing and developing
at every stage, until its body reacheth the age of
maturity. Having arrived at this stage it acquireth
the capacity to manifest spiritual and intellectual
perfections. The lights of comprehension, intelligence and knowledge become perceptible in it
and the powers of its soul unfold. Similarly, in
the contingent world, the human species hath
undergone progressive physical changes and, by
a slow process, hath scaled the ladder of civilization, realizing in itself the wonders, excellencies
and gifts of humanity in their most glorious form,
until it gained the capacity to express the splendors of spiritual perfections and divine ideals and
became capable of hearkening to the call of God.
Then at last the call of the Kingdom was raised,
the spiritual virtues and perfections were revealed,
the Sun of Reality dawned, and the teachings of

the Most Great Peace, of the oneness of the world of humanity and of the universality of men, were promoted. We hope that the effulgence of these rays shall become more and more intense, and the ideal virtues more resplendent, so that the goal of this universal human process will be attained and the love of God will appear in the utmost grace and beauty and bedazzle all hearts.

O ye beloved of God! Know ye, verily, that the 225.10 happiness of mankind lieth in the unity and the harmony of the human race, and that spiritual and material developments are conditioned upon love and amity among all men. Consider ye the living creatures, namely those which move upon the earth and those which fly, those which graze and those which devour. Among the beasts of prey each kind liveth apart from other species of its genus, observing complete antagonism and hostility; and whenever they meet they immediately fight and draw blood, gnashing their teeth and baring their claws. This is the way in which ferocious beasts and bloodthirsty wolves behave, carnivorous animals that live by themselves and fight for their lives. But the docile, good-natured and gentle animals, whether they belong to the flying or grazing species, associate with one another in complete affinity, united in their flocks, and living their lives with enjoyment, happiness and contentment. Such are the birds that are satisfied with and grateful for a few grains; they live in complete gladness, and break into rich and melodious song while soaring over meadows, plains, hills and mountains. Similarly those animals which graze, like the sheep, the antelope and the gazelle, consort in the greatest amity, intimacy and unity while living in their plains and prairies in a condition of complete contentment. But dogs, wolves, tigers, hyenas and those other beasts of prey, are alienated from each other as they hunt and roam about alone. The creatures of the fields and birds of the air do not even shun or molest one another when they come upon their mutual grazing and resting grounds but accept each other with friendliness, unlike the devouring beasts who immediately tear each other apart when one intrudes upon the other's cave or lair; yea, even if one merely passeth by the abode of another the latter at once rusheth out to attack and if possible kill the former.

225.11 Therefore, it hath been made clear and manifest that in the animal kingdom also love and affinity are the fruits of a gentle disposition, a pure nature and praiseworthy character, while discord and isolation are characteristic of the fierce beasts of the wild.

The Almighty hath not created in man the claws and teeth of ferocious animals, nay rather hath the human form been fashioned and set with the most comely attributes and adorned with the most perfect virtues. The honor of this creation and the worthiness of this garment therefore require man to have love and affinity for his own kind, nay rather, to act towards all living creatures with justice and equity. 225.12

Similarly, consider how the cause of the welfare, happiness, joy and comfort of humankind are amity and union, whereas dissension and discord are most conducive to hardship, humiliation, agitation and failure. 225.13

But a thousand times alas, that man is negligent and unaware of these facts, and daily doth he strut abroad with the characteristics of a wild beast. Lo! At one moment he turneth into a ferocious tiger; at the next he becometh a creeping, venomous viper! But the sublime achievements of man reside in those qualities and attributes that exclusively pertain to the angels of the Supreme Concourse. Therefore, when praiseworthy qualities and high morals emanate from man, he becometh a heavenly being, an angel of the Kingdom, a divine reality and a celestial effulgence. On the other hand, 225.14

when he engageth in warfare, quarrelling and bloodshed, he becometh viler than the most fierce of savage creatures, for if a bloodthirsty wolf devoureth a lamb in a single night, man slaughtereth a hundred thousand in the field of battle, strewing the ground with their corpses and kneading the earth with their blood.

225.15 In short, man is endowed with two natures: one tendeth towards moral sublimity and intellectual perfection, while the other turneth to bestial degradation and carnal imperfections. If ye travel the countries of the globe ye shall observe on one side the remains of ruin and destruction, while on the other ye shall see the signs of civilization and development. Such desolation and ruin are the result of war, strife and quarrelling, while all development and progress are fruits of the lights of virtue, cooperation and concord.

225.16 If one were to travel through the deserts of Central Asia he would observe how many cities, once great and prosperous like Paris and London, are now demolished and razed to the ground. From the Caspian Sea to the River Oxus there stretch wild and desolate plains, deserts, wildernesses and valleys. For two days and two nights the Russian railway traverseth the ruined cities and uninhabited villages of that wasteland. Formerly that plain bore the fruit of the finest civilizations of the past. Tokens of development and refinement were apparent all around, arts and sciences were well protected and promoted, professions and industries flourished, commerce and agriculture had reached a high stage of efficiency, and the foundations of government and statesmanship were laid on a strong and solid basis. Today that vast stretch of land hath become mostly the shelter and asylum of Turkoman tribes, and an arena for the ferocious display of wild beasts. The ancient cities of that plain, such as Gurgán, Nissá, Abívard and Shahristán, famous throughout the world for their arts, sciences, culture, industry, and well known for their wealth, greatness, prosperity and distinction, have given way to a wilderness wherein no voice is heard save the roaring of wild beasts and where bloodthirsty wolves roam at will. This destruction and desolation was brought about by war and strife, dissension and discord between the Persians and the Turks, who differed in their religion and customs. So rigid was the spirit of religious prejudice that the faithless leaders sanctioned the shedding of innocent blood, the ruin of property and the desecration of family honor. This is to cite only one illustration.

Consequently, when thou traversest the regions of the world, thou shalt conclude that all progress is the result of association and cooperation, while 225.17

ruin is the outcome of animosity and hatred. Notwithstanding this, the world of humanity doth not take warning, nor doth it awake from the slumber of heedlessness. Man is still causing differences, quarrels and strife in order to marshal the cohorts of war and, with his legions, rush into the field of bloodshed and slaughter.

225.18 Then again, consider the phenomenon of composition and decomposition, of existence and nonexistence. Every created thing in the contingent world is made up of many and varied atoms, and its existence is dependent on the composition of these. In other words, through the divine creative power a conjunction of simple elements taketh place so that from this composition a distinct organism is produced. The existence of all things is based upon this principle. But when the order is deranged, decomposition is produced and disintegration setteth in, then that thing ceaseth to exist. That is, the annihilation of all things is caused by decomposition and disintegration. Therefore attraction and composition between the various elements is the means of life, and discord, decomposition and division produce death. Thus the cohesive and attractive forces in all things lead to the appearance of fruitful results and effects, while estrangement and alienation of things lead to disturbance and annihilation.

Through affinity and attraction all living things like plants, animals and men come into existence, while division and discord bring about decomposition and destruction.

Consequently, that which is conducive to asso- 225.19 ciation and attraction and unity among the sons of men is the means of the life of the world of humanity, and whatever causeth division, repulsion and remoteness leadeth to the death of humankind.

And if, as thou passest by fields and planta- 225.20 tions, thou observest that the plants, flowers and sweet-smelling herbs are growing luxuriantly together, forming a pattern of unity, this is an evidence of the fact that that plantation and garden is flourishing under the care of a skilful gardener. But when thou seest it in a state of disorder and irregularity thou inferrest that it hath lacked the training of an efficient farmer and thus hath produced weeds and tares.

It therefore becometh manifest that amity and 225.21 cohesion are indicative of the training of the Real Educator, and dispersion and separation a proof of savagery and deprivation of divine education.

A critic may object, saying that peoples, races, 225.22 tribes and communities of the world are of different and varied customs, habits, tastes, character, inclinations and ideas, that opinions and thoughts are contrary to one another, and how, therefore, is it possible for real unity to be revealed and perfect accord among human souls to exist?

225.23　　In answer we say that differences are of two kinds. One is the cause of annihilation and is like the antipathy existing among warring nations and conflicting tribes who seek each other's destruction, uprooting one another's families, depriving one another of rest and comfort and unleashing carnage. The other kind which is a token of diversity is the essence of perfection and the cause of the appearance of the bestowals of the Most Glorious Lord.

225.24　　Consider the flowers of a garden: though differing in kind, color, form and shape, yet, inasmuch as they are refreshed by the waters of one spring, revived by the breath of one wind, invigorated by the rays of one sun, this diversity increaseth their charm, and addeth unto their beauty. Thus when that unifying force, the penetrating influence of the Word of God, taketh effect, the difference of customs, manners, habits, ideas, opinions and dispositions embellisheth the world of humanity. This diversity, this difference is like the naturally created dissimilarity and variety of the limbs and organs of the human body, for each one contributeth to the beauty, efficiency and perfection of the whole. When these different limbs and organs come under the influence of man's sovereign soul, and the soul's power pervadeth the limbs and members, veins and arteries of the body, then difference reinforceth harmony, diversity strengtheneth love, and multiplicity is the greatest factor for coordination.

How unpleasing to the eye if all the flowers and plants, the leaves and blossoms, the fruits, the branches and the trees of that garden were all of the same shape and color! Diversity of hues, form and shape, enricheth and adorneth the garden, and heighteneth the effect thereof. In like manner, when divers shades of thought, temperament and character, are brought together under the power and influence of one central agency, the beauty and glory of human perfection will be revealed and made manifest. Naught but the celestial potency of the Word of God, which ruleth and transcendeth the realities of all things, is capable of harmonizing the divergent thoughts, sentiments, ideas, and convictions of the children of men. Verily, it is the penetrating power in all things, the mover of souls and the binder and regulator in the world of humanity. 225.25

Praise be to God, today the splendor of the Word of God hath illumined every horizon, and from all sects, races, tribes, nations, and communities souls have come together in the light of the Word, as- 225.26

sembled, united and agreed in perfect harmony. Oh! What a great number of meetings are held adorned with souls from various races and diverse sects! Anyone attending these will be struck with amazement, and might suppose that these souls are all of one land, one nationality, one community, one thought, one belief and one opinion; whereas, in fact, one is an American, the other an African, one cometh from Asia and another from Europe, one is a native of India, another is from Turkestan, one is an Arab, another a Tajik, another a Persian and yet another a Greek. Notwithstanding such diversity they associate in perfect harmony and unity, love and freedom; they have one voice, one thought and one purpose. Verily, this is from the penetrative power of the Word of God! If all the forces of the universe were to combine they would not be able thus to gather a single assemblage so imbued with the sentiments of love, affection, attraction and enkindlement as to unite the members of different races and to raise up from the heart of the world a voice that shall dispel war and strife, uproot dissension and disputation, usher in the era of universal peace and establish unity and concord amongst men.

225.27   Can any power withstand the penetrative influence of the Word of God? Nay, by God! The proof is clear and the evidence is complete! If anyone looketh with the eyes of justice he shall be struck with wonder and amazement and will testify that all the peoples, sects and races of the world should be glad, content and grateful for the teachings and admonitions of Bahá'u'lláh. For these divine injunctions tame every ferocious beast, transform the creeping insect into a soaring bird, cause human souls to become angels of the Kingdom, and make the human world a focus for the qualities of mercy.

Furthermore each and every one is required to show obedience, submission and loyalty towards his own government. Today no state in the world is in a condition of peace or tranquillity, for security and trust have vanished from among the people. Both the governed and the governors are alike in danger. The only group of people which today submitteth peacefully and loyally to the laws and ordinances of government and dealeth honestly and frankly with the people, is none other than this wronged community. For while all sects and races in Persia and Turkestan are absorbed in promoting their own interests and only obey their governments either with the hope of reward or from fear of punishment, the Bahá'ís are the well-wishers of the government, obedient to its laws and bearing love towards all peoples. 225.28

Such obedience and submission is made incumbent and obligatory upon all by the clear Text of the Abhá Beauty. Therefore the believers, in obedi- 225.29

ence to the command of the True One, show the utmost sincerity and goodwill towards all nations; and should any soul act contrary to the laws of the government he would consider himself responsible before God, deserving divine wrath and chastisement for his sin and wrongdoing. It is astonishing that, in spite of this, some of the officials of the government consider the Bahá'ís to be ill-wishers while they regard the members of other communities as their well-wishers. Gracious God! Recently, when there was general revolution and agitation in Ṭihrán and in other provinces of Persia, it was proven that not a single Bahá'í had taken part nor intervened in these affairs. For this reason they were reproached by the ignorant because they had obeyed the command of the Blessed Perfection and refrained absolutely from interference in political matters. They were not associated with any party, but busied themselves with their own affairs and professions and discharged their own duties.

225.30   All the friends of God bear witness to the fact that 'Abdu'l-Bahá is, from every standpoint, the well-wisher of all governments and nations, and prayeth sincerely for their progress and advancement, especially for the two great states of the east, for these two countries are the native land and the place of exile of Bahá'u'lláh. In all epistles and writings he hath commended and praised these two governments and hath supplicated divine confirmations for them from the Threshold of the One true God. The Abhá Beauty—may my life be a sacrifice for His loved ones—hath offered prayers on behalf of Their Imperial Majesties. Gracious God! How strange that, notwithstanding these conclusive proofs, every day some event transpireth and difficulties arise. But we, and the friends of God, should on no account slacken our efforts to be loyal, sincere and men of good will. We should at all times manifest our truthfulness and sincerity, nay rather, we must be constant in our faithfulness and trustworthiness, and occupy ourselves in offering prayers for the good of all.

O ye beloved of God, these are days for stead- 225.31
fastness, for firmness and perseverance in the Cause of God. Ye must not focus your attention upon the person of 'Abdu'l-Bahá, for erelong he will bid you farewell. Rather must ye fix your gaze upon the Word of God. If the Word of God is being promoted, rejoice and be happy and thankful, though 'Abdu'l-Bahá himself be threatened by the sword or burdened by the weight of chains and fetters. For the Holy Temple of the Cause of God is important, not the physical body of 'Abdu'l-Bahá. The friends of God must arise with such stead-

fastness that if, at any moment, a hundred souls like 'Abdu'l-Bahá become the target for the arrows of affliction, they will not shift or waver in their resolve, their determination, their enkindlement, their devotion and service in the Cause of God. 'Abdu'l-Bahá is himself a servant at the Threshold of the Blessed Beauty and a manifestation of pure and utter servitude at the Threshold of the Almighty. He hath no other station or title, no other rank or power. This is my ultimate Purpose, my eternal Paradise, my holiest Temple and my Sadratu'l-Muntahá. With the Abhá Blessed Beauty and the Exalted One, His Herald—may my life be a sacrifice for Them both—hath ended the appearance of God's independent and universal Manifestation. And for a thousand years all shall be illumined by His lights and be sustained by the ocean of His favors.

225.32   O ye lovers of God! This, verily, is my last wish and my admonition unto you. Blessed, therefore, is he who is aided by God to follow that which is inscribed upon this scroll whose words are sanctified from the symbols current amongst men.

226.1   226. O thou servant of God! Thy letter was received, and was the cause of gladness. Thou hast expressed thine ardent wish that I should attend the Peace Congress. I do not present myself at such political conferences, for the establishment of peace is unachievable save through the power of the Word of God. When a conference is convened, representative of all nations and working under the influence of the Word of God, then universal peace will be established but otherwise it is impossible.

At present it is certain that temporary peace is established but it is not lasting. All governments and nations have become tired of war, of the difficulties of travel, of huge expenditures, of the loss of life, of the affliction of women, of the great number of orphans, and they are driven by force to peace. But this peace is not permanent, it is temporary. 226.2

We hope that the power of the Word of God will establish a peace that shall eternally remain effective and secure. 226.3

227.* O ye esteemed ones who are pioneers among the well-wishers of the world of humanity! 227.1

The letters which ye sent during the war were not received, but a letter dated February 11th, 1916, has just come to hand, and immediately an answer is 227.2

---

* This is the first part of 'Abdu'l-Bahá's reply to a letter addressed to Him by the Executive Committee of the Central Organization for a Durable Peace. The Tablet, described by Shoghi Effendi in *God Passes By* as of "far reaching importance," and dated December 17, 1919, was dispatched to the Committee at The Hague by the hands of a special delegation.

being written. Your intention deserves a thousand praises, because you are serving the world of humanity, and this is conducive to the happiness and welfare of all. This recent war has proved to the world and the people that war is destruction while universal peace is construction; war is death while peace is life; war is rapacity and bloodthirstiness while peace is beneficence and humaneness; war is an appurtenance of the world of nature while peace is of the foundation of the religion of God; war is darkness upon darkness while peace is heavenly light; war is the destroyer of the edifice of mankind while peace is the everlasting life of the world of humanity; war is like a devouring wolf while peace is like the angels of heaven; war is the struggle for existence while peace is mutual aid and cooperation among the peoples of the world and the cause of the good pleasure of the True One in the heavenly realm.

227.3   There is not one soul whose conscience does not testify that in this day there is no more important matter in the world than that of universal peace. Every just one bears witness to this and adores that esteemed Assembly because its aim is that this darkness may be changed into light, this bloodthirstiness into kindness, this torment into bliss, this hardship into ease and this enmity and hatred into fellowship and love. Therefore, the effort of those esteemed souls is worthy of praise and commendation.

But the wise souls who are aware of the essen- 227.4 tial relationships emanating from the realities of things consider that one single matter cannot, by itself, influence the human reality as it ought and should, for until the minds of men become unit- ed, no important matter can be accomplished. At present universal peace is a matter of great impor- tance, but unity of conscience is essential, so that the foundation of this matter may become secure, its establishment firm and its edifice strong.

Therefore Bahá'u'lláh, fifty years ago, expound- 227.5 ed this question of universal peace at a time when He was confined in the fortress of 'Akká and was wronged and imprisoned. He wrote about this important matter of universal peace to all the great sovereigns of the world, and established it among His friends in the Orient. The horizon of the East was in utter darkness, nations displayed the utmost hatred and enmity towards each other, religions thirsted for each other's blood, and it was dark- ness upon darkness. At such a time Bahá'u'lláh shone forth like the sun from the horizon of the east and illumined Persia with the lights of these teachings.

227.6   Among His teachings was the declaration of universal peace. People of different nations, religions and sects who followed Him came together to such an extent that remarkable gatherings were instituted consisting of the various nations and religions of the East. Every soul who entered these gatherings saw but one nation, one teaching, one pathway, one order, for the teachings of Bahá'u'lláh were not limited to the establishment of universal peace. They embraced many teachings which supplemented and supported that of universal peace.

227.7   Among these teachings was the independent investigation of reality so that the world of humanity may be saved from the darkness of imitation and attain to the truth; may tear off and cast away this ragged and outgrown garment of a thousand years ago and may put on the robe woven in the utmost purity and holiness in the loom of reality. As reality is one and cannot admit of multiplicity, therefore different opinions must ultimately become fused into one.

227.8   And among the teachings of Bahá'u'lláh is the oneness of the world of humanity; that all human beings are the sheep of God and He is the kind Shepherd. This Shepherd is kind to all the sheep, because He created them all, trained them, provided for them and protected them. There is no doubt that the Shepherd is kind to all the sheep and should there be among these sheep ignorant ones, they must be educated; if there be children, they must be trained until they reach maturity; if there be sick ones, they must be cured. There must be no hatred and enmity, for as by a kind physician these ignorant, sick ones should be treated.

And among the teachings of Bahá'u'lláh is that religion must be the cause of fellowship and love. If it becomes the cause of estrangement then it is not needed, for religion is like a remedy; if it aggravates the disease then it becomes unnecessary. 227.9

And among the teachings of Bahá'u'lláh is that religion must be in conformity with science and reason, so that it may influence the hearts of men. The foundation must be solid and must not consist of imitations. 227.10

And among the teachings of Bahá'u'lláh is that religious, racial, political, economic and patriotic prejudices destroy the edifice of humanity. As long as these prejudices prevail, the world of humanity will not have rest. For a period of 6,000 years history informs us about the world of humanity. During these 6,000 years the world of humanity has not been free from war, strife, murder and bloodthirstiness. In every period war has been waged in one country or another and that war was due to 227.11

either religious prejudice, racial prejudice, political prejudice or patriotic prejudice. It has therefore been ascertained and proved that all prejudices are destructive of the human edifice. As long as these prejudices persist, the struggle for existence must remain dominant, and bloodthirstiness and rapacity continue. Therefore, even as was the case in the past, the world of humanity cannot be saved from the darkness of nature and cannot attain illumination except through the abandonment of prejudices and the acquisition of the morals of the Kingdom.

227.12   If this prejudice and enmity are on account of religion consider that religion should be the cause of fellowship, otherwise it is fruitless. And if this prejudice be the prejudice of nationality consider that all mankind are of one nation; all have sprung from the tree of Adam, and Adam is the root of the tree. That tree is one and all these nations are like branches, while the individuals of humanity are like leaves, blossoms and fruits thereof. Then the establishment of various nations and the consequent shedding of blood and destruction of the edifice of humanity result from human ignorance and selfish motives.

227.13   As to the patriotic prejudice, this is also due to absolute ignorance, for the surface of the earth is one native land. Every one can live in any spot on the terrestrial globe. Therefore all the world is man's birthplace. These boundaries and outlets have been devised by man. In the creation, such boundaries and outlets were not assigned. Europe is one continent, Asia is one continent, Africa is one continent, Australia is one continent, but some of the souls, from personal motives and selfish interests, have divided each one of these continents and considered a certain part as their own country. God has set up no frontier between France and Germany; they are continuous. Yet, in the first centuries, selfish souls, for the promotion of their own interests, have assigned boundaries and outlets and have, day by day, attached more importance to these, until this led to intense enmity, bloodshed and rapacity in subsequent centuries. In the same way this will continue indefinitely, and if this conception of patriotism remains limited within a certain circle, it will be the primary cause of the world's destruction. No wise and just person will acknowledge these imaginary distinctions. Every limited area which we call our native country we regard as our motherland, whereas the terrestrial globe is the motherland of all, and not any restricted area. In short, for a few days we live on this earth and eventually we are buried in it, it is our eternal tomb. Is it worth while that we should engage in bloodshed and tear one another to pieces for this eternal tomb? Nay, far from it, neither is God pleased with such conduct nor would any sane man approve of it.

227.14 Consider! The blessed animals engage in no patriotic quarrels. They are in the utmost fellowship with one another and live together in harmony. For example, if a dove from the east and a dove from the west, a dove from the north and a dove from the south chance to arrive, at the same time, in one spot, they immediately associate in harmony. So is it with all the blessed animals and birds. But the ferocious animals, as soon as they meet, attack and fight with each other, tear each other to pieces and it is impossible for them to live peaceably together in one spot. They are all unsociable and fierce, savage and combative fighters.

227.15 Regarding the economic prejudice, it is apparent that whenever the ties between nations become strengthened and the exchange of commodities accelerated, and any economic principle is established in one country, it will ultimately affect the other countries and universal benefits will result. Then why this prejudice?

227.16 As to the political prejudice, the policy of God must be followed and it is indisputable that the policy of God is greater than human policy. We must follow the Divine policy and that applies alike to all individuals. He treats all individuals alike: no distinction is made, and that is the foundation of the Divine Religions.

And among the teachings of Bahá'u'lláh is the origination of one language that may be spread universally among the people. This teaching was revealed from the pen of Bahá'u'lláh in order that this universal language may eliminate misunderstandings from among mankind. 227.17

And among the teachings of Bahá'u'lláh is the equality of women and men. The world of humanity has two wings—one is women and the other men. Not until both wings are equally developed can the bird fly. Should one wing remain weak, flight is impossible. Not until the world of women becomes equal to the world of men in the acquisition of virtues and perfections, can success and prosperity be attained as they ought to be. 227.18

And among the teachings of Bahá'u'lláh is voluntary sharing of one's property with others among mankind. This voluntary sharing is greater than equality, and consists in this, that man should not prefer himself to others, but rather should sacrifice his life and property for others. But this should not be introduced by coercion so that it becomes a law and man is compelled to follow it. Nay, rather, 227.19

man should voluntarily and of his own choice sacrifice his property and life for others, and spend willingly for the poor, just as is done in Persia among the Bahá'ís.

227.20 And among the teachings of Bahá'u'lláh is man's freedom, that through the ideal Power he should be free and emancipated from the captivity of the world of nature; for as long as man is captive to nature he is a ferocious animal, as the struggle for existence is one of the exigencies of the world of nature. This matter of the struggle for existence is the fountain-head of all calamities and is the supreme affliction.

227.21 And among the teachings of Bahá'u'lláh is that religion is a mighty bulwark. If the edifice of religion shakes and totters, commotion and chaos will ensue and the order of things will be utterly upset, for in the world of mankind there are two safeguards that protect man from wrongdoing. One is the law which punishes the criminal; but the law prevents only the manifest crime and not the concealed sin; whereas the ideal safeguard, namely, the religion of God, prevents both the manifest and the concealed crime, trains man, educates morals, compels the adoption of virtues and is the all-inclusive power which guarantees the felicity of the world of mankind. But by religion is meant that which is ascertained by investigation and not that which is based on mere imitation, the foundations of Divine Religions and not human imitations.

And among the teachings of Bahá'u'lláh is that 227.22 although material civilization is one of the means for the progress of the world of mankind, yet until it becomes combined with Divine civilization, the desired result, which is the felicity of mankind, will not be attained. Consider! These battleships that reduce a city to ruins within the space of an hour are the result of material civilization; likewise the Krupp guns, the Mauser rifles, dynamite, submarines, torpedo boats, armed aircraft and bombers— all these weapons of war are the malignant fruits of material civilization. Had material civilization been combined with Divine civilization, these fiery weapons would never have been invented. Nay, rather, human energy would have been wholly devoted to useful inventions and would have been concentrated on praiseworthy discoveries. Material civilization is like a lamp-glass. Divine civilization is the lamp itself and the glass without the light is dark. Material civilization is like the body. No matter how infinitely graceful, elegant and beautiful it may be, it is dead. Divine civilization is like the spirit, and the body gets its life from the spirit, otherwise it becomes a corpse. It has thus been made evident that the world of mankind is in need of the breaths of the Holy Spirit. Without the spirit the world of mankind is lifeless, and without this light the world of mankind is in utter darkness. For the world of nature is an animal world. Until man is born again from the world of nature, that is to say, becomes detached from the world of nature, he is essentially an animal, and it is the teachings of God which convert this animal into a human soul.

227.23 And among the teachings of Bahá'u'lláh is the promotion of education. Every child must be instructed in sciences as much as is necessary. If the parents are able to provide the expenses of this education, it is well, otherwise the community must provide the means for the teaching of that child.

227.24 And among the teachings of Bahá'u'lláh are justice and right. Until these are realized on the plane of existence, all things shall be in disorder and remain imperfect. The world of mankind is a world of oppression and cruelty, and a realm of aggression and error.

227.25 In fine, such teachings are numerous. These manifold principles, which constitute the greatest basis for the felicity of mankind and are of the bounties of the Merciful, must be added to the matter of universal peace and combined with it, so that results may accrue. Otherwise the realization of universal peace by itself in the world of mankind is difficult. As the teachings of Bahá'u'lláh are combined with universal peace, they are like a table provided with every kind of fresh and delicious food. Every soul can find, at that table of infinite bounty, that which he desires. If the question is restricted to universal peace alone, the remarkable results which are expected and desired will not be attained. The scope of universal peace must be such that all the communities and religions may find their highest wish realized in it. The teachings of Bahá'u'lláh are such that all the communities of the world, whether religious, political or ethical, ancient or modern, find in them the expression of their highest wish.

For example, the people of religions find, in the 227.26 teachings of Bahá'u'lláh, the establishment of Universal Religion—a religion that perfectly conforms with present conditions, which in reality effects the immediate cure of the incurable disease, which relieves every pain, and bestows the infallible antidote for every deadly poison. For if we wish to arrange and organize the world of mankind in accordance with the present religious imitations and thereby to establish the felicity of the world of mankind, it is impossible and impracticable—for example, the enforcement of the laws of the Torah and also of the other religions in accordance with present imitations. But the essential basis of all the Divine Religions which pertains to the virtues of the world of mankind and is the foundation of the welfare of the world of man, is found in the teachings of Bahá'u'lláh in the most perfect presentation.

227.27 Similarly, with regard to the peoples who clamor for freedom: the moderate freedom which guarantees the welfare of the world of mankind and maintains and preserves the universal relationships, is found in its fullest power and extension in the teachings of Bahá'u'lláh.

227.28 So with regard to political parties: that which is the greatest policy directing the world of mankind, nay, rather, the Divine policy, is found in the teachings of Bahá'u'lláh.

227.29 Likewise with regard to the party of "equality" which seeks the solution of the economic problems: until now all proposed solutions have proved impracticable except the economic proposals in the teachings of Bahá'u'lláh which are practicable and cause no distress to society.

227.30 So with the other parties: when ye look deeply into this matter, ye will discover that the highest aims of those parties are found in the teachings of

Bahá'u'lláh. These teachings constitute the all-inclusive power among all men and are practicable. But there are some teachings of the past, such as those of the Torah, which cannot be carried out at the present day. It is the same with the other religions and the tenets of the various sects and the different parties.

For example, the question of universal peace, 227.31 about which Bahá'u'lláh says that the Supreme Tribunal must be established: although the League of Nations has been brought into existence, yet it is incapable of establishing universal peace. But the Supreme Tribunal which Bahá'u'lláh has described will fulfill this sacred task with the utmost might and power. And His plan is this: that the national assemblies of each country and nation—that is to say parliaments—should elect two or three persons who are the choicest of that nation, and are well informed concerning international laws and the relations between governments and aware of the essential needs of the world of humanity in this day. The number of these representatives should be in proportion to the number of inhabitants of that country. The election of these souls who are chosen by the national assembly, that is, the parliament, must be confirmed by the upper house, the congress and the cabinet and also by the president or monarch so these persons may be the elected ones of all the nation and the government. The Supreme Tribunal will be composed of these people, and all mankind will thus have a share therein, for every one of these delegates is fully representative of his nation. When the Supreme Tribunal gives a ruling on any international question, either unanimously or by majority rule, there will no longer be any pretext for the plaintiff or ground of objection for the defendant. In case any of the governments or nations, in the execution of the irrefutable decision of the Supreme Tribunal, be negligent or dilatory, the rest of the nations will rise up against it, because all the governments and nations of the world are the supporters of this Supreme Tribunal. Consider what a firm foundation this is! But by a limited and restricted League the purpose will not be realized as it ought and should. This is the truth about the situation, which has been stated. . . .

228.1   228. O Servant of the Threshold of Bahá'u'lláh! Thy letter dated 14 June 1920 hath been received. A letter from some of the members of the Peace Committee hath also been received and an answer hath been written to them. Deliver it to them.

228.2   It is evident that this meeting is not what it is reputed to be and is unable to order and arrange affairs in the manner which is befitting and necessary. However that may be, the matter in which they are engaged is nevertheless of the greatest importance. The meeting at The Hague should have such power and influence that its word will have an effect on the governments and nations. Point out to the revered members gathered there that the Hague Conference held before the war had as its President the Emperor of Russia, and its members were men of the greatest eminence. Nevertheless this did not prevent such a terrible war. Now how will it be? For in the future another war, fiercer than the last, will assuredly break out; verily, of this there is no doubt whatever. What can the Hague meeting do?

But the fundamental principles laid down by Bahá'u'lláh are day by day spreading. Deliver the answer to their letter and express the greatest love and kindness, and leave them to their own affairs. In any case they ought to be pleased with you, and subject to their approval you may print and distribute that detailed epistle of mine which hath already been translated into English. 228.3

As to the Esperantists, associate with them. Whenever you find one with capacity, convey to him the fragrances of Life. In all the meetings converse about the teachings of Bahá'u'lláh, because this will be effec- 228.4

tive today in the western countries. And if they ask regarding your belief in Bahá'u'lláh, you should reply that we consider Him as the foremost Teacher and Educator of the world in this age, and make clear, explaining in detail, that these teachings regarding universal peace and other subjects were revealed by the pen of Bahá'u'lláh fifty years ago and have already been published in Persia and India and spread abroad throughout the whole world. In the beginning all were incredulous about the idea of universal peace, considering it an impossibility. Further, speak of the greatness of Bahá'u'lláh, of the events that took place in Persia and Turkey, of the astonishing influence that He exerted, of the contents of the Epistles which He addressed to all the sovereigns, and of their fulfillment. Also speak of the spread of the Bahá'í Cause. Associate with the Committee of Universal Peace at The Hague as much as possible, showing them every courtesy.

228.5   It is evident that the Esperantists are receptive and thou art familiar with and expert in their language. Communicate also with the Esperantists of Germany and other places. The literature which thou circulatest should deal only with the teachings. The dissemination of other literature is at present not advisable. My hope is that the divine confirmations may continually assist thee. . . .

Grieve not over the apathy and coldness of the 228.6
Hague meeting. Put thy trust in God. Our hope
is that among the people the Esperanto language
may hereafter have a powerful effect. Thou hast
now sown the seed. Assuredly it will grow. Its
growth dependeth upon God.

229. O sincere servant of the True One! I hear 229.1
thou art grieved and distressed at the happenings of the world and the vicissitudes of fortune.
Wherefore this fear and sorrow? The true lovers of
the Abhá Beauty, and they that have quaffed the
Cup of the Covenant fear no calamity, nor feel depressed in the hour of trial. They regard the fire of
adversity as their garden of delight, and the depth
of the sea the expanse of heaven.

Thou who art neath the shelter of God, and 229.2
under the shadow of the Tree of His Covenant,
why sorrow and repine? Rest thou assured and feel
confident. Observe the written commandments
of thy Lord with joy and peace, with earnestness
and sincerity; and be thou the well-wisher of thy
country and thy government. His grace shall assist
thee at all times, His blessings shall be bestowed
upon thee, and thy heart's desire shall be realized.

By the Ancient Beauty!—may my life be a 229.3
sacrifice for His loved ones—Were the friends to

realize what a glorious sovereignty the Lord hath destined for them in His Kingdom, surely they would be filled with ecstasy, would behold themselves crowned with immortal glory and carried away with transports of delight. Erelong it shall be made manifest how brilliantly the light of His bountiful care and mercy hath shone upon His loved ones, and what a turbulent ocean hath been stirred in their hearts! Then will they clamor and exclaim: Happy are we; let all the world rejoice!

230.1   230. O respected personage! Thy second letter dated 19 December 1918 was received. It was the cause of great joy and gladness, for it showed thy firmness and steadfastness in the Covenant and Testament and thy yearning to raise the call of the Kingdom of God. Today the call of the Kingdom is the magnetic power which draweth to itself the world of mankind, for capacity in men is great. Divine teachings constitute the spirit of this age, nay rather the sun of this age. Every soul must endeavor that the veils that cover men's eyes may be torn asunder and that instantly the sun may be seen and that heart and sight may be illumined thereby.

230.2   Now, through the aid and bounty of God, this power of guidance and this merciful bestowal are found in thee. Arise, therefore, in the utmost Power that thou mayest bestow spirit upon moldering bones, give sight to the blind, balm and freshness to the depressed, and liveliness and grace to the dispirited. Every lamp will eventually be extinguished save the lamp of the Kingdom, which increaseth day by day in splendor. Every call shall ultimately weaken except the call to the Kingdom of God, which day unto day is raised. Every path shall finally be twisted except the road of the Kingdom, which straighteneth day by day. Undoubtedly heavenly melody is not to be measured with an earthly one, and artificial lights are not to be compared with the heavenly Sun. Hence one must exert endeavor in whatever is lasting and permanent so that one may more and more be illumined, strengthened and revived. . . .

I pray and supplicate the Divine Kingdom that 230.3 thy father, mother and brother may, through the light of guidance, enter the Kingdom of God.

231. O thou blossom on the Tree of Life! Happy 231.1 art thou to have girded thy loins in service; to have risen with all thy power in the promulgation of the divine teachings, to have convened gatherings and to have striven for the exaltation of the Word of God.

231.2   In this mortal world every important matter hath an end; and every remarkable achievement a termination; none having permanent existence. For instance, consider how the important achievements of the ancient world have been totally exterminated and not a trace remaineth therefrom save the great Cause of the Kingdom of God, which hath no beginning and will have no end. At most, it is only renewed. At the beginning of each renewal it commandeth no attention in the sight of the people, but when once definitely established, it will daily advance and in its daily exaltation will reach the supreme heavens.

231.3   For instance, consider the day of Christ, which was the day of the renewal of the Kingdom of God. The people of the world attached no importance to it and did not realize its significance to such an extent that the sepulchre of Christ remained lost and unknown for three hundred years, until the maidservant of God, Helen, the mother of Constantine arrived and discovered the sacred spot.

231.4   My purpose in all this is to show how unobservant are the people of the world and how ignorant, and on the day of the establishment of the Kingdom, they remain heedless and negligent.

231.5   Erelong the power of the Kingdom will encompass all the world and then they will be awakened and will cry and lament over those who were oppressed and martyred, and will sigh and moan. Such is the nature of people.

232. As to President Wilson, the fourteen principles which he hath enunciated are mostly found in the teachings of Bahá'u'lláh and I therefore hope that he will be confirmed and assisted. Now is the dawn of universal peace; my hope is that its morn will fully break, converting the gloom of war, of strife and of wrangling among men into the light of union, of harmony and of affection.   232.1

233. O ye faithful friends, O ye sincere servants of Bahá'u'lláh! Now, in the midwatches of the night, when eyes are closed in slumber and all have laid their heads upon the couch of rest and deep sleep, 'Abdu'l-Bahá is wakeful within the precincts of the Hallowed Shrine and, in the ardor of his invocation uttereth this, his prayer: 233.1

O Thou kind and loving Providence! The east is astir and the west surgeth even as the eternal billows of the sea. The gentle breezes of holiness are diffused and, from the Unseen Kingdom, the rays of the Orb of Truth shine forth resplendent. The anthems of divine unity are being chanted and the ensigns of celestial might are waving. The angelic Voice is raised   233.2

and, even as the roaring of the leviathan, soundeth the call to selflessness and evanescence. The triumphal cry *Yá Bahá'u'l-Abhá* resoundeth on every side, and the call *Yá 'Alíyyu'l-A'lá* ringeth throughout all regions. No stir is there in the world save that of the Glory of the One Ravisher of Hearts, and no tumult is there save the surging of the love of Him, the Incomparable, the Well-Beloved.

233.3 The beloved of the Lord, with their musk-scented breath, burn like bright candles in every clime, and the friends of the All-Merciful, even as unfolding flowers, can be found in all regions. Not for a moment do they rest; they breathe not but in remembrance of Thee, and crave naught but to serve Thy Cause. In the meadows of truth they are as sweet-singing nightingales, and in the flower garden of guidance they are even as brightly colored blossoms. With mystic flowers they adorn the walks of the Garden of Reality; as swaying cypresses they line the riverbanks of the Divine Will. Above the horizon of being they shine as radiant stars; in the firmament of the world they gleam as resplendent orbs. Manifestations of celestial grace are they, and daysprings of the light of divine assistance.

Grant, O Thou Loving Lord, that all may 233.4
stand firm and steadfast, shining with everlasting splendor, so that, at every breath, gentle breezes may blow from the bowers of Thy loving-kindness, that from the ocean of Thy grace a mist may rise, that the kindly showers of Thy love may bestow freshness, and the zephyr waft its perfume from the rose garden of divine unity.

Vouchsafe, O Best Beloved of the World, 233.5
a ray from Thy Splendor. O Well-Beloved of mankind, shed upon us the light of Thy Countenance.

O God Omnipotent, do Thou shield us and 233.6
be our refuge and, O Lord of Being, show forth Thy might and Thy dominion.

O Thou loving Lord, the movers of sedition 233.7
are in some regions astir and active, and by night and day are inflicting a grievous wrong.

Even as wolves, tyrants are lying in wait, 233.8
and the wronged, innocent flock hath neither help nor succor. Hounds are on the trail of the gazelles of the fields of divine unity, and the pheasant in the mountains of heavenly guidance is pursued by the ravens of envy.

O Thou divine Providence, preserve and 233.9
protect us! O Thou Who art our Shield, save

us and defend us! Keep us beneath Thy Shelter, and by Thy Help save us from all ills. Thou art, indeed, the True Protector, the Unseen Guardian, the Celestial Preserver, and the Heavenly Loving Lord.

233.10 O ye beloved of the Lord! On one side the standard of the One True God is unfurled and the Voice of the Kingdom raised. The Cause of God is spreading, and manifest in splendor are the wonders from on high. The east is illumined and the west perfumed; fragrant with ambergris is the north, and musk-scented the south.

233.11 On the other side the faithless wax in hate and rancor, ceaselessly stirring up grievous sedition and mischief. No day goeth by but someone raiseth the standard of revolt and spurreth his charger into the arena of discord. No hour passeth but the vile adder bareth its fangs and scattereth its deadly venom.

233.12 The beloved of the Lord are wrapped in utter sincerity and devotion, unmindful of this rancor and malice. Smooth and insidious are these snakes, these whisperers of evil, artful in their craft and guile. Be ye on your guard and ever wakeful! Quick-witted and keen of intellect are the faithful, and firm and steadfast are the assured. Act ye with all circumspection!

"Fear ye the sagacity of the faithful, for he seeth   233.13
with the divine light!"

Beware lest any soul privily cause disruption or   233.14
stir up strife. In the Impregnable Stronghold be
ye brave warriors, and for the Mighty Mansion a
valiant host. Exercise the utmost care, and day and
night be on your guard, that thereby the tyrant
may inflict no harm.

Study the Tablet of the Holy Mariner that ye   233.15
may know the truth and consider that the Blessed
Beauty hath fully foretold future events. Let them
who perceive take warning. Verily in this is a bounty for the sincere!

Even as dust upon the Sacred Threshold, in utter   233.16
humility and lowliness, 'Abdu'l-Bahá is engaged in
the promulgation of His signs in the daytime and
in the night season. Whensoever he findeth time
he prayeth ardently, and beseecheth Him tearfully
and fervently, saying:

O Thou divine Providence, pitiful are we,   233.17
grant us Thy succor; homeless wanderers, give
us Thy shelter; scattered, do Thou unite us;
astray, gather us to Thy fold; bereft, do Thou
bestow upon us a share and portion; athirst, lead
us to the wellspring of Life; frail, strengthen us
that we may arise to help Thy Cause and offer

ourselves as a living sacrifice in the pathway of guidance.

233.18   The faithless, however, by day and night, openly and privily do their utmost to shake the foundations of the Cause, to root out the Blessed Tree, to deprive this servant of service, to kindle secret sedition and strife and to annihilate 'Abdu'l-Bahá. Outwardly they appear as sheep, yet inwardly they are naught but ravening wolves. Sweet in words, they are but at heart a deadly poison.

233.19   O ye beloved ones, guard the Cause of God! Let no sweetness of tongue beguile you—nay, rather consider the motive of every soul, and ponder the thought he cherisheth. Be ye straightway mindful and on your guard. Avoid him, yet be not aggressive! Refrain from censure and from slander, and leave him in the Hand of God. Upon you rest the Glory of Glories.

234.1   234. O thou who art enraptured by the sweet breathings of the Lord! I have noted the contents of thine eloquent letter, and have learned that thou sheddest tears and thy heart is afire from grieving over the imprisonment of 'Abdu'l-Bahá.

234.2   O thou handmaid of God! This prison is sweeter to me and more to be desired than a garden of flowers; to me, this bondage is better than the freedom to go my way, and I find this narrow place more spacious than wide and open plains. Do not grieve over me. And should my Lord decree that I be blessed with sweet martyrdom's cup, this would but mean receiving what I long for most.

Fear not if this Branch be severed from this material world and cast aside its leaves; nay, the leaves thereof shall flourish, for this Branch will grow after it is cut off from this world below, it shall reach the loftiest pinnacles of glory, and it shall bear such fruits as will perfume the world with their fragrance. 234.3

235. O God, my God! Illumine the brows of Thy true lovers and support them with angelic hosts of certain triumph. Set firm their feet on Thy straight path, and out of Thine ancient bounty open before them the portals of Thy blessings; for they are expending on Thy pathway what Thou hast bestowed upon them, safeguarding Thy Faith, putting their trust in their remembrance of Thee, offering up their hearts for love of Thee, and withholding not what they possess in adoration for Thy Beauty and in their search for ways to please Thee. 235.1

O my Lord! Ordain for them a plenteous share, a destined recompense and sure reward. 235.2

235.3   Verily, Thou art the Sustainer, the Helper, the Generous, the Bountiful, the Ever-Bestowing.

236.1   236. O Thou, my God, Who guidest the seeker to the pathway that leadeth aright, Who deliverest the lost and blinded soul out of the wastes of perdition, Thou Who bestowest upon the sincere great bounties and favors, Who guardest the frightened within Thine impregnable refuge, Who answerest, from Thine all-highest horizon, the cry of those who cry out unto Thee. Praised be Thou, O my Lord! Thou hast guided the distracted out of the death of unbelief, and hast brought those who draw nigh unto Thee to the journey's goal, and hast rejoiced the assured among Thy servants by granting them their most cherished desires, and hast, from Thy Kingdom of beauty, opened before the faces of those who yearn after Thee the gates of reunion, and hast rescued them from the fires of deprivation and loss—so that they hastened unto Thee and gained Thy presence, and arrived at Thy welcoming door, and received of gifts an abundant share.

236.2   O my Lord, they thirsted, Thou didst lift to their parched lips the waters of reunion. O Tender One, Bestowing One, Thou didst calm their pain with the balm of Thy bounty and grace, and didst heal their ailments with the sovereign medicine of Thy compassion. O Lord, make firm their feet on Thy straight path, make wide for them the needle's eye, and cause them, dressed in royal robes, to walk in glory for ever and ever.

Verily art Thou the Generous, the Ever-Giving, 236.3 the Precious, the Most Bountiful. There is none other God but Thee, the Mighty, the Powerful, the Exalted, the Victorious.

O my spiritual loved ones! Praise be to God, 236.4 ye have thrust the veils aside and recognized the compassionate Beloved, and have hastened away from this abode to the placeless realm. Ye have pitched your tents in the world of God, and to glorify Him, the Self-Subsistent, ye have raised sweet voices and sung songs that pierced the heart. Well done! A thousand times well done! For ye have beheld the Light made manifest, and in your reborn beings ye have raised the cry, "Blessed be the Lord, the best of all creators!" Ye were but babes in the womb, then were ye sucklings, and from a precious breast ye drew the milk of knowledge, then came ye to your full growth, and won salvation. Now is the time for service, and for servitude unto the Lord. Release yourselves from all distracting thoughts, deliver the Message with an eloquent tongue, adorn your assemblages with praise of the Beloved, till bounty shall descend in overwhelming floods and dress the world in fresh greenery and blossoms. This streaming bounty is even the counsels, admonitions, instructions, and injunctions of Almighty God.

236.5   O ye my loved ones! The world is wrapped in the thick darkness of open revolt and swept by a whirlwind of hate. It is the fires of malevolence that have cast up their flames to the clouds of heaven, it is a blood-drenched flood that rolleth across the plains and down the hills, and no one on the face of the earth can find any peace. Therefore must the friends of God engender that tenderness which cometh from Heaven, and bestow love in the spirit upon all humankind. With every soul must they deal according to the Divine counselings and admonitions; to all must they show forth kindness and good faith; to all must they wish well. They must sacrifice themselves for their friends, and wish good fortune to their foes. They must comfort the ill-natured, and treat their oppressors with loving-kindness. They must be as refreshing water to the thirsty, and to the sick, a swift remedy, a healing balm to those in pain and a solace to every burdened heart. They must be a guiding light to those who have gone astray, a sure leader for the lost. They must be seeing eyes to the blind, hearing ears to the deaf, and to the dead eternal life, and to the despondent joy forever.

Let them willingly subject themselves to every 236.6 just king, and to every generous ruler be good citizens. Let them obey the government and not meddle in political affairs, but devote themselves to the betterment of character and behavior, and fix their gaze upon the Light of the world.

237. *Whoso reciteth this prayer with lowliness* 237.1
and fervor will bring gladness and joy to
the heart of this Servant; it will be even
as meeting Him face to face.

He is the All-Glorious! 237.2

O God, my God! Lowly and tearful, I raise my 237.3 suppliant hands to Thee and cover my face in the dust of that Threshold of Thine, exalted above the knowledge of the learned, and the praise of all that glorify Thee. Graciously look upon Thy servant, humble and lowly at Thy door, with the glances of the eye of Thy mercy, and immerse him in the Ocean of Thine eternal grace.

Lord! He is a poor and lowly servant of Thine, 237.4 enthralled and imploring Thee, captive in Thy hand, praying fervently to Thee, trusting in Thee, in tears before Thy face, calling to Thee and beseeching Thee, saying:

237.5 O Lord, my God! Give me Thy grace to serve Thy loved ones, strengthen me in my servitude to Thee, illumine my brow with the light of adoration in Thy court of holiness, and of prayer to Thy Kingdom of grandeur. Help me to be selfless at the heavenly entrance of Thy gate, and aid me to be detached from all things within Thy holy precincts. Lord! Give me to drink from the chalice of selflessness; with its robe clothe me, and in its ocean immerse me. Make me as dust in the pathway of Thy loved ones, and grant that I may offer up my soul for the earth ennobled by the footsteps of Thy chosen ones in Thy path, O Lord of Glory in the Highest.

237.6 With this prayer doth Thy servant call Thee, at dawntide and in the night-season. Fulfill his heart's desire, O Lord! Illumine his heart, gladden his bosom, kindle his light, that he may serve Thy Cause and Thy servants.

237.7 Thou art the Bestower, the Pitiful, the Most Bountiful, the Gracious, the Merciful, the Compassionate.

GLOSSARY

ABHÁ *Most Glorious.* See **Alláh-u-Abhá; Yá Bahá'-u'l-Abhá.**

ABHÁ BEAUTY A translation of *Jamál-i-Abhá,* a title of **Bahá'u'lláh.**

ABHÁ KINGDOM *The Most Glorious Kingdom:* the spiritual world beyond this world.

AFNÁN *Twigs:* the Báb's kindred; specifically, descendants of His three maternal uncles and His wife's two brothers.

AGHSÁN *Branches:* the sons and male descendants of Bahá'u'lláh.

ALLÁH-U-ABHÁ *God is Most Glorious:* the **Greatest Name,** also adopted as a greeting among Bahá'ís during the period of Bahá'u'lláh's exile in Adrianople (1863–68).

ANCIENT BEAUTY A translation of *Jamál-i-Qadím,* a name of God that is also used as a title of Bahá'u'lláh, Who is the latest Manifestation of God to humankind.

ANCIENT OF DAYS See **Ancient Beauty.**

BAHÁ'U'LLÁH *The Glory of God:* title of Mírzá Ḥusayn-'Alí Núrí (12 November 1817–29 May 1892), Founder of the Bahá'í Faith. For accounts of His life, see Shoghi Effendi, *God Passes By;* Nabíl, *Dawn-Breakers;* and Balyuzi, *Bahá'u'lláh: The King of Glory.* Bahá'u'lláh is referred to by a variety of titles, including the Promised One of All Ages, the Blessed Beauty, the Blessed Perfection, the Morn of Truth, the Abhá Luminary, the Dayspring of the Most Divine Essence, the Ancient Beauty, the Ancient Root, the Ancient of Days, the Author of the Bahá'í Revelation, the Mystic Dove, the Sovereign Revealer, the Judge, the Redeemer, the Divine Physician, the Prince of Peace, the Pen of Glory, the Pen of the Most High, the Supreme Pen, the Lord of Hosts, and the Lord of the Age.

BAYÁN *Exposition, explanation, lucidity, eloquence, utterance:* the title given by the Báb to two of His major works, one in Persian, the other in Arabic. It is also used sometimes to denote the entire body of His writings.

BEST BELOVED See Ancient Beauty.

BLESSED BEAUTY A translation of *Jamál-i-Mubárak*, a title of Bahá'u'lláh. See also **Ancient Beauty**.

CENTER OF THE COVENANT A title of **'Abdu'l-Bahá** referring to His appointment by Bahá'u'lláh as the successor to whom all must turn after Bahá'u'lláh's passing. See also **Covenant**.

CONCOURSE ON HIGH The company of holy souls of the spiritual world.

COVENANT Generally, an agreement or contract between two or more people, usually formal, solemn, and binding. A religious covenant is "a binding agreement between God and man, whereby God requires of man certain behavior in return for which He guarantees certain blessings, or whereby He gives man certain bounties in return for which He takes from those who accept them an undertaking to behave in a certain way." There are two types of religious covenant: "There is . . . the Greater Covenant which every Manifestation of God makes with His followers, promising that in the fullness of time a new Manifestation will be sent, and taking from them the undertaking to accept Him when this occurs. There is also the Lesser Covenant that a Manifestation of God makes with His followers that they will accept His appointed successor after Him. If they do so, the Faith can remain united and pure. If not, the Faith becomes divided and its force spent." In the Bahá'í Dispensation the Greater Covenant refers to the renewal of God's ancient Covenant through the appearance of the twin Manifestations of God, the **Báb** and **Bahá'u'lláh**, and the promise of another Manifestation to come in the future after the passage of at least one thousand years. The Lesser Covenant, in this case, refers to Bahá'u'lláh's Covenant with His followers, which establishes **'Abdu'l-Bahá** as the Center of the Covenant. It confers upon 'Abdu'l-Bahá the authority to interpret Bahá'u'lláh's writings in order "to perpetuate the influence" of the Faith and to "insure its integrity, safeguard it from schism, and stimulate its world-wide expansion." The Lesser Covenant also establishes the Guardianship and the Universal House of Justice as the twin successors of Bahá'u'lláh and 'Abdu'l-Bahá.

COVENANT-BREAKER A Bahá'í who attempts to disrupt the unity of the Faith by defying and opposing the authority of Bahá'u'lláh as the Manifestation of God for this Age, or His appointed successor, 'Abdu'l-Bahá, or after Him, the Guardian and the Universal House of Justice. Bahá'ís who continue, despite remonstrances, to violate the Covenant are expelled from the Faith by the Universal House of Justice. This provision preserves the unity of the Faith, which is essential to achieving its cardinal purpose of unifying humankind. It also preserves the purity of Bahá'u'lláh's teachings from the disruptive influence of egoistic individuals who, in past Dispensations, have been responsible for dividing every religion into sects, disrupting its mission, and frustrating to a large degree the intention of its Founder. See also **Covenant.**

DAYSPRING OF DIVINE GUIDANCE Bahá'u'lláh.

DIVINE ESSENCE God.

DIVINE PEN A title of Bahá'u'lláh.

GREATEST NAME The name **Bahá'u'lláh** ("the Glory of God") and its derivatives, such as **Alláh-u-Abhá** ("God is Most Glorious"), *Bahá* ("glory," "splendor," or "light"), and **Yá Bahá'u'l-Abhá** ("O Thou the Glory of the Most Glorious!"). Also referred to as the Most Great Name.

KITÁB-I-AQDAS, THE *The Most Holy Book* (*Kitáb* means "book"; *Aqdas* means "Most Holy"): the chief repository of Bahá'u'lláh's laws and the Mother Book of His revelation. It was revealed by Bahá'u'lláh in 'Akká in 1873.

MANIFESTATION OF GOD Designation of a Prophet "endowed with constancy" Who is the Founder of a religious Dispensation, inasmuch as in His words, His person, and His actions He manifests the nature and purpose of God in accordance with the capacity and needs of the people to whom He comes.

MASHRIQU'L-ADHKÁR *The Dawning-place of the Praise of God:* a title designating a Bahá'í House of Worship or Temple. Houses of Worship have been constructed in Chicago, Illinois; Kampala, Uganda; Sydney, Australia; Frankfurt, Germany; Panama City, Panama; Apia, Western Samoa; and New Delhi, India.

MOST HOLY BOOK See **Kitáb-i-Aqdas, The**.

MOUNT CARMEL A mountain in Israel on which the Shrine of the Báb and the Bahá'í World Center are located. The home of the prophet Elijah, it is referred to by Bahá'u'lláh as "the Hill of God and His Vineyard" and was extolled by Isaiah as the "mountain of the Lord" to which "all nations shall flow." On it Bahá'u'lláh pitched His tent and revealed the **Tablet**

of Carmel, the charter of the world spiritual and administrative centers of the Bahá'í Faith.

NINETEEN DAY FEAST A Bahá'í institution inaugurated by the Báb and confirmed by Bahá'u'lláh in the Kitáb-i-Aqdas. It is held on the first day of every Bahá'í month, each consisting of nineteen days and bearing the name of one of the attributes of God. The Feast is the heart of Bahá'í community life at the local level and consists of devotional, consultative, and social elements.

RIḌVÁN The Islamic name of the gardener and custodian of Paradise. In Bahá'í terminology the word denotes both "garden" and "paradise"; however, it has also been used to denote God's good-pleasure and His divine acceptance. The Riḍván Festival, the holiest and most significant of all Bahá'í festivals, commemorates Bahá'u'lláh's declaration of His mission to His companions in the Garden of Riḍván in Baghdad in 1863. It is a twelve-day period celebrated annually, 21 April–2 May. It is also called the Most Great Festival. During each Riḍván Festival Local and National Spiritual Assemblies are elected, and, once every five years, the Universal House of Justice is elected.

SADRATU'L-MUNTAHÁ Refers to a tree planted by the Arabs in early times at the end of a road to serve as a guide. Here the term symbolizes the Manifestations of God.

SHRINE The original meaning of the word is a casket or case for books, but it later acquired the special meaning of a casket containing sacred relics, and thence a tomb of a saint, a chapel with special associations, or a place hallowed by some memory. It is used to denote the latter in Bahá'í terminology. The term "Holy Shrines," for example, refers to the burial places of Bahá'u'lláh, the Báb, and 'Abdu'l-Bahá.

TABLETS Refers to letters revealed by Bahá'u'lláh, the Báb, and 'Abdu'l-Bahá.

WILL AND TESTAMENT OF 'ABDU'L-BAHÁ is a document that serves as the charter of the Administrative Order of the Bahá'í Faith. Written, signed, and sealed by 'Abdu'l-Bahá, the Will and Testament consists of three sections written at three different times between 1901 and the year of His passing. The Will and Testament affirms "the two-fold character of the Mission of the Báb," which was to bring an independent revelation from God and to herald the coming of another, greater revelation through Bahá'u'lláh. It also "discloses the full station of" Bahá'u'lláh as the "Supreme Manifestation of God," declares the fundamental beliefs of the Bahá'í Faith, establishes the institution of the Guardianship, and appoints Shoghi Effendi as Guardian. It provides for the election of the Universal House of Justice and defines its scope. It also creates the institution of the National Spiritual Assembly, provides for the appointment of the Hands of the Cause of God and prescribes their obligations, and exposes the conduct of the Covenant-breakers.

YÁ 'ALÍYYU'L-A'LÁ *O Thou the Exalted, the Most Exalted!* A form of the **Báb**'s name that is used as an invocation.

YÁ BAHÁ'U'L-ABHÁ *O Thou the Glory of the Most Glorious!* A form of **Bahá'u'lláh**'s name (the **Greatest Name**) that is used as an invocation.

NOTES ON TRANSLATIONS

PASSAGES TRANSLATED
BY THE GUARDIAN

Whenever a passage in one of the Tablets has been translated by the Guardian, that translation has been used. These are identified below. Extensive use has also been made, especially in those sections retranslated by the Committee, of very early translations and notes made by Shoghi Effendi during the lifetime of 'Abdu'l-Bahá.

Section.paragraph no.

2.16	"The most vital duty . . ." to "of every living man."
5.3	"Let not your hearts . . ." to ". . . Our favored angels."
5.4	"Be not dismayed . . ." to "Word amongst men."
12.1–4	Whole Section
15.6	"In cycles gone by . . ." to ". . . merged into one."
15.6	"In like manner all the . . ." to ". . . their realization."
20.1–3	Whole Section

35.5	"O army of God! Through . . ." to ". . . Covenant and Testament of God."
38.5	"These Spiritual Assemblies are aided . . ." to ". . . under all conditions."
42.4–5	"Whenever ye enter . . ." to ". . . the Compassionate."
43.1	Whole Section
44.1	Whole Section
45.1	Whole Section except from "is that the members" which is a Committee translation.
52.1–3	Whole Section
175.1	Whole Section
176.1–3	Whole Section
194.1–3	Whole Section
198.5	"I never passed a tree . . ." to ". . . crucified upon thee."
202.14	"The Balkans will remain . . ." to ". . . influence will spread."
204.1–4	Whole Section
208.1	Whole Section
214.2	"Not everything . . ." to ". . . of those who hear it."[1]
218.3	"We behold you . . ." to ". . . favored angels."
222.1–3	Whole Section
225.24	"Consider the flowers . . ." to ". . . unto their beauty."
225.25	"How unpleasing . . ." to ". . . the children of men."
229.1–3	Whole Section
234.3	"Fear not . . ." to ". . . with their fragrance."
237.1–7	Whole Section

1. This is a tradition which is quoted by Bahá'u'lláh (see *Gleanings from the Writings of Bahá'u'lláh*, item LXXXIX) and is also quoted by 'Abdu'l-Bahá in a Tablet which appears in the compilation of the Universal House of Justice on "Teaching."

Sections Translated by Marzieh Gail.

1–4	76	148–163
6–10	79	174
15–17	84–87	181–182
19	90–92	188
21–29	94–97	190–191
31	99–111	193
33	113–114	195–196
35–42	118–119	198–203
47–51	121–123	205–207
53–61	129	209–210
64–65	134	216–221
72–74	137–146	234–236

Sections Translated by a Committee at the World Center, based on earlier Translations.

5	34	80–83
11	46	88–89
13–14	62–63	93
18	66–71	98
30	75	112
32	77–78	115–17
120	164–173	197
124–128	177–180	211–215
130–133	183–187	223–228
135–136	189	230–233
147	192	

INDEX